A Laboratory Course

in C++

Nell Dale

University of Texas, Austin

JONES AND BARTLETT PUBLISHERS

Sudbury, Massachusetts

BOSTON   TORONTO   LONDON   SINGAPORE

World Headquarters

Jones and Bartlett Publishers
40 Tall Pine Drive
Sudbury, MA 01776
978-443-5000
info@jbpub.com
www.jbpub.com

Jones and Bartlett Publishers Canada
P.O. Box 19020
Toronto, ON M5S 1X1
CANADA

Jones and Bartlett Publishers International
Barb House, Barb Mews
London W6 7PA
UK

Library of Congress Cataloging-in-Publication Data

Dale, Nell.
    A laboratory course in C++ / Nell Dale.
       p.   cm.
    ISBN 0-7637-0247-1
    1. C++ (Computer program language)   I. Title.
QA76.73.C153D336   1996
005.13'3--dc20   96-32748
                                   CIP

Acquisitions Editor: David Geggis
Developmental Editor: Karen Jolie
Production Editor: Marilyn E. Rash
Manufacturing Manager: Dana L. Cerrito
Cover Design: Hannus Design Associates
Cover Printing: John P. Pow Company
Printing and Binding: Edwards Brothers, Inc.

Printed in the United States of America

00 99 98   10 9 8 7 6

Contents

17   Pointers, Dynamic Data, and Reference Types   343

18   Linked Structures   365

19   Recursion   383

Appendixes   397

Glossary   403

Preface

Need for Support in Learning C++

For the last 16 years, the introductory computer science course has been taught mostly in Pascal. Over the last two to three years there has been a move toward C++ in place of Pascal. Even the strongest advocates for the change realize that C++ is going to be more difficult than Pascal for most beginning students to learn.

C and later C++ were designed for systems programming. Systems programmers are assumed to know what they mean and mean what they say. Therefore, C++ has very little runtime error checking and compiles some very weird code. Beginning students, on the other hand, often do not know what they mean and even more often do not mean what they say. Hence, it is essential that students understand the syntax and semantics of each construct as they go along. Closed laboratory activities seem an ideal way to make this happen.

Closed Laboratories in Computer Science

The Denning Report[1] introduced the term *closed laboratories* without defining exactly what they were. At least four different definitions subsequently surfaced.

1. A scheduled time when students work on their programming assignments under supervision.
2. A scheduled drill and practice time when students work on mini-problems under supervision.
3. The use of specially prepared laboratory materials where students interact with the computer as they would a microscope or Bunsen burner. The labs should help the student discover principles and solutions under supervision. This definition is closest to the spirit of the Denning Report.
4. A combination of two or more of the above.

With the publication of the Curriculum '91[2] report, laboratory exercises were suggested for many of the knowledge units. However, a precise definition of what constituted a closed laboratory activity was not included. And, in fact, many of the activities suggested could be done equally well in a nonsupervised (or open) setting.

Laboratory activities as defined in this manual are a combination of definitions 2 and 3.

---

[1] Denning, P. J. (chair) "Computing as a Discipline." *Communications of the ACM*, Vol. 32, No. 1, pp. 9-23.

[2] Tucker, A. B. (Ed.) "Computing Curricula 1991: Report of the ACM/IEEE-CS Joint Curriculum Task Force." Final Draft, December 17, 1991. ACM Order Number 201910. IEEE Computer Society Press Order Number 2220.

Open versus Closed Laboratories

Although the Denning Report and Curriculum '91 imply that laboratory exercises should be done under supervision, we do not feel that this is essential. Our view is that closed laboratory exercises are valuable for two reasons: the exercises themselves and the extra contact time with a faculty member or a teaching assistant. If a closed laboratory environment is not an option, the students can still benefit from working the exercises on their own.

Organization of the Manual

Each chapter contains three types of activities: Prelab, Inlab, and Postlab. The Prelab activities include a reading review assignment and simple paper and pencil exercises. The Inlab activities are broken into lessons, each of which represents a concept covered in the chapter. Each lesson is broken into exercises that thoroughly demonstrate the concept. The Postlab exercises are a collection of outside programming assignments appropriate for each chapter. Each exercise requires that the students apply the concepts covered in the chapter.

When this manual is being used in a closed-laboratory setting, we suggest that the Prelab activities be done before the students come to lab. The students can spend the first few minutes of the laboratory checking their answers (Lesson 1 for each chapter). The Inlab activities are designed to take approximately two hours, the usual time for a closed laboratory. However, an instructor can tailor the chapter to the level of the class by only assigning a partial set of exercises or by shortening the time allowed.

The Postlab activities present a selection of programming projects. We do not suggest that all of them be assigned. In most cases, one should be sufficient, unless there are several related problems.

If the manual is not being used in a closed-laboratory setting, an instructor can assign all or a selection of the Inlab activities to be done independently (see the section "Flexibility" below). In either a closed or open setting, many of the Inlab and Postlab activities can be done in groups.

Theoretical Basis for the Activities

The decision to break each chapter in three types of activities is based on the work of Benjamin Bloom, who developed a taxonomy of six increasingly difficult levels of achievement in the cognitive domain.[3] In developing the activities for this manual, we combined Bloom's six categories into three. These categories are defined below in terms of the concrete example of learning an algorithm (or language-related construct).

Recognition The student can trace the algorithm and determine what the output should be for a given data set (no transfer).

Generation The student can generate a very similar algorithm (near transfer).

---

[3]Bloom, Benjamin *Taxonomy of Educational Objectives—Handbook I: Cognitive Domain.* New York: David McKay, 1956.

Projection The student can modify the algorithm to accomplish a major change (far transfer), can apply the algorithm in a different context, can combine related algorithms, and can compare algorithms.

The Prelab activities are at the recognition level. Most of the Inlab activities are at the generation level with a few projection-level activities included where appropriate. The Postlab activities are projection-level activities.

The activities are also influenced by the work of Kolb and others on how students learn.[4] The more actively involved students are in the learning process, the more they learn. Reading and writing are forms of active involvement. Therefore, the Prelab activities begin with a reading review, and many of the exercises ask the students to write explanations of what happened. Just watching a program run and looking at the answer is a passive activity, but having to write the answer down transforms the exercise into an active one.

Flexibility

A Laboratory Course in C++ is designed to allow the instructor maximum flexibility. Each chapter has an assignment cover sheet that provides a checklist in tabular form. The first column of the table in the Assignment Cover Sheet lists the chapter activities, in the second column students check which activities have been assigned, in the third column they record what output is to be turned in, and the fourth column is for the instructor to use for grading. The pages are perforated so that students can easily tear out sheets to turn in.

Student Disk

The accompanying disk contains the programs, program shells (partial programs), and data files. A copy of most of the programs or program shells is listed before the exercises that use the program or program shell. Programs used for debugging exercises are not shown, however. Because some of the exercises ask the student to go back to the original version a previous program or program shell, we suggest that the student copy the disk and work from the copy.

The disk is divided into subdirectories, one for each chapter. The programs and program shells are stored in files under the program name with a **.cpp** extension. Header files are stored with a **.h** extension.

---

[4]Svinicki, Marilla D., and Dixon Nancy M. "The Kolb Model Modified for Classroom Activities." *College Teaching*, Vol. 35, No. 4: Fall, pp. 141-146.

Acknowledgments

No author writes in a vacuum. There is always formal and informal feedback from colleagues. Thanks to those of you in my department who patiently answered "by the way" questions about C++. Thanks also to the following colleagues who wrote formal reviews of the manuscript: Mary D. Medley, Augusta College; Susan Wallace, University of North Florida; Paul Ross, Millersville University of Pennsylvania; Jeanine Ingber, University of New Mexico, Albequerque; James C. Miller, Bradley University; Ed Korntved, Northwest Nazarene College; Charles Dierbach, Towson State University; Mansar Zand, and University of Nebraska, Omaha. My special thanks to Mark Headington, University of Wisconsin, La Crosse, who must be the world's most meticulous reviewer and proofreader.

I want to add a special word of thanks to Porter Scobey at Saint Mary's University who discovered that there was a problem with recognizing the end of line under certain systems and then helped us solve the problem.

To Karen Jolie, a long-time colleague who always has the right answers; to Dianne Cannon Wood, who did a masterful job of copyediting; to Marilyn Rash, the production editor; and to all the staff at Jones and Bartlett: thank you. I trust that this is the beginning of a long and rewarding association.

1

Overview of Programming and Problem Solving

OBJECTIVES

- To be able to log on to a computer.
- To be able to do the following tasks on a computer.
  - Change the active (work) directory.
  - List the files in a directory.
- To be able to do the following tasks using an editor and a C++ compiler.
  - Load a file containing a program.
  - Alter a file containing a program.
  - Save a file.
  - Compile a program.
  - Run a program.
  - Change a program and rerun it.
  - Correct a program with errors.
  - Enter and run a program.
  - Exit the system.

Chapter 1: Assignment Cover Sheet

Name _____   Date _____

Section _____

Fill in the following table showing which exercises have been assigned for each lesson and check what you are to submit: (1) lab sheets, (2) listings of output files, and/or (3) listings of programs. Your instructor or teaching assistant (TA) can use the Completed column for grading purposes.

Activities	Assigned: Check or list exercise numbers	Submit (1)	(2)	(3)	Completed
Prelab					
Review					
Prelab Assignment					
Inlab					
Lesson 1-1: Check Prelab Exercises					
Lesson 1-2: Basic File Operations					
Lesson 1-3: Compiling and Running a Program					
Lesson 1-4: Editing, Running, and Printing a Program File					
Lesson 1-5: Running a Program with an Error					
Lesson 1-6: Entering, Compiling, and Running a New Program					
Postlab					

Prelab Activities

Review

A computer is a programmable electronic device that can store, retrieve, and process data. The verbs *store*, *retrieve*, and *process* relate to the five basic physical components of the computer: the memory unit, the arithmetic/logic unit, the control unit, input devices, and output devices. These physical components are called computer *hardware*. The programs that are available to run on a computer are called *software*. Writing the programs that make up the software is called *programming*.

Programming

A program is a sequence of instructions written to perform a specific task. Programming is the process of defining the sequence of instructions. There are two phases in this process: determining the task that needs doing and expressing the solution in a sequence of instructions.

The process of programming always begins with a problem. Programs are not written in isolation; they are written to solve problems. Determining what needs to be done means outlining the solution to the problem. This first phase, then, is the problem-solving phase.

The second phase, expressing the solution in a sequence of instructions, is the implementation phase. Here, the general solution outlined in the problem-solving phase is converted into a specific solution (a program in a specific language). Testing is part of both phases. The general solution must be shown to be correct before it is translated into a program.

Let's demonstrate the process with the following problem.

Problem: Calculate the average rainfall over a period of days.

Discussion: To do the job "by hand," you would write down the number of inches of rain that had fallen each day. Then you would add the figures up and divide the total by the number of days. This is exactly the algorithm we use in the program.

Algorithm (on next page):

Average Rainfall

```
Get total inches of rain
if total is zero then
    There wasn't any rain
otherwise
    Average <- total / number of days
```

Selection construct.

One thing is done if
there is no rain;
another thing is done
if there is rain.

Function construct.

The task of getting the total number of inches is stated in the
main algorithm without saying how it is done. This task is
expanded separately as a subalgorithm.

Get Total Inches of Rain

```
for number of days
    Get inches
    Add to total
```

Loop construct.

The task of getting the number
of inches and adding it to the
total is repeated for each day.

Sequence construct.

The task of getting inches is followed immediately
by the task of adding the inches to the total.

The C++ program that implements this algorithm is given below. Don't worry
if you don't understand it. At this stage, you're not expected to. Before long, you
will be able to understand all of it.

Incidentally, the information between the symbols /* and the symbols */ is
meant for the human reader of the program. This kind of information is called a
comment and is ignored by the C++ compiler. Information from // to the end of a
line is also a comment.

```cpp
// Program Rain calculates the average rainfall over a period
// of days.  The number of days and the rain statistics are in
// file Rain.in.

#include <iostream.h>
#include <fstream.h>
#include <iomanip.h>

void GetInches(ifstream&, int&, float&);
// Rain statistics are read from a file; the average is
// returned.

int main()
{
    float  average;            // average rainfall
    float totalRain;           // total accumulated rain
    int numberOfDays;          // number of days in calculation
    ifstream  rainFile;        // data file
    cout.setf(ios::fixed, ios::floatfield);
    cout.setf(ios::showpoint);
```

```
        rainFile.open("Rain.In");
        GetInches(rainFile, numberOfDays, totalRain);

        if (totalRain == 0.0)
            cout  << "There was no rain during this period."
                  << endl;
        else
        {
            average = totalRain / numberOfDays;
            cout  << "The average rain fall over "
                  << numberOfDays;
            cout  << " days is " << setw(1)  << setprecision(3)
                  << average  << endl;
        }

        return 0;
}


//*******************************************************

void  GetInches(ifstream& rainFile, int& numberOfDays,
        float& totalRain)
// Pre:  rainFile has been opened.
//       numberOfDays is the first value on rainFile, followed
//       by numberOfDays real values representing inches of
//       rain.
// Post: numberOfDays is read from rainFile.
//       Number of inches of rain for numberOfDays are read
//       and their sum is returned in totalRain.

{
    float  inches;          // Day's worth of rain
    int  counter;           // loop control variable

    rainFile >> numberOfDays;
    totalRain = 0.0;
    counter = 1;
    while (counter <= numberOfDays)
    {
        rainFile >> inches;
        totalRain = totalRain + inches;
        counter++;
    }
}
```

Getting Started

Certain C++ systems provide an integrated environment for the creation and execution of C++ programs. For example, Turbo C++, which runs on IBM-compatible PCs, provides such an environment. The compiler, the editor, and the runtime system are all bundled together into one system. Other C++ compilers come separately so that you must use a general-purpose editor to enter your program. You compile the program and then run it. There are far too many systems for us to describe any of them in detail. Therefore, we use an analogy to describe the process of entering and running your program.

When you first get on a machine (*log in*), the *operating system* is the software that is running. You can think of the operating system as a hallway that connects all the other pieces of software. You enter the name of the software you want to use, and the operating system provides it. When you finish using the software, you must come back to the operating system (the hallway) before you can use another piece of software.

Each piece of software is like a doorway. The operating system opens the door and ushers you into the room where the software you want to use is kept. In the *editor*, you create a file of written information. This file may contain a program or data for a program.

An editor is a program that allows you to use your keyboard and screen like a very smart electronic typewriter. A *file* is the information that you type in through the keyboard. You see what you type on the screen. Commands to the editor do what you would do "by hand" with a typewriter. These allow you to change and rearrange letters, words, and sentences. A file resides in an area in secondary storage that has a name and is used to hold a collection of data. The data itself also is referred to as a file.

When you are satisfied with what you've typed, you give your file a name and tell the editor to save it for you. Giving a file a name is like putting information into a folder with a label on it. You can pick up the file and carry it with you from one room to another.

When you leave the editor, the operating system comes back with a prompt that says it's ready for you to tell it where you want to go next. If you've created a C++ program, you say that you want to *compile* (translate) your file (go to the C++ room). The operating system opens the door, and you hand your file folder to the C++ compiler.

The C++ compiler attempts to translate your program. If the program contains grammatical errors (errors in syntax), the compiler tells you so. You then have to go back to the editing room to correct the mistakes. When your C++ program finally compiles correctly, the C++ compiler leaves the object program (the translated code) in a file.

You tell the operating system that you are ready to run the object program. The file containing the translated program is taken into the execute room, where it is run. It's here, in the execute room, that the problem your program was written to solve actually gets solved.

When you're finished and ready to quit (*log out*), you tell the operating system. It opens the door marked exit, and you can leave.

Some systems bundle the editing room, the compiling room, and the executing room into one luxurious suite. For example, in Turbo C++ you enter this suite by saying "TC" to the operating system. You are then handed a menu of the things that you can do: create a new file, modify an old file, compile a program, or run a program. You even have the option of asking for help. You make a choice either by using a mouse (a pointing device) or by pressing a function key on the keyboard. Several of these choices then provide you with a second menu from which to choose. Integrated systems are *user-friendly* systems: you are never left stranded; you are always guided through the input (edit), compile, and run cycle by the use of these menus that appear at the top of your screen.

Chapter 1: Prelab Assignment

Name _____   Date _____

Section _____

Your instructor should provide a handout describing the system that you are using.

Exercise 1:   What computer are you using?

Exercise 2:   What operating system are you using?

Exercise 3:   What C++ system are you using?

Exercise 4:   Is your C++ system an integrated system, or is the editor separate from the compiler?

Exercise 5:   If your editor is separate, which editor are you using?

Lesson 1-1: Check Prelab Exercises

Name _____   **Date** _____

Section _____

Exercise 1:   What computer are you using? IBM-compatible PCs, Macintosh computers, and Digital Equipment computers are common in this course. You also might be using a terminal to a computer network.

Exercise 2:   What operating system are you using?   Windows '95, DOS, Macintosh, and UNIX are common operating systems.

Exercise 3:   What C++ system are you using? There are lots of choices, but it must be compatible with the operating system that you are using.

Exercise 4:   Is your C++ system an integrated system, or is the editor separate from the compiler? You only have two choices here: either it is integrated or it is not.

Exercise 5:   If your editor is separate, which editor are you using? Word and WordPerfect are two common editors on PCs. Emacs and vi are two editors for UNIX machines.

Lesson 1-2: Basic File Operations

Name _____   **Date** _____

Section _____

Exercise 1:   Follow your instructor's instructions on how to log on to the system.

Exercise 2:   Regardless of the system you are using, the memory should be divided up into hierarchical subsections called directories. At any one time, you are in a directory. List all the contents of the directory you are in when you log on to the system. (Hint: The command to list a directory on PC compatibles is **dir**; on UNIX machines it is **ls** . In a Windows system, you click on the directory name.)

Exercise 3:   Enter the editor. Type your name on the screen and save the file.

Exercise 4:   Bring file **rain.cpp** into your editor. Look through it carefully; it contains the C++ program shown in the review. Save the file.

Exercise 5:   Bring file **rain2.cpp** into your editor. Examine it carefully. It is the same as file **rain.cpp** with the formatting changed. (Which is easier for the human to read?) Save the file.

Lesson 1-3: Compiling and Running a Program

Name _____   **Date** _____

Section _____

Exercise 1:   Compile and run program **Rain** in file **rain.cpp**.   How many inches of rain were there?

Exercise 2:   Compile and run program **Rain** in file **rain2.cpp**.   How many inches of rain were there?

Exercise 3:   Are you surprised that the results were the same in Exercises 1 and 2? What does that tell you about the differences between how the compiler views the text of a program and how the user views the text of a program?

Exercise 4:   Compile and run program **FirstOne**.   What is printed on the screen?

Lesson 1-4: Editing, Running, and Printing a Program File

Name _____   **Date** _____

Section _____

Exercise 1:   Bring file **firstone.cpp** to the screen. Replace the name Nell Dale with your own name. Compile and run the program. What is printed on the screen?

Exercise 2:   Did you notice that there is no period after the name and that the line of asterisks is not even? Go back and edit this program so that a period follows the name and the two lines contain the same number of asterisks. Compile and run your program. What is printed on the screen?

Exercise 3:   Save your changed file.

Exercise 4:   You now need to print out a copy of your changed file from Exercise 3 to turn in to your instructor. Follow your instructor's instructions on how to print a file.

Lesson 1-5: Running a Program with an Error

Name _____   **Date** _____

Section _____

Exercise 1:   Compile program **Error** in file **Error.cpp**. The error message you get and what happens when this occurs depends on the C++ compiler you are using. What was the error message and what happened?

Exercise 2:   Go back into the editor and correct the error. (There is a semicolon missing.) Compile and run your program. What is the output?

Lesson 1-6: Entering, Compiling, and Running a New Program

Name _____   Date _____

Section _____

Exercise 1:   Get into the editor and enter the following program. You are not expected to understand what it does; just copy it exactly as shown.

```
// Program Area calculates the area of a square.
// The user is prompted to enter the number of
// inches on each side.

#include <iostream.h>
int main ()
{
   int inches;

   cout << "Enter the number of inches on a side "
      << endl1;
   cout << "Press the return key."
      << endl;
   cin >> inches;
   cout << endl
       << "The area is " << inches * inches <<"."
      << endl;
   return 0;
}
```

Exercise 2:   When you have finished keying in this program, try to compile it. If you have made any typing errors, correct them and try to compile the program again.

Exercise 3:   When the program compiles without any errors, you are ready to run it. When the program is running, you are asked to input a number. Enter a number between 1 and 150. What number did you input? What was written on the screen?

Exercise 4:   Exit the system.

----

[1]Note that these are the letters *e*, *n*, *d*, and *l*. That last character is not the number 1, but a lowercase *l* as in love.

Postlab Activities

Exercise 1:   Key in the following program, compile it, and run it.

```
// Program Stars prints three rows of asterisks.

#include <iostream.h>

int main ()
{
    cout  << "***********"  << endl;
    cout  << " ********* "  << endl;;
    cout  << "  *******  "  << endl;;
    return 0;
}
```

Exercise 2:   Edit program **Stars** so that it prints five asterisks centered on the fourth line, three asterisks centered on the fifth line, and one asterisk centered on the sixth line. Compile and run your program.

Exercise 3:   Using program **Stars** as a model, write a program that prints the same pattern on the screen but with the symbol a dollar sign rather than an asterisk.

2

C++ Syntax and Semantics, and the Program Development Process

OBJECTIVES

- To be able to compile and run a C++ program from disk.
- To be able to modify the various parts of a program and observe what these changes do to the program's output.
- To be able to construct output statements that send information to the output stream.
- To be able to construct assignment statements to accomplish a stated task.
- To be able to debug a program with syntax errors.
- To be able to debug a program with logic errors.

Chapter 2: Assignment Cover Sheet

Name _____   **Date** _____

Section _____

Fill in the following table showing which exercises have been assigned for each lesson and check what you are to submit: (1) lab sheets, (2) listings of output files, and/or (3) listings of programs. Your instructor or TA can use the Completed column for grading purposes.

Activities	Assigned: Check or list exercise numbers	Submit (1)	(2)	(3)	Completed
Prelab					
Review					
Prelab Assignment					
Inlab					
Lesson 2-1: Check Prelab Exercises					
Lesson 2-2: Components of a Program					
Lesson 2-3: Sending Information to the Output Stream					
Lesson 2-4: Working with Numeric Expressions					
Lesson 2-5: Debugging					
Postlab					

Prelab Activities

Review

There are two basic parts to a C++ program: (1) instructions to the C++ preprocessor and compiler and (2) instructions that describe the processing to be done. However, before we can describe these instructions, we must have a way of naming things so that we can tell the compiler about them and describe what we want to have done to them.   We name things (data types, data objects, and actions) by giving them an *identifier*. An identifier is made up of letters, numbers, and underscores, but must begin with a letter or an underscore. We use the words *identifier* and *name* interchangeably.

Beware: C++ is case sensitive. This means that Value, VALUE, value, and vaLue are four separate identifiers. In fact, we can construct 32 distinct identifiers from these five letters by varying the capitalization.

Program Structure

Let's examine the following C++ program. We have numbered the lines so that we can discuss them.

```
1.   // Program Lunch calculates the number of calories in
2.   // a cheese sandwich.

3.   #include <iostream.h>

4.   const int BREAD = 63;       // calories in a slice of bread
5.   const int CHEESE = 106;     // calories in a slice of cheese
6.   const int MAYONNAISE = 49;  // calories in mayonnaise
7.   const int PICKLES = 25;     // calories in pickles

8.   int main()
9.   {
10.      int totalCalories;

11.      totalCalories = 2 * BREAD + CHEESE
                         + MAYONNAISE + PICKLES;
12.      cout << "There were " << totalCalories;
13.      cout << " calories in my lunch yesterday." << endl;
14.      cout << "What is for lunch today?" << endl;
15.      return 0;
16. }
```

Lines 1 and 2 begin with a double slash (**//**) and are ignored by the translation system. Such lines are called *comments* and are meant for the reader of the program. They tell the user what the program is going to do. Comments begin with **//** and extend to the end of the line. Another way of entering comments into the program is to insert them between **/*** and ***/**. Comments between **/*** and ***/** can extend across any number of lines.

Line 3 is a directive to the C++ preprocessor. The preprocessor scans the program for lines beginning with a hash mark (**#**).   The words "**include**

<iostream.h>" tell the preprocessor to insert the contents of the file **iostream.h** in place of the directive. The angle brackets around the file name indicate that the file is in the standard *include directory*. This file includes constant, variable, and function declarations needed by the program.

Lines 4 through 7 instruct the compiler to assign the identifier on the left of the equal sign a place in memory and to store the value on the right of the equal sign in that place. A constant declaration is made up of the reserved word **const** followed by the data type identifier **int**. **int** says that the value to be stored in the constant is an integer value. The data type identifier is followed by the name to be given to the constant: in this case, **BREAD**. The constant name is followed by an equal sign and the value to be stored there. By convention, most C++ programmers use all uppercase for constant identifiers.

Line 8 contains the words that begin the executable part of the program—that is, the part that contains statements that describe what you want to have done. A function performs an action and returns a result. The data type identifier **int** says that the value returned by function **main** is an integer. The compiler knows that **main** is a function because it is followed by a pair of parentheses. All C++ programs must have an **int** function **main**. Line 9 contains only one character: the left brace (**{**). This character begins a block that is the body of the function. The right brace (**}**)on line 16 is the closing brace of the block; it ends the body of the function. The body of the function contains the statements that are translated by the compiler and executed when the program is run.

Line 10 contains the declaration of **totalCalories**, an integer variable. The compiler assigns a memory location to **totalCalories**. Nothing is stored in **totalCalories** yet. When values are stored there, they must be values of type **int**.

Line 11 is an assignment statement. The expression on the right side of the equal sign is evaluated, and the result is stored in the variable whose identifier is on the left of the equal sign. Therefore, 306 is stored in **totalCalories**.

Lines 12 through 14 cause information to be written on the screen. **cout**, which is defined in file **<iostream.h>**, is a predefined variable that denotes an *output stream*. An output stream is just what it sounds like: a stream of characters sent to some output device. The operator **<<** (double less-than signs) is called the *insertion operator*. The stream of characters described on the right of the insertion operator is sent to the output stream named on the left of the insertion operator. Let's look at line 12 (repeated below) in detail.

```
12.      cout << "There were "  << totalCalories;
```

The collection of characters that appear between the double quotes is called a *string*. The leftmost insertion operator sends the string to **cout**; that is, the characters that make up the string are printed on the screen. The next insertion operator sends the value stored in variable **totalCalories** to **cout**.

Line 13 has two insertion operators: the first sends a string to **cout** and the second sends a special feature called a *manipulator* to the output stream. **endl** is a manipulator that tells the output stream to go to a new line by writing the end-of-line marker. Thus, anything written after this statement begins on the next line of output. Line 14 sends another string and the end-of-line manipulator to **cout**.

We said that the executable part of the program is **int** function **main**. Because **main** is an **int** function, it must return an integer value. Line 15 says to return the value zero. By convention, **main** returns zero when the program executes with no errors. Line 16 ends function **main** and thus the program. The output from this program is:

```
There were 306 calories in my lunch yesterday.
What is for lunch today?
```

Data Types

A data type is a set of values and a set of operations on these values. In the preceding program, we used the data type identifier **int**. In the discussion we called **totalCalories** (declared as type **int**) an integer variable. In C++ there are four integral types that can be used to refer to an integer value (whole numbers with no fractional parts). These types are **char**, **short**, **int**, and **long** and are intended to represent integers of different sizes. Although the actual number of bits used to represent each of these types varies from one computer to another, the number of digits that can be represented increases from **char** (the smallest) to **long** (the largest). The set of values for each of these integral data types is the range of numbers from the smallest value that can be represented through the largest value that can be represented. The operations on these values are the standard arithmetic operations allowed on integer values.

float, double, and **long double** are data type identifiers that refer to floating point numbers; that is, numbers with a whole and a fractional part. Again, the set of values is defined by the range of the minimum value through the maximum value that can be represented. The operations are the standard arithmetic operators allowed on decimal values.

In addition to the standard arithmetic operators, C++ provides an *increment* operator and a *decrement* operator. The increment operator **++** adds one to its operand; the decrement operator **--** subtracts one from its operand.

Data type **char**, the smallest integral data type, has an additional use: to describe one alphanumeric character. Each machine has a character set made up of all the alphanumeric characters that can be represented. If we need to represent a character in a program, we enclose it in single quotes. The following are seven alphanumeric characters available in all character sets.

```
'A'   'a'   '0'   ' '   '*'   '$'   '9'
```

Although arithmetic operations are defined on alphanumeric characters because they are type **char** (an integral type), such operations would not make any sense to us at this point. However, there is a collating sequence defined on each character set, so we can ask if one character comes before another character. Fortunately, the uppercase letters, the lowercase letters, and the digits are in order in all character sets. The relationship between these groups varies, however. We discuss manipulating **char** data in Chapter 5.

Operator Symbols

Here is a table of the C++ equivalent of the standard arithmetic operators and the other operators defined in this chapter.

Operator   Meaning

+	Unary plus
–	Unary minus
+	Addition
–	Subtraction
*	Multiplication
/	Floating point operands: floating point result Integer operands: quotient Mixed operands: floating point result
%	Modulus (remainder from integer division, operands must be integral)
++	Increment by one; can be prefix or postfix
– –	Decrement by one; can be prefix or postfix
=	Assignment; evaluate expression on right and store in the variable named on the left
<<	Insertion; insert the characters (if a string) or the value (if a variable or constant) into the output stream named on the left of the first insertion operator

Words and Symbols with Special Meanings

Certain words have predefined meanings within the C++ language; these are called *reserved words*. For example, the names of data types are reserved words. In program **Lunch**, there are three reserved words: **const, int**, and **return**. **const** directs the compiler to set up a constant; **int** is a data type identifier for an integral value; and **return** signals the end of the function and usually sends back a value.

A hash mark followed by the word **include** and a file name is an instruction to the C++ preprocessor. It directs the preprocessor to insert the contents of the file into the program at that point.

Two slashes (**/ /**) signal that the characters from that point to the end of the line are comments and are to be ignored by the compiler. Characters written between **/ *** and ***** / are also comments and ignored by the compiler.

The statements that define constants (lines 4 through 7) and variables (line 10) are called *declarations*. A C++ program is made up of declarations and one or more function definitions. A function definition is made up of a heading and a block. Line 8 is the function heading. The block begins with the left brace on line 9 and ends with the right brace on line 16.

Semicolons terminate statements in the C++ language. There are ten semicolons in program **Lunch**, so there are ten statements in the program: four statements in the declaration section and six statements in the block of function **main**.

Chapter 2: Prelab Assignment

Name _____   **Date** _____

Section _____

Examine the following program and answer Exercises 1 through 5.

```
// Program Schedule prints a daily schedule with the
// amount of time spent on each task.

#include <iostream.h>

const int DRESS = 45;
const int EAT   = 30;
const int DRIVE = 30;
const int CLASS = 60;

int main()
{
    int  totalMinutes;

    totalMinutes = DRESS + 3*EAT + 2*DRIVE + 4*CLASS;
    cout << "You spend " << totalMinutes / 60
         << " hours and "  << totalMinutes % 60
         << " minutes a day on scheduled activities."
         << endl;
    return 0;
}
```

Exercise 1: What is written by program **Schedule**?

Exercise 2: List the identifiers that are defined in progam **Schedule**.

Exercise 3: Which of these identifiers are named constants?

Exercise 4: List the literal constants.

Exercise 5: List the identifiers that are defined in **<iostream.h>**.

Lesson 2-1: Check Prelab Exercises

Name _____   **Date** _____

Section _____

Exercise 1:   Run program **Schedule** to check your answer to Prelab Exercise 1. Was your answer completely correct? If it was not, explain where you made your mistake.

Exercise 2:   The identifiers are **totalMinutes**, **DRESS**, **EAT**, **DRIVE**, and **CLASS**.

Exercise 3:   The named constants are **DRESS**, **EAT**, **DRIVE**, and **CLASS**.

Exercise 4:   **0, 2, 3, 4, 30, 45, 60** are the numeric literal constants. "**You spend** ", "**hours and** ", and " **minutes a day on scheduled activities.**" are string literals.

Exercise 5:   **cout** and **endl** are defined in **<iostream.h>**.

Lesson 2-2: Components of a Program

Name _____   **Date** _____

Section _____

This lesson uses program **Convert**. Compile and rerun the program after each modification.

```
// Program Convert takes a value in inches and converts it
// to feet and inches.

#_____
_____ int INCHES = 136;

_____ _____ ()
{
    _____ << INCHES << " inches is " << INCHES ___ 12
             << " feet and " << INCHES ___ 12
             << " inches.";
        _____ ;
}
```

Exercise 1:   Program **Convert** changes inches to feet and inches. However, it is missing certain identifiers, reserved words, and operators that are necessary for it to compile. Replace each blank with the appropriate identifier, reserved word, or operator and run the program. Record the output.

Exercise 2:   Replace the named constant with a value of your choice that is an even multiple of 12. Run the program and record the value and the output.

Exercise 3:   Replace the named constant with a value of your choice that is not an even multiple of 12. Run the program and record the value and the output.

Exercise 4:   The output from the last several runs may all run together on a line. If this happens, you can correct it by putting an end-of-line marker as the last item sent to the output stream. Make this change and rerun your program twice. Record any change you observe.

Lesson 2-3: Sending Information to the Output Stream

Name _____   **Date** _____

Section _____

Lesson 2-3 focuses on constructing output statements. Program **Shell** is the outline of a program. Use this shell for Exercises 1 through 3.

```
// Program Shell

#include <iostream.h>

int main ()
{

    return 0;

}
```

Exercise 1:   Write a program to print the following information single spaced on the screen. Use literal constants in the output statements themselves for each of the data items to be written on the screen. Run your program to verify that the output is as specified.

a.   your name (last name, comma, first name)
b.   today's date (month:day:year)

Exercise 2:   Change your program so that there is a space between the two lines of output.

Exercise 3:   Change your program so that your first name is printed followed by your last name with a blank in between.

Lesson 2-4: Working with Numeric Expressions

Name _____   **Date** _____

Section _____

Lesson 2-4 focuses on constructing numeric expressions. Program **Shell2** is the outline of a program. Use this shell for Exercises 1 through 4.

```
// Program Shell2
#include <iostream.h>

const int  VALUE = 5;

int main ()
{
    int  intValue;

    cout << intValue;
    return 0;
}
```

Exercise 1:   Add two assignment statements to program **Shell2**: one that stores **VALUE** into **intValue** and one that increments **intValue** by 1 using the plus operator (+). Run your program and record the results.

Exercise 2:   Replace the plus operator in the program in Exercise 1 with the double plus operator and rerun your program. Are the results the same?

Exercise 3:   Change the program in Exercise 2 so that it decrements **intValue** rather than incrementing it. You may use either the negative operator or the double negative operator. Record your results.

Exercise 4:   Add the statements necessary to print the result of applying the division operator and the modulus operator to **intValue**. Show integer division by 2, integer remainder of division by 2, and floating point division by 2.0. Send each of these values to the output stream with an accompanying comment. Record your results.

Lesson 2-5: Debugging

Name _____   **Date** _____

Section _____

Exercise 1: Program **Ounces** converts a value in ounces to cups, quarts, and gallons. Compile and run this program. Be forewarned: a few bugs are lurking in the code. The elements (definitions, statements, and symbols) of the program are numbered on the left in comments. Fill in the chart to show the syntactic errors and what you did to correct them. (This time you do not get a printed copy; you must use only the file.)

#	OK	Error	Correction (if error)
1			
2			
3			
4			
5			
6			
7			
8			
9			
10			
11			
12			
13			
14			
15			

Exercise 2:   Now that program **Ounces** compiles and runs, you must check the output for logic errors. List the logic errors that you find and indicate what you did to correct them. Run your corrected program.

Exercise 3:   Compare your final program in Exercise 2 with program **Ounces2.cpp**. Did you catch all the logic errors? Explain.

Postlab Activities

Exercise 1:   Write a program to print out the following lines from Dr. Seuss's *Horton Hatches the Egg*.[1]

I meant what I said
and I said what I meant
An elephant's faithful
one hundred percent

Put a border of asterisks around the entire quotation (all four sides). Each line of the quotation should be sent to the output stream in the same statement.

Exercise 2:   Write a program that produces a cover sheet for your laboratory assignments. It should have the chapter number, the lessons that have been assigned, your instructor's name, your name, the date, and any other information that your instructor has requested.

Exercise 3:   Write a program that converts a constant, **PENNIES**, to dollars and cents. Set the constant **PENNIES** to a value that is evenly divisible by 100, run your program, and show your output. Change the constant to a value that is not evenly divisible by 100, run your program, and show your output. Be sure to label your output appropriately.

Exercise 4:   Set **PENNIES** to zero and rerun your program. Describe what happens.

---

[1] Dr. Seuss, *Horton Hatches the Egg* (New York: Random House, 1940).

3

Arithmetic Expressions, Function Calls, and Output

OBJECTIVES

- To be able to write simple arithmetic expressions to accomplish a specified task.
- To be able to convert a value from one numeric type to another numeric type.
- To be able to write output statements that format data in specified ways.
- To be able to use value-returning library functions.
- To be able to debug a program with syntax errors.
- To be able to debug a program with logic errors.

Chapter 3: Assignment Cover Sheet

Name _____   **Date** _____

Section _____

Fill in the following table showing which exercises have been assigned for each lesson and check whether you are to submit (1) lab sheets, (2) listings of output files, and (3) listings of programs. Your instructor or TA can use the Completed column for grading purposes.

Activities	Assigned: Check or list exercise numbers	Submit (1)	(2)	(3)	Completed
Prelab					
Review					
Prelab Assignment					
Inlab					
Lesson 3-1: Check Prelab Exercises					
Lesson 3-2: Arithmetic Operations					
Lesson 3-3: Formatting Output					
Lesson 3-4: Value-Returning Functions					
Lesson 3-5: Debugging					
Postlab					

Prelab Activities

Review

In Chapter 2, we showed how identifiers are constructed and said they name data types, data objects, and actions. We used the following two statements.

```
const  int BREAD = 63;
int   totalCalories;
```

The first named a constant, **BREAD**, and stored the value **63** into it. The second named a variable **totalCalories**, into which a value of type **int** can be stored.

We also said that variables and constants of integral and floating point types can be combined into expressions using arithmetic operators. The operations between constants or variables of these types are addition (**+**), subtraction (**−**), multiplication (*****), and division (**/**). If the operands of the division operation are integral, the result is the integral quotient; if the operands are floating point types, the result is a floating point type with the division carried out to as many decimal places as the type allows. There is an additional operator for integral types, the modulus operator (**%**). This operator returns the remainder from integer division.

Precedence Rules

The precedence rules of arithmetic apply to arithmetic expressions in a program. That is, the order of execution of an expression that contains more than one operation is determined by the precedence rules of arithmetic. These rules state the parentheses have the highest precedence, multiplication, division, and modulus have the next highest precedence, and addition and subtraction have the lowest. Because parentheses have the highest precedence, they can be used to change the order in which operations are executed.

Converting Numeric Types

If an integral and a floating point variable or constant are mixed in an operation, the integral value is changed temporarily to its equivalent floating point representation before the operation is executed. This automatic conversion of an integral value to a floating point value is called *type coercion*. Type coercion also occurs when a floating point value is assigned to an integral variable. Coercion from an integer to a floating point is exact. Although the two values are represented differently in memory, both representations are exact. However, when a floating point value is coerced into an integral value, loss of information occurs unless the floating point value is a whole number. That is, 1.0 can be coerced into 1, but what about 1.5? Is it coerced into 1 or 2? In C++ when a floating point value is coerced into an integral value, the floating point value is truncated. Thus, the floating point value 1.5 is coerced into 1.

Type changes can be made explicit by placing the value to be changed in parentheses and placing the name of the new type before it. That is,

```
intValue = 10.66;
```

and

```
intValue = int(10.66);
```

produce the same results. The first is implicit; the second is explicit. Explicit type changing is called *type casting* or *type conversion,* as opposed to implicit type changing, which is called *type coercion.* Explicit type conversion is more self-documenting and is therefore better style.

Value-Returning Functions

Every C++ program must have an **int** function **main** that forms the main program. That is, **main** is the name of the function that calculates what we want to have done (the action). We can also use functions to do specific tasks within our function **main**. When we want the task to be executed, we use the function name in an expression.

C++ provides a wealth of preprogrammed functions to use. These functions are collected into files and made available through the **#include** directive. For example the **<math.h>** file includes such useful functions as **cos** and **sin** that calculate the cosine and sine of a variable in radians, **pow** that raises a value to a power, and **sqrt** that takes the square root of a floating point value. These functions are all value-returning functions and are executed by using their names in an expression. Here is an example.

```
#include <math.h>
#include <iostream.h>

cout  << pow(3.0, 4.0)  << sqrt(81.0)  << endl;
```

pow(3.0,   4.0) returns the value **81.0**; this value is written on the screen. **sqrt(81.0)** returns the value **9.0**, which is written on the screen. The values in the parentheses to the right of the function names are called *parameters* to the function. Parameters are the values that the functions use as input. In the case of **pow**, the first value is the one to be taken to a power and the second is the power. The parameter to **sqrt** is the value for which the square root is calculated.

You can write your own value-returning functions as well. Look at the following program.

```
// Program Miles prints miles in kilometers.

#include <iostream.h>

float  kilometers(int);

int main ()
{
    cout  << "One mile is " << kilometers(1)
          << " kilometers."  << endl;
    cout  << "Ten miles is " << kilometers(10)
          << " kilometers."  << endl;
```

```
    cout   << "One hundred miles is  << kilometers(100)
           << " kilometers."  << endl;
    return 0;
}

float  kilometers(int miles)
{
    const  KILO = 1.609;
    return KILO * float(miles);
}
```

Function **kilometers** is a user-defined value-returning function. It takes one **int** parameter that represents miles and returns that value expressed in kilometers. Function **kilometers** is invoked by using its name in an output statement. That is, the value returned from the function is sent to the output stream. We discuss how to write value-return functions in depth in Chapter 8.

Void Functions

C++ provides another type of function called a *void function*. A void function is the name of an action that does not return a single value. Value-returning functions like **main** have the data type of the value being returned before the name of the function (**int main**, for example). Void functions have the word **void** before the name of the function to indicate that they are not returning a single value. Rather than being used in an expression, void functions are used as statements in the body of other functions. We discuss void functions at great length in Chapter 7.

Output Formatting

We can control the vertical spacing of lines on the screen (or page) by using the **endl** manipulator described in Chapter 2. **endl** inserts an end-of-line character and forces the next output to begin on the next line. We can use successive **endl**'s to create blank lines. For example, the first of the following two statements creates three blank lines and writes the message "Happy New Year" on the fourth line.

```
cout  << endl  << endl  << endl  << "Happy New Year";
cout  << "!"
```

Where does the exclamation point go? Immediately following the *r* in *Year*. Characters are streamed to **cout** without line breaks unless **endl** is inserted into the stream.

We can put blanks in a line by including them within the strings that we are writing. For example, we can put extra blanks before and after the message as follows:

```
cout  << endl  << endl  << endl  <<    "  Happy New Year  ";
```

Note that we also added extra blanks before the double quote. These extra blanks have no effect on the output whatsoever. Only blanks within the strings are sent to **cout**.

When outputting numbers, it is useful to be able to state how many column positions the number should occupy. We can do this with another manipulator called **setw**. This manipulator (available in file **<iomanip.h>**) states how many columns the following data value is to occupy. For example,

```
intValue = 5;
cout  << setw(4)  << intValue;
```

prints the contents of **intValue** right-justified in four columns. The parameter to **setw** is an integer expression called the *fieldwidth*. If the fieldwidth is not large enough to contain the digits in the number, it is automatically expanded to the appropriate size. You specify the fieldwidth for floating point numbers the same way (don't forget to include the decimal point in your fieldwidth count). You can set the number of decimal places to be shown by the manipulator **setprecision** (also in file **<iomanip.h>**). For example,

```
realValue = 3.14159;
cout << setprecision(3) << realValue;
```

prints **3.142**. Note that the last digit printed has been rounded. **setprecision(3)** remains in effect until the next **setprecision** is used, but **setw** applies only to the value immediately following.

Because the default spacing for floating point outut may be different on different systems, you can ensure that your floating point output looks the same by including the following two statements in your program before sending any floating point values to the output stream. Don't try to figure out what these statements mean now; just use them.

```
cout.setf(ios::fixed, ios::floatfield);
cout.setf(ios::showpoint);
```

Chapter 3: Prelab Assignment

Name _____   **Date** _____

Section _____

Examine the following program carefully and answer the question in Exercise 1.

```
// Program Pres demonstrates the precedence of operators.

#include <iostream.h>

int main ()
{
    cout.setf(ios::fixed, ios::floatfield);
    cout.setf(ios::showpoint);
    cout << 4 + 3 * 5  << endl;
    cout << (4 + 3) * 5  <<endl;
    cout << 4 * 5 % 3 + 2  << endl;
    cout << (4 * (5 / 3) + 2)  << endl;
    return 0;
}
```

Exercise 1:   Show what is written by each of the output statements.

Examine the following program carefully and then answer the questions in Exercises 2 and 3.

```
// Program Format demonstrates the use of fieldwidth
// specifications.

#include <iostream.h>
#include <iomanip.h>

const int   INT_NUMBER = 1066;
const float  FLT_NUMBER = 3.14159;

main ()
{
    float   fltValue;
    int     intValue;
```

```
    cout.setf(ios::fixed, ios::floatfield);
    cout.setf(ios::showpoint);

    intValue = INT_NUMBER + FLT_NUMBER;
    fltValue = float(INT_NUMBER) + FLT_NUMBER;
    cout << INT_NUMBER  << endl;
    cout << intValue  << endl;
    cout << setw(10)  << intValue;
    cout << setw(10)  << intValue  << intValue /10  << endl;
    cout << setw(10)  << fltValue  << endl;
    cout << setprecision(10)  << fltValue  << endl
    cout << setw(10)  << setprecision(3)  << fltValue
        << endl;
    cout << fltValue << endl;
    cout << intValue  << setw(3)  << intValue  << setw(7)
        << intValue
        << endl;
    return 0;
}
```

Exercise 2:   Show what is written by each of the output statements.

Exercise 3:   Circle a statement that contains type conversion, and underline a statement that contains type coercion.

Lesson 3-1: Check Prelab Exercises

Name _____   **Date** _____

Section _____

Exercise 1:   Run program **Pres** to check your answers. Were your answers completely correct? If they were not, explain what was wrong.

Exercise 2:   Run program **Format** to check your answers Were your answers completely correct? If they were not, explain what was wrong.

Exercise 3:

```
 intValue = INT_NUMBER + FLT_NUMBER;

 fltValue = float(INT_NUMBER) + FLT_NUMBER;
```

Lesson 3-2: Arithmetic Operations

Name _____   **Date** _____

Section _____

Use program **Convert** for Exercises 1 through 5. Study this program carefully.
It converts a temperature from Fahrenheit to Celsius and a temperature from
Celsius to Fahrenheit.

```
// Program Convert converts a temperature in Fahrenheit to
// Celsius and a temperature in Celsius to Fahrenheit.

#include <iostream.h>

const int TEMP_IN_F = 32;
const int TEMP_IN_C = 0;

int main ()
{
    int fToC; // Place to store Celsius answer
    int cToF; // Place to store the Fahrenheit answer

    cToF = (9 * TEMP_IN_C / 5) + 32;
    fToC = 5 * (TEMP_IN_F - 32) / 9;
    cout << TEMP_IN_F  << " in Fahrenheit is "  << fToC
         << " in Celsius. "  << endl;
    return 0;
}
```

Exercise 1:   Compile and run program **Convert**. What value is written out for
fToC?

Exercise 2:   Notice that the program computes two values (**cToF** and **fToC**) but
only one value is written on the screen. Insert a second output statement that prints
the value of **cToF** immediately below the value of **fToC**. Compile and run the
program. (If you have trouble compiling your program, check to be sure that you
have a semicolon after the second output statement.)

What was the output from your additional statement?

Exercise 3:   Change the values for constants **TEMP_IN_F** and **TEMP_IN_C** to the following values and compile and rerun the program after each change. Record the values for **fToC** and **cToF** for each set of values.

TEMP_IN_F	TEMP_IN_C	fToC	cToF
a. 212	100	_____	_____
b. 100	50	_____	_____
c. 122	37	_____	_____
d. _____	_____	_____	_____

(You choose.)

Exercise 4:   Examine the output from b and c. There seems to be an inconsistency. Describe the inconsistency and make a hypothesis to explain it.

Exercise 5:   Change the integer constants and variables to type **float** and rerun the program with the same data you used in parts b and c in Exercise 3. Do the results confirm your hypothesis? Explain.

Exercise 6:   Remove the parentheses from both assignment statements and rerun the program using the values that you used in part c in Exercise 3.

What values are printed?   **fToC** _____ **cToF** _____

These are not the same values that were printed in Exercise 5. Why?

Lesson 3-3: Formatting Output

Name _____ **Date** _____

Section _____

Use the following program shell for Exercises 1 through 4.

```
// Program Numbers sends numbers to the output stream in
// specified formats.

#include <iostream.h>
#include <iomanip.h>

int main ()
{
    cout.setf(ios::fixed, ios::floatfield);
    cout.setf(ios::showpoint);

    return 0;
}
```

Exercise 1: Write a program to print the following numbers right-justified in a column on the screen. Make the values named constants.

```
1066   1492   512   1   -23
```

Exercise 2: Add two statements to your program. Calculate the floating point result from dividing the sum of the first two values by the sum of the last three values and store it in **answer**. The second statement should write the contents of **answer** on the screen to four decimal places. (Do not forget to declare **answer**.)

The answer is _____.

Exercise 3: Write the following numbers right-justified in a column on the screen. Each of the data values should be written in formatted floating point notation with two decimal places. Use fieldwidth specifications rather than listing the numbers in your program with the proper formatting. You may use either literal constants or named constants.

```
23.62   46.0   43.4443   100.1   98.98
```

Exercise 4: Add two statements to your program for Exercise 3. The first statement should calculate the sum of the numbers and store the result in variable **sum**. The second statement should write **sum** on the screen, properly labeled.

The sum of the numbers is _____.

Use the following program shell for Exercises 5 and 6.

```
// Program Center sends strings to the output stream in
// specified formats.

#include <iostream.h>
#include <iomanip.h>

int main ()
{

    return 0;
}
```

Exercise 5: Add the statements necessary to print the following strings centered in fields of 20 characters all on one line: "Good Morning", "Sarah", and "Sunshine!". Do not use manipulators. Compile and run your program; show your output.

Exercise 6: Repeat Exercise 5 using manipulators to help center your strings. Compile and run your program. Your output should be the same.

Exercise 7: Change the program in Exercise 6 so that the three strings print on three separate lines with a blank line in between each string.

Lesson 3-4: Value-Returning Functions

Name _____ **Date** _____

Section _____

Use the following shell for Exercises 1 and 2.

```
// Program Function demonstrates the use of library and
// user-defined functions.

#include <iostream.h>
#include <math.h>

float answer(float, float, float);

int main ()
{
    cout.setf(ios::fixed, ios::floatfield);
    cout.setf(ios::showpoint);

    cout  << answer(_____, _____, _____);
    return 0;
}

float answer(float one, float two, float three)
{
    return ((- two + sqrt(pow(two, _____)
        - (4.0 * one * three))) / (2.0 * one));
}
```

Exercise 1: Fill in the blanks in function **answer** such that the value stored in parameter **two** is taken to the second power. Fill in the blanks in function **main** so that function **answer** is invoked with **10.0** as the first parameter, **20.0** as the second parameter, and **5.0** as the third parameter. What is printed?

Exercise 2: Change the program in Exercise 1 so that function **answer** is invoked with **5.0** as the first parameter, **20.0** as the second parameter, and **10.0** as the third parameter. What is printed?

Exercise 3:   Change the program in Exercise 1 so that function **answer** is invoked with **5.0** as the first parameter, **10.0** as the second parameter, and **20.0** as the third parameter . What happens? Explain why.

Exercise 4:   Do you know the name of the formula that function **answer** is calculating?

Lesson 3-5: Debugging

Name _____   **Date** _____

Section _____

Exercise 1:   Program **Typos** contains syntax errors.   Correct the program, describe the errors, and show what is printed.

List the syntax errors.

Show what is printed.

Exercise 2:   The output from program **Typos** looks strange! Clearly, there are logic bugs lurking in the code. Find and correct these errors.

List the logic errors.

Show what is printed.

Postlab Activities

Exercise 1:   Write a program that prints the hundreds digit in a series of integer constants.   For example, if constants **ONE** and **TWO** are **1456** and **254** respectively, your program should print 4 and 2.   You may choose the integers yourself.   Your output should include the original number followed by the digit in the hundreds position.   Label your output appropriately.

Exercise 2:   Write a program that prints the number 1349.9431 with three decimal places, with two decimal places, and with one decimal place.

Exercise 3:   Write a program that prints each of the following values in two columns: 1234, 45, 7, 87, 99999.   The first column is left-justified and the second column is right-justified.

4

Program Input and the Software Design Process

OBJECTIVES

- To be able to determine how data must be input in order for a program to run correctly.
- To be able to examine the input data to a program and the results and deduce the form of the input statements.
- To be able to create a data file.
- To be able to take a program that extracts data from the keyboard and change it to extract data from a file.
- To be able to construct input and output statements that take their input from a file and send their output to a file.
- To be able to take a problem statement and construct a top-down design for the problem, code the design in C++, and run the program.
- To be able to debug a program that inputs data from the keyboard and a file.

Chapter 4: Assignment Cover Sheet

Name _____   **Date** _____

Section _____

Fill in the following table showing which exercises have been assigned for each lesson and check what you are to submit: (1) lab sheets, (2) listings of output files, and/or (3) listings of programs. Your instructor or TA can use the Completed column for grading purposes.

Activities	Assigned: Check or list exercise numbers	Submit (1) (2) (3)			Completed
Prelab					
Review					
Prelab Assignment					
Inlab					
Lesson 4-1: Check Prelab Exercises					
Lesson 4-2: Input Statement and Data Consistency					
Lesson 4-3: Input and Output with Files					
Lesson 4-4: Top-Down Programming					
Lesson 4-5: Debugging					
Postlab					

Prelab Activities

Review

Chapter 4 contains a great deal of new material: reading data from the keyboard, reading data from a file, creating a file, and learning a methodology for writing solutions to problems. Mastering these concepts here, before you go on to the next chapter, will save you much grief later. We promise!

Input Streams

There are four ways that a value can be stored in a place in memory. You have already seen two methods in Chapter 2: a value can be stored by the compiler as the result of a constant declaration, or it can be stored as the result of an assignment statement. Chapter 4 introduces a third way: a value can be read into the program while the program is being executed. (We show you the fourth way in Chapter 8.)

In Chapter 2, we said that **cout** was an output stream. Characters inserted into this stream appear on the screen. That is, the insertion operator (**<<**) inserts strings and values from within the program into the output stream that appears on the screen. In an analogous fashion, we can extract data values from an input stream prepared at the keyboard and store them in variables in our program. **cin** is the input stream from the keyboard, and **>>** is the extraction operator.

cout is of type **ostream**, and **cin** is of type **istream**. **istream**, **ostream**, **cin**, and **cout** are defined in file **<iostream.h>** and accessed by using the preprocessor directive **#include <iostream.h>**. Whereas statements using **cout** and the insertion operator (**<<**) place values in the output stream, statements using **cin** and the extraction operator (**>>**) take values from the input stream and place them in variables in the program.

The data type of the place in which a value is stored determines how the value is read. If you are reading numeric data, whitespace characters are skipped and an inappropriate character ends the input of the number. Whitespace characters are blanks and certain nonprintable characters like end-of-line. If you are reading data into a variable of type **char**, whitespace characters are skipped and one character is read.

There are as many values read from the input stream as there are extraction operator/place name pairs to the right of **cin**. The values are extracted one at a time from the input stream and stored in the places named in order. The first value read goes into the first place listed, the second value read goes into the second place listed, etc. The values read must be of the same type as the places in which they are to be stored with the exception that a floating point value can be keyed as an integral value without a decimal point. The decimal point is automatically inserted in this case.

Because there are times when you do not want to skip whitespace before inputting a character, the **istream** data type provides a function to input the next character in the stream regardless of what it is. The function is named **get** and is applied as shown.

```
cin.get(character);
```

The next character in the input stream is returned in **char** variable **character**. If the previous input was a numeric value, **character** contains whatever inappropriate character ended the inputting of the value.

There are also times when you want to skip the rest of the values on a line and go to the beginning of the next line. There is a function called **ignore** defined in file **<iostream.h>** that allows you to do this. It has two parameters. The first is an **int** expression and the second is a character. This function skips the number of characters specified in the first parameter or all the characters up to and including the character specified in the second parameter, whichever comes first. For example,

```
cin.ignore(80, '\n');
```

skips 80 characters or skips to the beginning of the next line depending on whether a newline character is encountered before 80 characters are skipped (read and discarded).

Keyboard Input Prompts

If your input is coming from the keyboard, someone is sitting at the keyboard waiting to enter the values at the proper time. The program should prompt the person to enter the values when it is ready to read them. For example, if the program needs the number of gallons of paint purchased and the price of a gallon, the person at the keyboard should be prompted with a message string something like this:

"Enter the number of gallons of paint (whole number) followed by the cost of a gallon (dollars and cents). Press return."

The statement that reads in the values follows the statement that writes the prompting message to the screen.

Files

If you want to prepare the input data ahead of time and store it on a file, or store output data on a file to use later, you may direct the program to read the data from a file or write data to a file by doing the following things:

1. Request the preprocessor to include file **<fstream.h>** as well as file **<iostream.h>**. The former contains the declarations for defining input and output streams other than **cin** and **cout**.
2. Declare an input stream to be of type **ifstream** or an output stream to be of type **ofstream** (or both).
3. Prepare the streams for use by using the function named **open** provided in file **<fstream.h>**. The parameter for function **open** is the external name of the file. The external name is the name under which the file is stored on the disk.
4. Put the file name to the left of the insertion or extraction operator.

Here is an example program that reads four floating point data values from a file and writes them to another file in reverse order.

```
// Program IODemo demonstrates how to use files.

#include <iostream.h>
#include <fstream.h>

int main()
{
    float val1, val2, val3, val4;      // declares 4 variables
    ifstream inData;                   // declares input stream
    ofstream outData;                  // declares output stream

    outData.setf(ios::fixed, ios::floatfield);
    outData.setf(ios::showpoint);

    inData.open("Data.In");
    // binds program variable inData to file "Data.In"
    outData.open("Data.Out");
    // binds program variable outData to file "Data.Out"

    inData  >> val1 >> val2 >> val3
            >> val4;                           // inputs 4 values
    outData  << val4  << endl;
    outData  << val3  << endl;
    outData  << val2  << endl;
    outData  << val1  << endl;                 // outputs 4 values
    return 0;
}
```

Each file in your program has both an internal name and an external name. The internal name is what you call it in your program; the external name is the name the operating system knows it by. Somehow these two names must be associated with one another. This association is called *binding* and is done in function **open**. Notice that **inData** and **outData** are identifiers declared in your program; "**Data.In**" and "**Data.Out**" are character strings. **Data.In** is the name that was used when the input data file was created; **Data.Out** is the name of the file where the answers are stored.

Input Failure

The key to reading data in correctly (from either the keyboard or a file) is to make sure that the order and the form in which the data are keyed are consistent with the order and type of the identifiers on the input stream extraction statement. If your data and your input statements are not consistent, your program does not crash or give an error message, but every subsequent stream operation is ignored. An error causes the stream to enter the fail state, and any further references to a stream in the fail state are ignored. If you misspell the name of the file that is the parameter to function **open** (**In.dat** instead of **Data.In**, for example), the stream enters the fail state. Your program continues to operate, but all references to **inData** are ignored.

Creating a Data File

If you are using an integrated environment, such as Turbo C++, in which an editor is provided for you to write your program, you may use the same editor to create a data file. That is, instead of writing a C++ program, you just key in the data you want the program to read.

If you are using a general-purpose word processor to create your programs, such as Word or WordPerfect, you need to save both your programs and your data files in text mode. General-purpose word processors have formatting information at the beginning of the file that you cannot see on the screen. This information must be removed from the file before the compiler can compile the program or the program can read data correctly. If the program file has formatting information, the compiler cannot compile the program and alerts you that there is a problem. If the data file has formatting information, you simply get the wrong answer.

Top-Down Design

Writing a top-down design is like writing an outline for a paper. The main subheadings are listed, and then each subhead is further divided until no more subheadings are needed. However, in a top-down design the main subheadings are the tasks that must be accomplished for the problem to be solved. Each task (subheading) is further divided into the subtasks that must be accomplished before it is complete. Each subtask is further divided into the tasks necessary to complete its job. A task (or subtask) needs no further division when it becomes a concrete step, that is, when the task (or subtask) can be directly coded into a C++ statement.

Object-Oriented Design

Object-oriented design is a methodology developed for large-scale programming projects. The solution to a problem using this technique is expressed in terms of self-contained entities composed of both data and operations on the data. The entities are called *objects*. Top-down design focuses on the tasks to be completed; object-oriented design focuses on the data objects that the tasks manipulate. We have much more to say about object-oriented design in Chapter 15.

Chapter 4: Prelab Assignment

Name _____   **Date** _____

Section _____

Exercise 1:   If file **Data.In** contains the values shown below, what does program **IODemo** write on file **Data.Out**?

```
5.5
6.6
7.7
8.8
```

Program **Frame**   is an interactive program that reads the dimensions of a print and calculates the amount of wood needed to make a frame for it. Examine it carefully and then complete Exercises 2 through 6.

```
// Program Frame prompts the user to input values representing
// the dimensions of a print.  The amount of wood needed for
// the frame is calculated and printed on the screen.

#include <iostream.h>

int main ()
{
    int  side;              // vertical dimension in inches
    int  top;               // horizontal dimension in inches
    int  inchesOfWood;      // inches of wood needed


    cout  << "Enter the vertical dimension of your print."
          << endl;
    cout  << "The dimension should be in whole inches. "
          << "Press return."  << endl;
    cin  >> side;

    cout  << "Enter the horizontal dimension of your print."
          << endl;
    cout  << "The dimension should be in whole inches. "
          << "Press return."  << endl;
    cin  >> top;

    inchesOfWood = top + top + side + side;
    cout << "You need "  << inchesOfWood
         <<" inches of wood."  << endl;
    return 0;
}
```

Exercise 2:   Program **Frame** prompts for and reads the vertical dimension of the print and then prompts for and reads the horizontal dimension of the print. How many lines of input does program **Frame** expect? Explain.

What happens if you key both values at the same time with a blank between them?

Exercise 3:   Hand-simulate program **Frame** with the following three sets of input values; record the value for **inchesOfWood**.

top	*side*	*inchesOfWood*
10	20	_____
13	5	_____
12	12	_____

Exercise 4:   If the program is reorganized so that the prompts are together before the first input statement, what happens under the following reads? (The prompts are unchanged and the user follows them.)

```
a. cin  >> side  >> top;
```

```
b. cin >> side;
   cin >> top;
```

Exercise 5:   What happens if you forget to put a space between the values for **side** and **top** in the input stream?

Exercise 6:   Program **Frame** is to be changed to read from file **data**. Mark all the changes on program **Frame**.

Lesson 4-1: Check Prelab Exercises

Name _____   **Date** _____

Section _____

Exercises1: Run program **IODemo** and check your answer. Did one of the answers surprise you? Can you explain it?

Exercises 2 and 3: Program **Frame** expects two lines of input. You can tell because there are two accesses to **cin** with an output statement in between. Now, run program **Frame** to check the rest of your answers to Exercises 2 and 3 and answer the following questions.

What happened when you keyed both numbers on the same line?

Were your hand simulations correct? If not, why not?

Exercise 4:   Programs **Frame2** and **Frame3** input the data as described in parts a and b of this exercise, respectively. Run programs **Frame2** and **Frame3** to check your answers. Were your answers completely correct? If not, explain where you made your mistake(s).

Exercise 5:   The program would input the combined numbers as one and store it in the first place named on the input statement (**side**). The program would then wait for the next value to be input.

Exercise 6:   Compare your answers with program **Frame4**, which has the changes requested. (You will use this program later.)

Lesson 4-2: Input Statement and Data Consistency

Name _____ **Date** _____

Section _____

Exercises 1 through 3 use program shell **ReadData**.

```
// Program ReadData is a test bed for you to try various
// combinations of input statements with different data
// configurations.
// It determines the cost of a sheet of glass given the
// dimensions and the price per square foot of glass.

#include <iostream.h>
#include <iomanip.h>

const  int inchesInSqFt = 144;

int main ()
{
    int   length;               // measured in inches
    int   width;                // measured in inches
    float  price;               // sold by square foot
    float  cost;
    cout.setf(ios::fixed, ios::floatfield);
    cout.setf(ios::showpoint);

    /*  TO BE FILLED IN. */

    cout  << "Width: "  << setw(5)  << width
          << " Length: "  << setw(5)  << length
          << " Price: "  << setw(6)  << setprecision(2)
          << price  << endl;
    cost = ((width * length) / inchesInSqFt) * price;
    cout  << "The cost of the glass is $"  << setw(6)
          << cost  << endl;
    return 0;
}
```

Exercise 1: Write the appropriate prompts and input statements. (The data values should be keyed on one line with blanks between them.) Run program **ReadData** with the following data values and show the result.

Length	*Width*	*Price*
36	24	25.25

Exercise 2: Key in the values for **length** and **width** in reverse order. What happens?

Exercise 3: Key in the values for **price** and **length** in reverse order. What happens? Is the situation in Exercise 3 different from the situation in Exercise 2?

Exercise 4: Program **InOut** reads values from the keyboard but does not give any prompts. Compile and execute this program. Enter the following values from the keyboard exactly as shown. *Do not look at the code.*

```
11   12   13   14
21   22
31   32
41
51
```

What values are printed?

a _____   b _____   c _____   d _____   e _____
f _____   g _____   h _____

This program contains five input-related statements. What must these statements be to give the results shown?

Exercise 5: The input values that have been read in the previous tasks have all been numeric. This exercise uses program **CharRead** to read character variables.

```
// Program CharRead prompts for and reads four characters
// from the keyboard and then prints them.

#include <iostream.h>
```

```
int main ()
{
    char   char1;
    char   char2;
    char   char3;
    char   char4;
    cout  << "Input four characters.  Press Return."  << endl;
    cin  >> char1  >> char2  >> char3  >> char4;
    cout  << char1  << char2  << char3  << char4;
    return 0;
}
```

Compile and run this program four times using the four sets of data values listed below. Key these values exactly as shown, including blanks.

Input Data   *What Is Printed*

```
abcd              _____
a  b  c  d        _____
      1b2c        _____
31  45            _____
```

Examine the results carefully. Do any of the results surprise you? (Remember that the extraction operator skips whitespace.)

Exercise 6:   This exercise also reads character data.

```
// Program Char2Rd prompts for and reads four characters
// from the keyboard and then prints them.

#include <iostream.h>

int main ()
{
    char   char1;
    char   char2;
    char   char3;
    char   char4;

    cout  << "Input four characters.  Press Return."  << endl;
    cin.get(char1);
    cin.get(char2);
    cin.get(char3);
    cin.get(char4);
    cout  << char1  << char2  << char3  << char4;
    return 0;
}
```

Compile and run this program four times using the four sets of data values listed below. Key these values exactly as shown, including blanks.

Input Data   *What Is Printed*

abcd   _____
a b c d   _____
        1b2c   _____
31 45   _____

Examine the results carefully. Do any of the results surprise you? (Remember that the function **get** does not skip whitespace.)

Lesson 4-3: Input and Output with Files

Name _____   **Date** _____

Section _____

Program **Frame4** gets its input from a file.

```
// Program Frame4 reads input values that represent the
// dimensions of a print from a file and calculates and
// prints the amount of wood needed for a frame.

#include <iostream.h>
#include <fstream.h>

int main ()
{
    ifstream  din;          // input stream
    int   side;             // vertical dimension in inches
    int   top;              // horizontal dimension in inches
    int   inchesOfWood;         // inches of wood needed

    din.open("Frame.In");
    din >> side >> top;
    cout << "Dimensions are " << top  << " and "
         << side << "."  << endl;
    inchesOfWood = top + top + side + side;
    cout << "You need "  << inchesOfWood
         <<" inches of wood."  << endl;
    return 0;
}
```

Exercise 1:   Create a data file on the same directory as program **Frame4**, and name it **Frame.In**. Make the values in the file consistent with the input statements. Run program **Frame4** and record the output below.

Exercise 2:   Why are there no prompts in program **Frame4**?

Exercise 3:   Change program **Frame4** so that the output goes to file **dout**; **dout**'s external name should be **Frame.Out**. You must do the following tasks:

- Declare **dout** to be of type **ofstream**.
- Invoke function **open** to associate the internal name and the external name.
- Send the output to stream **dout**.

Run your changed program. Show what was written on file **Frame.Out**.

Lesson 4-4: Top-Down Programming

Name _____   **Date** _____

Section _____

Exercise 1:   Write a top-down design for the following problem. Maggie, your Labrador puppy, has eaten a hole in the carpet in the dining room. How much will it cost to replace the carpet? The input to your program should be the dimensions of the room and the price of carpet. The output should be the cost written to the screen. Be sure to include prompts and echo-print the input along with the answer appropriately labeled.

Top-Down Design

Main   *Level 0*

```
┌──────────────────────────────────────────────────────────────────────────┐
│                                                                            │
│                                                                            │
│                                                                            │
│                                                                            │
│                                                                            │
│                                                                            │
│                                                                            │
└──────────────────────────────────────────────────────────────────────────┘
```

On a separate sheet of paper, fill in as many levels of detail as are needed to make each statement a concrete step.

Exercise 2:   Translate your top-down design into C++ code and run your program.

Show your input.

How much does it cost to recarpet the dining room?

Lesson 4-5: Debugging

Name _____   **Date** _____

Section _____

Exercise 1.   Program **FourVals** reads four **int** values from a file and writes them out with exactly one blank between them.   The program doesn't even compile! Correct the syntax errors and run the program. Show your output.

Exercise 2:   Now the program runs, but the output does not meet its specifications. Describe this logic error, correct it, and rerun the program. Show your output.

Exercise 3:   Run your program using file **Four2Val.in**.   Describe what happens.

Exercise 4:   Program **FourVals** makes an assumption about the data that is not stated in the problem.

What is this assumption?

How would you have to change program **FourVals** in order for it to work properly on file **Four2Val.in**?

Postlab Activities

Exercise 1:   The dining room looks so nice with the new carpet that you decide to repaint the room. Write a top-down design for a program that takes as input the dimensions of the room, the price of a gallon of paint, and the number of square feet that a gallon of paint covers. The output is what it will cost to paint the dining room. Echo your input and the answer on the screen, all appropriately labeled.

Exercise 2:   Translate your design into a C++ program and run it.

Exercise 3:   Write a top-down design for a program to calculate how many calories your lunch contained. The input is on three lines: a character, M(eat), V(eggie), D(esert), followed by the associated calories. Read and echo-print the input. Write out the total number of calories in your lunch.

Exercise 4:   Translate your design into a C++ program and run it.

5

Conditions, Logical Expressions, and Selection Control Structures

OBJECTIVES

- To be able to construct Boolean expressions to evaluate a given condition.
- To be able to construct If-Then statements to perform a specified task.
- To be able to construct If-Then-Else statements to perform a specified task.
- To be able to constructed nested If statements to perform a specified task.
- To be able to design and implement a test plan.
- To be able debug a program with a selection control structure.

Chapter 5: Assignment Cover Sheet

Name _____   **Date** _____

Section _____

Fill in the following table showing which exercises have been assigned for each lesson and check what you are to submit: (1) lab sheets, (2) listings of output files, and/or (3) listings of programs. Your instructor or TA can use the Completed column for grading purposes.

Activities	Assigned: Check or list exercise numbers	Submit (1)	(2)	(3)	Completed
Prelab					
Review					
Prelab Assignment					
Inlab					
Lesson 5-1: Check Prelab Exercises					
Lesson 5-2: Boolean Expressions					
Lesson 5-3: If-Then Statements					
Lesson 5-4: If-Then-Else Statements					
Lesson 5-5: Nested Logic					
Lesson 5-6: Test Plan					
Lesson 5-7: Debugging					
Postlab					

Prelab Activities

Review

The physical order of a program is the order in which the statements are *listed*. The logical order of a program is the order in which the statements are *executed*. In this chapter, you learn to ask questions in your program and change the order in which the statements are executed depending on the answer to your question.

Boolean Data Type

To ask a question in a program, you make a statement. If your statement is true, the answer to the question is yes. If your statement is not true, the answer to the question is no. You make these statements in the form of *Boolean expressions*. A Boolean expression asserts (states) that something is true. The assertion is evaluated and if it is true, the Boolean expression is true. If the assertion is not true, the Boolean expression is false.

Many programming languages have a data type Boolean with two values, *true* and *false*, but at present C++ does not. In C++, Boolean values are declared to be of type **int**; the value zero represents *false*, and any nonzero value represents *true*. However, we can simulate the Boolean data type in C++ with the following declarations:

```
typedef int Boolean;
const Boolean   TRUE = 1;
const Boolean   FALSE = 0;
```

typedef is a statement that allows us to give a new name to an existing type. Here we are saying that **Boolean** is a new name for **int**. When the program is compiled, the word **int** is substituted for the word **Boolean** throughout the program. We have defined two constants, **TRUE** and **FALSE**, which are synonyms for one and zero, respectively. Now we can write our program using **TRUE** and **FALSE** rather than the integers one and zero.

Why do we go to all this trouble when one and zero work just fine? Because Boolean values are logically different from integer values. C++ encodes true as nonzero and false as zero, but conceptually the logical values true and false are not numbers. By using the constants **TRUE** and **FALSE** we make that distinction clear—both to ourselves and to anyone reading the program. From now on, we assume these declarations are in all our programs that work with Boolean data.

Boolean Expressions

A Boolean expression can be a simple Boolean variable or constant or a more complex expression involving one or more of the relational operators. Relational operators take two operands and test for a relationship between them. Here are the relational operators and the C++ symbols that stand for them.

C++ Symbol	Relationship
==	Equal to
!=	Not equal to
>	Greater than
<	Less than
>=	Greater than or equal to
<=	Less than or equal to

For example, the Boolean expression

number1 < number2

is evaluated to **TRUE** if the value stored in **number1** is less than the value stored in **number2**, and evaluated to **FALSE** otherwise.

When a relational operator is applied between variables of type **char**, the assertion is in terms of where the two operands fall in the collating sequence of a particular character set. For example,

character1 < character2

is evaluated to true if the character stored in **character1** comes before the character stored in **character2** in the collating sequence of the machine on which the expression is being evaluated. Although the collating sequence varies among machines, you can think of it as being in alphabetic order. That is, *A* always comes before *B* and *a* always before *b*, but the relationship of *A* to *a* may vary.

We must be careful when applying the relational operators to floating point operands, particularly equal (==) and not equal (!=). Integer values can be represented exactly; floating point values with fractional parts often are not exact in the low-order decimal places. Therefore, you should compare floating point values for near equality. We have more to say about the problem of representing floating point values in Chapter 10. For now, *do not compare floating point numbers for equality.*

A simple Boolean expression is either a Boolean variable or constant or an expression involving the relational operators that evaluates to either true or false. These simple Boolean expressions can be combined using the logical operations defined on Boolean values. There are three Boolean operators: AND, OR, and NOT. Here is a table showing the meaning of these operators and the symbols that are used to represent them in C++.

C++ *Symbol* *Meaning*

C++ Symbol	Meaning
& &	AND is a binary Boolean operator. If both operands are true, the result is true. Otherwise, the result is false.
| |	OR is a binary Boolean operator. If at least one of the operands is true, the result is true. Otherwise, the result is false.
!	NOT is a unary Boolean operator. NOT changes the value of its operand: if the operand is true, the result is false; if the operand is false, the result is true.

If both relational operators and Boolean operators are combined in the same expression in C++, the Boolean operator NOT (!) has the highest precedence, the relational operators have next higher precedence, and the Boolean operators AND (&&) and OR (||) come last (in that order). Expressions in parentheses are always evaluated first.

For example, given the following expression (**stop** is a **Boolean** variable)

```
count <= 10 && sum >= limit || !stop
```

!stop is evaluated first, the expressions involving the relational operators are evaluated next, the **& &** is applied, and finally the **| |** is applied. C++ uses *short-circuit evaluation*. The evaluation is done in left-to-right order and halts as soon as the result is known. For example, in the above expression if both of the arithmetic expressions are true, the evaluation stops because the left operand to the OR operation (**| |** operator) is true. There is no reason to evaluate the rest of the expression: true**| |** anything is true.

The precedence of all the operators we have seen so far is summarized in the following table.

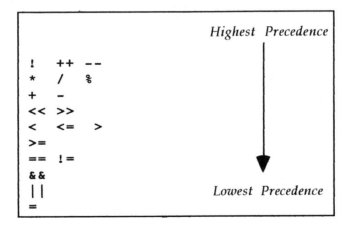

If-Then and If-Then-Else Statements

The If statement allows the programmer to change the logical order of a program; that is, make the order in which the statements are executed differ from the order in which they are listed in the program.

The If-Then statement uses a Boolean expression to determine whether to execute a statement or to skip it.

```
if (number < 0)
    number = 0;
sum = sum + number;
```

The expression **(number < 0)** is evaluated. If the result is true, the statement **number = 0** is executed. If the result is false, the statement is skipped. In either case, the next statement to be executed is **sum = sum + number**. The statement that is either executed or skipped may be a *block*. A block is a group of statements in the action part of the program enclosed in braces.

The If-Then-Else statement uses a Boolean expression to determine which of two statements to execute.

```
cout << "Today is a ";
if (temperature <= 32)
    cout << "cold ";
else
    cout << "nice ";
cout << "day." << end
```

The characters "**Today is a** " are sent to the output stream. The expression **(temperature <= 32)** is evaluated. If the result is true, the characters "**cold** " are sent to the output stream. If the result is false, the characters "**nice** " are sent to the output stream. In either case, the next statement to be executed sends the characters "**day.**" to the output stream. Either of the statements may be a block (compound statement) as shown in the following example.

```
if (temperature <= 32)
{
    cout << "Today is a cold day." << endl;
    cout << "Sitting by the fire is appropriate." << endl;

}
else
{
    cout << "Today is a nice day." << endl;
    cout << "How about taking a walk?" << endl;
}
```

There is a point of C++ syntax that you should note: there is never a semicolon after the right brace of a block (compound statement).

Nested Logic

An If-Then statement uses a Boolean expression to determine whether to execute a statement or skip it. An If-Then-Else statement uses a Boolean expression to determine which of two statements to execute. The statements to be executed or skipped can be simple statements or blocks (compound statements). There is no constraint on what the statements can be. This means that the statement to be skipped in an If-Then statement can be another If statement. In the If-Then-Else statement, either or both of the choices can be another If statement. An If statement within another If statement is called a *nested* If statement.

The following is an example of a nested If statement.

```
cout << "Today is a ";
if (temperature <= 32)
    cout << "cold ";
else if (temperature <= 85)
    cout << "nice ";
else
    cout << "hot ";
cout << "day." << endl;
```

Notice that the nested If statement does not have to ask if the temperature is greater than 32 because we do not execute the **else** branch of the first If statement if the temperature is less than or equal to 32.

In nested If statements, there may be confusion over which **if** an **else** belongs. In the absence of braces, the compiler pairs an **else** with the most recent **if** that doesn't have an **else**. You can override this pairing by enclosing the preceding **if** in braces to make the **then** clause of the outer If statement complete.

State of an I/O Stream

In Chapter 4, we said that all references to an input or output stream are ignored if the stream is in the fail state. The fail state is entered if the file that is the parameter to the **open** operation isn't found, if you try to input from a stream after all the values have been read, or if invalid data is encountered in the input stream. C++ provides a way to test the state of a stream: the stream name used in an expression returns true if the state if okay and false if the stream is in the fail state. Look at the following example.

```
// Program Area demonstrates stream testing.
#include <iostream.h>
#include <fstream.h>

int main()
{
    int side1;              // one side of a rectangle
    int side2;              // the other side of a rectangle
    ifstream inData;        // file stream
    int area;               // area of rectangle

    inData.open("myData.dat");
```

```
        if (!inData)
        {
            cout  << "Input file not found." << endl;
            return 1;
        }
        inData  >> side1  >> side2;
        if (!inData)
        {
            cout  << "Data format incorrect.";
            return 2;
        }
        area = side1 * side2;
        cout  << "Area is "  << area  << endl;
        return 0;
}
```

If the input file **myData.dat** cannot be found, **1** is returned to the operating system. If the data format on file **inData** is incorrect, **2** is returned to the operating system. If there are no input errors, **0** is returned to the operating system. Notice that the function **main** is exited as soon as a value is returned. Therefore, there are three ways that this function can be completed: two with an error (return **1** or **2**) and one with no error (return **0**). Returning **0** means normal completion of a program; returning any other value signals an error. When you are writing your program, you may choose the values to return to indicate different error conditions.

Test Plans

How do you test a specific program to determine its correctness? You design and implement a *test plan*. A test plan for a program is a document that specifies the test cases that should be run, the reason for each test case, and the expected output from each case. The test cases should be chosen carefully. The *code-coverage* approach designs test cases to ensure that each statement in the program is executed. The *data-coverage* approach designs test cases to ensure that the limits of the allowable data are covered. Often testing is a combination of code and data coverage.

Implementing a test plan means that you run each of the test cases described in the test plan and record the results. If the results are not as expected, you must go back to your top-down design and find and correct the error(s). The process stops when each of the test cases gives the expected results. Note that an implemented test plan gives you a measure of confidence that your program is correct; however, all you know for sure is that your program works correctly on your test cases. Therefore, the quality of your test cases is extremely important.

An example of a test plan for the code fragment that tests temperatures is shown on the next page. We assume that the fragment is embedded in a program that reads in a data value that represents a temperature.

Reason for Test Case	Input Values	Expected Output	Observed Output
Test first end point	32	Today is a cold day.	
Test second end point	85	Today is a nice day.	
Test value below first end point	31	Today is a cold day.	
Test value between end points	45	Today is a nice day.	
Test value above second end point	86	Today is a hot day.	
Test negative value	-10	Today is a cold day.	

To implement this test plan, the program is run six times, once for each test case. The results are written in the Observed Output column.

Warning

The assignment operator (=) and the equality test operator (==) easily can be miskeyed one for the other. What happens if this occurs? Unfortunately, the program does not crash; it continues to execute but probably gives incorrect results. Look at the following two statements.

```
aValue == aValue + 1;     // aValue = aValue + 1 is meant

if (value1 = value2)      // if (value1 == value2) is meant
```

The first statement returns false: **aValue** can never be equal to **aValue + 1**. The semicolon ends the statement, so nothing happens to the value returned (**aValue + 1**) and execution continues with the next statement. **aValue** has not been changed. In the second case, although we think of **value1 = value2** as being an assignment statement, it is technically just an expression that does two things: it returns the value of the expression on the right of the equal sign, and it stores this value in the place on the left. Here, the value returned is the content of **value2**. If this value is not zero, true is returned; if **value2** contains zero, false is returned. We have more to say about the assignment statement actually being an expression in Chapter 11.

The moral of this story is to be very careful when you key your program. A simple keying error can cause logic errors that the compiler does not catch and that are very difficult for the user to find. Great care and a good test plan are essential to C++ programming.

Chapter 5: Prelab Assignment

Name _____   **Date** _____

Section _____

Examine program **Convert** and answer the questions in Exercises 1 through 3.

```
// Program Convert converts a temperature from Fahrenheit to
// Celsius or a temperature from Celsius to Fahrenheit
// depending on whether the user enters an F or a C.

#include <iostream.h>

int main ()
{
    char letter;            // Place to store input letter
    int tempIn;             // Temperature to be converted
    int tempOut;            // Converted temperature

    cout  <<"Input Menu"  << endl  << endl;
    cout  <<"F:  Convert from Fahrenheit to Celsius"  << endl;
    cout  <<"C:  Convert from Celsius to Fahrenheit"  << endl;
    cout  <<"Type a C or an F, then press return."  << endl;
    cout  <<"Type an integer number, then press return."
          << endl;

    cin  >> letter;
    cin  >> tempIn;

    if (letter == 'C')
        tempOut = (9 * tempIn / 5) + 32;
    else
        tempOut = 5 * (tempIn - 32) / 9;
    cout  << "Temperature to convert: "  << tempIn  << endl;
    cout  << "Converted temperature:  "  << tempOut << endl;

    return 0;
}
```

Exercise 1:   If the letter C and the value 100 are input, what is the output?

Exercise 2:   If the letter F and the value 32 are input, what is the output?

Exercise 3:   If the letter c and the value 0 are input, what is the output?

Exercise 4:   Examine the following pairs of expressions and determine if they are equivalent. Put a T in the Result column if they are the same and an F if they are not.

Expression 1	Expression 2	Result
! (A == B)	A != B	_____
! ((A == B) || (A == C))	(A != B) && (A != C)	_____
! ((A == B) && (C > D))	(A != B) || (C <= D)	_____

Exercise 5:   Examine the following pairs of expressions and determine if they are equivalent. Put a T in the Result column if they are the same and an F if they are not.

Expression 1	Expression 2	Result
!A && B	B && !A	_____
!A || B	B || !A	_____
!(A && B)	A || B	_____
A && B || C	A && (B || C)	_____
(A && B || C)	!(A || B && C)	_____

Lesson 5-1: Check Prelab Exercises

Name _____   **Date** _____

Section _____

Run program Convert to check your answers to Prelab Exercises 1 through 3 and answer the following questions.

Exercise 1:   Was your answer completely correct? If it was not, explain where you made your mistake.

Exercise 2:   Was your answer completely correct? If it was not, explain where you made your mistake.

Exercise 3:   Was your answer completely correct? If it was not, explain where you made your mistake.

Exercise 4 :   The answers are T, T, and T.

Exercise 5:   The answers are T, T, F, F, and F.

Lesson 5-2: Boolean Expressions

Name _____   **Date** _____

Section _____

Use program **Shell1** for Exercises 1 and 2.

```
// Program Shell1 prints appropriate messages based on a
// grade read from the keyboard.

#include <iostream.h>

int main ()
{
    int grade;

    cout  << "Enter an integer grade between 50 and 100."
          << "  Press return. "  << endl;
    cin  >> grade;

    if  /* TO BE FILLED IN  */
        cout  << "Congratulations!"  << endl;
    return 0;
}
```

Exercise 1: When completed, program **Shell1** reads an integer value and writes an appropriate message. Fill in the Boolean expression beside the **if** so that "Congratulations!" is written if the numeric grade is greater than or equal to 80. Run the program five times entering the following values for grade: 50, 100, 80, 81, and 79.

"Congratulations!" is printed _____ time(s) in the five runs.

Exercise 2: Change the Boolean expression in Exercise 1 so that "Try harder" is printed if the numeric grade is less than 70. Run the program with the same data listed for Exercise 1.

"Try harder" is printed _____ time(s) in the five runs.

Exercise 3: Change the Boolean expression so that "Average" is printed if the numeric grade is less than 80 but greater than 70. Run the program with the same data listed for Exercise 1.

"Average" is printed _____ time(s) in the five runs.

Lesson 5-3:   If-then Statements

Name _____   **Date** _____

Section _____

Use program **Shell2** for the exercises in this lesson. This program prompts for and reads an integer value, and then prints a message based on this value.

```
// Program Shell2 prints appropriate messages based on a
// pressure reading input from the keyboard.

#include <iostream.h>

main ()
{
    int  pressure;

    cout << "Enter an integer pressure reading. "
        << " Press Return."  << endl;
    cin >> pressure;
    /* FILL IN Code appropriate to exercise */
    return 0;
}
```

Exercise 1:   Insert a statement that writes the following warning to the screen i f the pressure reading is greater than 100.

"Warning!! Pressure reading above danger limit."

Run your program eight times using the following values as input: 5, 75, 80, 99, 0, 100, 110, 199

"Warning !! Pressure reading above danger limit." is printed _____ times.

If your answer is 2, your If statement is correct. If your answer is 3, the relational operator on your expression is incorrect. It should be greater than, not greater than or equal to. Rerun your corrected program.

Exercise 2:   Insert a statement in program **Shell2** that writes the following message if the pressure reading is lower than 100 but greater than 5.

"Everything seems normal."

Run your program eight times using the same data that you used in Exercise 1.

"Everything seems normal" is printed _____ times.

Lesson 5-4: If-Then-Else Statements

Name _____ **Date** _____

Section _____

Exercise 1: Take program **Shell2** in Lesson 5-3 and change it so that it prints the message in both Lesson 5-3, Exercise 1, and Lesson 5-3, Exercise 2. Run the program with the data set for Lesson 5-3, Exercise 1.

"Warning !! Pressure reading above danger limit." is printed _____ times.

"Everything seems normal" is printed _____ times.

Use program Shell3 for Exercises 2, 3, and 4.

```
// Program Shell3 calculates a person's percentage of
// calories from fat and prints an appropriate message.

#include <iostream.h>

int main ()
{
    char   c1, c2, c3, c4, c5, c6, c7, c8, c9, c10;
    int    gramsOfFat;
    int    calories;
    float  fatCalPercent;

    cout  << "Enter food name using exactly 10 letters."
          << "  Press return."  << endl;
    cin.get(c1);
    cin.get(c2);
    cin.get(c3);
    cin.get(c4);
    cin.get(c5);
    cin.get(c6);
    cin.get(c7);
    cin.get(c8);
    cin.get(c9);
    cin.get(c10);

    cout  << "Enter the grams of fat; press return."  << endl;
    cin   >> gramsOfFat;

    cout  << "Enter the number of calories; press return."
          << endl;
    cin   >> calories;

    /* TO BE FILLED IN */
    return 0;
}
```

Exercise 2: The American Heart Association recommends that no more than 30 percent of a person's daily calories come from fat. Each gram of fat is nine calories. Given the grams of fat and the number of calories in an item, we can calculate the percentage of calories that comes from fat. Add statements to program **Shell3** to print the item and the percentage of calories that come from fat (**fatCalPercent**). Run your program four times with the following data:

Item	Grams of Fat	Calories	Percent from Fat
Tuna	1	60	_____
Spaetzle	2	170	_____
V8	0	35	_____
CornedBeef	7	200	_____

Exercise 3: Add a statement to program **Shell3** from Exercise 2 that prints one of the following two messages depending on the percentage of calories from fat (value of **fatCalPercent**).

"This item is Heart Healthy!"
"This item is NOT Heart Healthy!!"

Run your program using the data in Exercise 2.

Which of the items listed are heart healthy?

Exercise 4: Your test should look like one of the following where **fatCalOK** is a **Boolean** variable:

```
fatCalOK = fatCalPercent <= 0.30;
if (fatCalOK)

if (fatCalPercent <= 0.30)

fatCalOK = fatCalPercent <= 0.30;
if (fatCalOK == TRUE)

if ((fatCalPercent <= 0.30) == TRUE)
```

Circle the one that you used in your program. If you used the first or the second, you understand Boolean expressions and If statements. If you used one of the others, you are correct, but you have redundant code. A Boolean variable contains one of the constants **TRUE** or **FALSE**, and a Boolean expression returns true or false. You do not need to compare the Boolean variable or expression with the value **TRUE**.

Lesson 5-5: Nested Logic

Name _____   **Date** _____

Section _____

Use the following shell for the exercises in this lesson.

```
// Program Shell4 reads in a temperature and prints an
// appropriate message.

#include <iostream.h>

int main ()
{
    int   temperature;

    cout  << "Enter the temperature in your room."  << endl;
    cin  >> temperature;

    /* TO BE FILLED IN */
    return 0;
}
```

Exercise 1:   Add five If-Then statements to program **Shell4** so that one of the following messages is printed based on the value of **temperature**.

Temperature	Message
> 90	"Visit a neighbor."
<= 90, > 80	"Turn on air conditioning."
<= 80, > 70	"Do nothing."
<= 70, >55	"Turn on heat."
<= 55	"Visit a neighbor."

Run your program as many times as it takes to write each message exactly once. What data values did you use?

Exercise 2:   Rewrite the program in Exercise 1 using nested logic (i.e., If-Then-Else where the Else branch is an If statement). Rerun the program with the same data. Did you get the same answers? Explain.

Exercise 3: Complete program **HiScore** so that it reads and prints three test scores, then labels and prints the largest of the three.

```
// Program HiScore reads and prints three test scores.
// The largest value of the three is printed with an
// appropriate message.
// Assumption:  The scores are unique.

#include <iostream.h>

int main ()
{
     int   test1Score;
     int   test2Score;
     int   test3Score;

     cout  << "Enter score for test 1; press return."  << endl;
     cin  >> test1Score;
     cout  << "Enter score for test 2; press return."  << endl;
     cin  >> test2Score;
     cout  << "Enter score for test 3; press return."  << endl;
     cin  >> test3Score;

     cout  << "The three test scores are: "  << endl;
     cout  << test1Score  << endl;
     cout  << test2Score  << endl;
     cout  << test3Score  << endl;

     /* TO BE FILLED IN */
     return 0;
}
```

Fill in the missing statement(s) in program **HiScore** so that the largest of the three input values (scores) is printed and labeled as the highest test score. You may use a nested If statement or a series of If statements. For example, if **test2Score** with a value of 98 is the largest, your output might look as follows:

```
The value for test 2 is the highest; it is 98.
```

Your message may be different, but it must include the largest value and which test had that value. Run your program three times using the three sets of input values listed below.

Input values	What Is printed
100 80 70	_____
70 80 100	_____
80 100 60	_____

Lesson 5-6:   Test Plan

Name _____   **Date** _____

Section _____

Exercise 1:   Design a test plan for program **HiScore** in Lesson 5-5. (Hint: there should be at least six test cases.)

Reason for Test Case	Input Values	Expected Output	Observed Output

Exercise 2:   Implement the test plan designed in Exercise 1. You may show the results in the chart in Exercise 1.

Lesson 5-7: Debugging

Name _____   **Date** _____

Section _____

Exercise 1:   Program **AddSub** is supposed to read in a letter and two integer values and print either the sum of the two values or the difference of the two values depending on the letter read. It is such a simple program, but it doesn't even compile! Correct the program and describe the errors.

Exercise 2:   Now that the program compiles, run it with the following sets of values.

Input Values	Means	What Is Printed
A 10 20	add 10 and 20	_____
A 20 10	add 20 and 10	_____
S 10 20	subtract 20 from 10	_____
S 20 10	subtract 10 from 20	_____

Exercise 3:   Unless you corrected the logic errors in Exercise 1, you answers are incorrect. Locate the logic errors and rerun you program until you get the correct answers. Describe the errors.

Postlab Activities

Exercise 1:   Your history instructor gives three tests worth 50 points each.   You can drop one of the first two grades.   The final grade is the sum of the best of the first two grades and the third grade.   Given three test grades, write a program that calculates the final letter grade using the following cut-off points.

>= 90	A
< 90, >= 80	B
< 80, >= 70	C
< 70, >= 60	D
< 60	F

Exercise 2:   Write a program to determine if the digits in a three-digit number are all odd, all even, or mixed odd and even.   Your program should prompt the user to input a three-digit number and echo-print the number.   If the digits in the number are all odd, write "This number contains all odd digits."   If the digits are all even, write "This number contains all even digits."   If the number contains both odd and even digits, write "This number contains both odd and even digits."   Use integer division and modulus to access the digits in the number.

Exercise 3:   The world outside of the United States has switched to Celsius.   You are going to travel in England, where the temperature is given in Celsius.   A friend said that a quick approximation of the Fahrenheit equivalent of a Celsius number is to take the number, double it, and add 32.   Write a program that takes as input a temperature in Celsius and calculates both the approximated Fahrenheit equivalent and the actual Fahrenheit equivalent.   Write out all three values.   If the approximation and the actual value are within two degrees, write out "Close enough."   If they are not within two degrees, write out "Will not do."

6

Looping

OBJECTIVES

- To be able to modify a program containing a While statement.
- To be able to construct a count-controlled loop to implement a specified task.
- To be able to construct an event-controlled loop to implement a specified task.
- To be able to construct a loop nested within another loop.
- To be able to test the state of an I/O stream.
- To be able to answer questions about a loop that you have implemented.

Chapter 6: Assignment Cover Sheet

Name _____   Date _____

Section _____

Fill in the following table showing which exercises have been assigned for each lesson and check what you are to submit: (1) lab sheets, (2) listings of output files, and/or (3) listings of programs. Your instructor or TA can use the Completed column for grading purposes.

Activities	Assigned: Check or list exercise numbers	Submit (1)	(2)	(3)	Completed
Prelab					
Review					
Prelab Assignment					
Inlab					
Lesson 6-1: Check Prelab Exercises					
Lesson 6-2: Count-Controlled Loops					
Lesson 6-3: Event-Controlled Loops					
Lesson 6-4: Nested Logic					
Lesson 6-5: Debugging					
Postlab					

Prelab Activities

Review

In Chapter 5, we looked at Boolean expressions and how they can be used in the If statement to make a choice. In this chapter, we examine how Boolean expressions can be used in a While statement to make the program repeat a statement or group of statements. Such repetitions are called *loops*.

While Statement

The If statement allows the program to skip the execution of a statement or choose between one of two statements to be executed based on the value of a Boolean expression. In contrast, the While statement allows a program to continue executing a statement as long as the value of a Boolean expression is true. When the Boolean expression becomes false, execution of the program continues with the statement immediately following the While statement. Look at the following code fragment.

```
sum = 0;
count = 1;
while (count <= 10)
{
    cin >> value;
    sum = sum + value;
    count++;
}
cout << "The sum of the 10 numbers is " << sum;
```

The variables **sum** and **count** are assigned the values **0** and **1** respectively. The Boolean expression **(count <= 10)** is evaluated. The value in **count** is less than or equal to 10, so the expression is true and the block (compound statement) associated with the While is executed. A number is extracted from the standard input stream and added to **sum**. The value in **count** is incremented by 1.

At this point, the logical order of the program diverges from the physical order. The While expression is evaluated again. Because the value stored in **count** is still less than or equal to 10, the compound statement associated with the While is executed again. This process continues until **count** contains the value 11. At that time, the expression is no longer true, the body of the While statement is not executed again, and execution continues with the statement immediately following the While statement that sends the labeled answer to the output stream.

Types of Loops

There are two basic types of loops: count-controlled and event-controlled. A *count-controlled loop* is one that is executed a certain number of times. The expression that controls the loop becomes false when the loop has executed the prescribed number of times. An *event-controlled loop* is one whose execution is controlled by the occurrence of an event within the loop itself. The previous example is a count-controlled loop that executes 10 times. Let's look at an example of an event-controlled loop that reads and sums values from **cin** until a negative value is encountered.

```
typedef int Boolean;
const Boolean TRUE = 1;
const Boolean FALSE = 0;
Boolean  moreData;

sum = 0;

cin  >> value;

// Set moreData to true if the first data item is not
// negative; false otherwise.
moreData = value >= 0;

while (moreData)
{
    sum = sum + value;
    cin  >> value;
    moreData = value >= 0;        // Reset moreData
}
cout  << "The sum of the values prior to a negative value is "
      << sum  << endl;
```

sum is set to zero and the first data item (**value**) is read outside of the loop. **value** is compared to zero and the result is stored in **moreData**. If the first data item is less than zero, **moreData** is **FALSE**, and the body of the loop is not executed. If the first data item is greater than or equal to zero, **moreData** is true, and the body of the loop is entered. **value** is added to **sum**, and the next data item is read. This new data item is compared to zero, and **moreData** is reset. The expression is tested again. This process continues until a value of less than zero is read and **moreData** becomes false. When this happens, the body of the While is not executed again, and the sum of the nonnegative numbers is sent to the output stream.

Reading the first value outside of the body of the loop is called a priming read. When a priming read is used before a loop, the input values are processed at the beginning of the loop body and a subsequent read occurs at the end of the loop body.

Notice the difference between these two loops. The first reads ten values and sums them; the second reads and sums values until a negative number if read. The first is count-controlled; the second is event-controlled. The second loop is called a sentinel-controlled loop because reading a sentinel (a negative number) is the event that controls it.

EOF Loops

In Chapter 5, we stated that running out of data puts the input stream into the fail state. We also said that the stream name can be used to test to see if the stream is in the fail state. We can put these two facts together to construct a very useful event-controlled loop for reading data values. We can read and process data values until the stream goes into the fail state. When the last data value has been read, the stream is at the end of the file (called EOF). The stream is fine until another data value is requested. At that point, the stream goes into the fail state. This means that we must try to read one more value than exists on the stream in order to let the fail state control the reading. The following loop reads and sums values until there is no more data.

```
sum = 0;
cin >> value;
while (cin)
{
    sum = sum + value;
    cin >> value;
}
```

Because **cin** does not go into the fail state until we try to access a value when the stream is at EOF, we must use a priming read as we did in the previous example. If there is a value, **(cin)** returns true and the body of the loop is entered where the value is added to **sum** and a new value is read. After the last value has been processed, the attempt to read one more value causes **cin** to enter the fail state. When the While expression is tested the last time, **(cin)** returns false and the loop is not repeated.

Proper Loop Operation

For obvious reasons, the While statement is called a loop or looping statement. The statement that is being executed within the loop is called the *body* of the loop.
There are three basic steps that must be done for a loop to operate properly.

1. The variables in the expression (the counter or event) must be set (initialized) before the While statement is executed the first time.
2. The expression must test the status of the counter or event correctly so that the body of the loop executes when it is supposed to and terminates at the proper time.
3. The counter or the event must be updated within the loop. If the counter or the event is not updated, the loop never stops executing. This situation is called an *infinite loop*.

Nested Loops

The body of the loop can contain any type of statement including another While statement. The following program counts the number of characters on each line in a file. We know that the manipulator **endl** forces the next characters sent to the output stream to begin a new line. How can we recognize a new line on the input stream? A new line begins following the symbol '**\n**'. We must be sure to use function **get** defined in file **<iostream.h>**, not the extraction operator, to input each character.

```
// Program LineCt counts the number of characters per line
// and the number of lines in a file.
// There is a '\n' before the EOF.

#include <iostream.h>
#include <fstream.h>
```

```
int main()
{
    int   lineNo;
    char character;
    int   number;
    fstream inData;

    inData.open("Data.In");
    lineNo = 0;
    inData.get(character);
    while (inData)
    {
        lineNo++;
        number = 0;
        while (character != '\n')
        {
            number++;
            inData.get(character);
        }
        cout  << "Line "  << lineNo  << " contains "
              << number  << " characters."  << endl;
        inData.get(character);
    }
    return 0;
}
```

Chapter 6: Prelab Assignment

Name _____   **Date** _____

Section _____

Read program **Count** carefully.

```
// Program Count prompts for, reads, echo prints, and sums a
// fixed number of integer values.  The sum is printed.

#include <iostream.h>

const int  LIMIT = 10;

int main ()
{
    int  counter;                 // loop-control variable
    int  sum;                     // summing variable
    int  dataValue;               // input value
    counter = 1;
    sum = 0;

    // Input and sum integer data values.
    while (counter <= LIMIT)
    {
        cout  << "Enter an integer value.  Press return."
            << endl;
        cin  >> dataValue;
        sum = sum + dataValue;
        counter++;
    }
    cout  << "Sum is "  << sum  << endl;
    return 0;
}
```

Exercise 1:   What is printed, if the following data values are entered as prompted?

8   5   3   -2   0   9   1   7   3   10

Exercise 2:   Is the loop in program **Count** a count-controlled loop or an event-controlled loop? Explain.

Read program **Count2** carefully.

```
// Program Count2 prompts for, reads, and sums integer
// values until a negative number is read.  The input
// values and the sum are printed.

#include <iostream.h>

int main ()
{
    int  sum;        // summing variable
    int  dataValue; // input value
    sum = 0;
    cout  << "To stop processing, enter a negative"
          << " value."  << endl;
    cout  << " Enter an integer value; press return."
          << endl;
    // Read first data value to prepare for loop.
    cin  >> dataValue;

    // Input and sum integer data values
    while (dataValue > 0)
    {
        sum = sum + dataValue;
        cout  << "Enter an integer value; press return."
              << endl;
        cin  >> dataValue;
    }
    cout  << "Sum is "  << sum  << endl;
    return 0;
}
```

Exercise 3:   What is printed, if the following data values are entered one per line?

```
8   5   3   -2   0   9   1   7   3   10
```

Exercise 4:   Is the loop in program **Count2** a count-controlled loop or an event-controlled loop? Explain.

Lesson 6-1: Check Prelab Exercises

Name _____   **Date** _____

Section _____

Exercise 1:   Run program **Count** to check your answers. Were they correct? If not, why not?

Exercise 2:   The loop in program **Count** is a count-controlled loop because the loop body is executed a specified number of times.

Exercise 3:   Run program **Count2** to check your answers. Were they correct? If not, why not?

Exercise 4:   The loop in program **Count2** is an event-controlled loop because input of a negative data value (the event) stops it.

Lesson 6-2: Count-Controlled Loops

Name _____   **Date** _____

Section _____

Exercise 1:   Change program **Count** so that the number of values to be read (**limit**) is input from the keyboard rather than being set as a named constant. Run your program using a value of 10 and entering the data listed for Prelab Exercise 1. (Don't forget to prompt for **limit**.) Your answer should be the same. If it is not, you have an error.

Run your program again entering a value of your choice for **limit**, followed by **limit** integer values.

List **limit**, your data, and the sum.

Exercise 2:   Run program **Count** entering one fewer data value than called for. What happens? Explain.

Exercise 3:   Run program **Count** entering one more data value than called for. What happens? Explain.

Exercise 4:   Examine program **Shell1**. When completed, program **Shell1** prompts for and reads a one-digit number, then adds the numbers from zero to the number, inclusive, and prints the sum.

```
// Program Shell1 prompts for and reads a one-digit number.
// Values between 0 and the digit (inclusive) are summed.

#include <iostream.h>

int main ()
{
    int   counter;    // loop-control variable
    int   sum;        // running sum
    int   digit;

    cout  << "Enter a one-digit number; press return."
          << endl;
    cin  >> digit;
    counter =  /* TO BE FILLED IN */
    sum     =  /* TO BE FILLED IN */

    while /* TO BE FILLED IN  */
    {
      /*  TO BE FILLED IN */
    }
    cout  << "Sum of digits between 0 and "
          << digit  << " is "  << sum  << endl;
    return 0;
}
```

Fill in the appropriate initializations and the body of the While loop so that the sum of the digits from zero through **digit** (the input value) is computed. Run your program four times using 0, 3, 7, and 9 as the input values.

Answer for 0: _____   Answer for 3: _____

Answer for 7: _____   Answer for 9: _____

Exercise 5: Program **Shell3** in Lesson 5-4 read and printed ten characters, each with a different identifier. Change your program so that only one **char** variable is used for this process. Run the program four times using the following data. Were your answers the same?

Item	Grams of Fat	Calories	Percent from Fat
Tuna	1	60	_____
Spaetzle	2	170	_____
V8	0	35	_____
CornedBeef	7	200	_____

Exercise 6: Exercise 5 asks you to run the program four times. What a waste of effort! Rewrite the program so that all the processing is done at one time. That is, enclose the entire program in a count-controlled loop that executes four times.

Lesson 6-3: Event-Controlled Loops

Name _____   **Date** _____

Section _____

Use program **Shell2** for Exercises 1 and 2.

```
// Program Shell2 counts the number of uppercase letters
// on a line.

#include <iostream.h>

int main ()
{
    char letter;
    int  letterCt;

    /* TO BE FILLED IN */
    return 0;
}
```

Exercise 1: Fill in the body of program **Shell2** so that the number of uppercase letters on a line of input is printed. Run your program with the following input and show the result. (Hint: Remember that relational operators can be applied between two variables of type **char**. The assertions being made relate to the variables' relative positions in the collating sequence. In Chapter 10, we show you a better way to work with character data.)

AbbaDabbaDoo

Exercise 2: Change program **Shell2** from Exercise 1 so that the counting stops if the input line contains a digit. Run your program with the following data and show the results.

ABBA1DABBA2Doo

Exercise 3: Change program **Shell2** from Exercise 1 so that it counts uppercase and lowercase letters. Run your program with the following data and show the result.

Abba#Dabba#2Doo

Exercise 4: In Exercise 5 in the last lesson, you modified **Shell3** from Chapter 5. Then, in Exercise 6, you enclosed the entire program in a loop that executes four times. Change your program so that characters are read and printed until the newline character ('\n') is encountered. Run your program using the following data. Are all three outputs the same? Explain.

Item	Grams of Fat	Calories	Percent from Fat
Tuna	1	60	_____
Spaetzle	2	170	_____
V8	0	35	_____
CornedBeef	7	200	_____

Lesson 6-4: Nested Logic

Name _____   **Date** _____

Section _____

Exercise 1:   Rewrite your solution to Lesson 6-2, Exercise 4, so that the processing is repeated until a negative digit is read. That is, embed your solution within another loop that continues to prompt for a digit and calculates the sum of the digits from zero through **digit** as long as **digit** is positive. The process stops when **digit** is negative. Be sure to add this information to the prompt. Rewrite the program documentation at the beginning of the program to reflect this change. Run your program once using the same data you used Lesson 6-2, Exercise 4.

What additional documentation did you include?

Is the outer loop a count-controlled loop or an event-controlled loop?

Exercise 2:   Examine program **Shell3**. When completed this program prompts for and reads an integer value and prints a warning message based on the input value.

Pressure	Message
< 0	"Error in input."
>= 0, < 50	"Pressure in the normal range."
>= 50, < 100	"Pressure on the high side."
> = 100	"Evacuate plant!!!!"

```
// Program Shell 3 prints appropriate messages based
// on a pressure reading read from a file.  Processing
// continues until the plant is evacuated because of
// a pressure reading over 100.


#include <iostream.h>
#include <fstream.h>
```

```
int main ()
{
    int  pressure;
    ifstream  data;
    data.open("Shell3.D1");

    /* LOOP TO BE FILLED IN */

        data  >> pressure;

        /* FILL IN Code to print the message */

    return 0;
}
```

What kind of a loop is being used?

How many times was each message printed?
"Error in input."
"Pressure in the normal range."   _____
"Pressure on the high side."   _____
"Evacuate plant!!!!"   _____
                                         _____

Exercise 3:   The program to check pressure readings (your solution to Exercise 2) continues to run as long as the pressure readings are within the safe range. The program only halts when an unsafe reading is read.   Plant maintenance has decided that the process should also be halted after 60 safe readings.   Rewrite your solution from Exercise 2 to end the program when a dangerous reading occurs or when 60 safe readings have been read.   Run your program twice, using **Shell3.D2** and **Shell3.D3** as input.

What was the result using **Shell3.D2**?

What was the result using **Shell3.D3**?

Exercise 4:   Program **Shell3** as modified in Exercise 3 seems to be both an event-controlled loop and a count-controlled loop.   However, we classify any loop that is not a pure count-controlled loop as an event-controlled loop.   Explain why.

Exercise 5: Plant maintenance has decided to add one more modification. If all the pressure readings are safe and there are less than 60 of them, stream **data** goes into the fail state. Rewrite the program so that it prints the message "Insufficient data." if there are less than 60 safe readings. Also print out how many pressure readings there were. Use the state of the input stream as the loop control. Run your program using **Shell3.D4**. How many pressure readings are there?

Lesson 6-5: Debugging

Name _____   **Date** _____

Section _____

Exercise 1:   Program **SumNums** reads and counts nonnegative integers until there are no more data values. You run the program using file **SumNums.D1**, and the program says that there are no values on the file. You know that there are nine values on the file and that seven of them are nonnegative. Locate the bug and describe it.

Exercise 2:   The program now runs, but it gives the wrong answer. Locate and describe this bug.

Exercise 3:   The answer is different but still wrong! Keep looking. Describe the error.

Postlab Activities

Exercise 1:   Write a program to print a triangle composed of a symbol. The number of lines in the triangle and the symbol should be entered as input from the keyboard. For example, if the input values are 7 and #, the output is as follows:

```
      #
     ###
    #####
   #######
  #########
 ###########
#############
```

In your program documentation, describe the loop(s) used as count-controlled or event-controlled.

Exercise 2:   File **History.d1** contains a brief history of computing. There are no indentations in this file. Write a program to read this file, inserting five blanks at the beginning of each paragraph. You can recognize a paragraph because a blank line appears before the first line of each paragraph. Write the changed file on **History.d2**. In your program documentation, describe the loop(s) used as count-controlled or event-controlled.

Exercise 3:   How many nonblank characters are there in file **History.d1**? Add a counter to your program from Exercise 2 that keeps track of the number of nonblank characters in the file. Print this number to the screen. Do not include '**\n**' in your nonblank count.

Exercise 4:   As a child, did you ever play the game "One potato, two potato, . . . " to determine who would be "it"? The complete rhyme is given below:

One potato, two potato, three potato, four;
Five potato, six potato, seven potato, more.
O U T spells "out you go."

A child is pointed to during each phrase. There are four phrases in lines 1 and 2 and seven phrases in line 3, so the last child pointed to is the 15th one. If there are fewer than 15 children, you go around the circle again. The child pointed to when the word *go* is said is "out." The game begins again with the remaining children, starting again with the first child. The last child remaining is "it."

Simulate this game in a computer program. The input is the number of children; the output is which child is "it."

Exercise 5:   Modify the game in Exercise 4 so that rather than beginning again with child number 1, you start again with the child following the last one out.

Exercise 6:   In Chapter 5, Postlab Exercise 3, you were asked to determine the accuracy of an approximation of a translation of a temperature from Celsius to Fahrenheit. The Fahrenheit approximation is the Celsius number doubled plus 32. Write a program that creates a table with three columns. The first column is temperatures in Celsius, the second is the Fahrenheit approximation, and the third is the actual Fahrenheit equivalent. Run your program using at least 10 data values. Examine your table and write a paragraph discussing the accuracy of the approximation.

Exercise 7:   There is a temperature for which Fahrenheit and Celsius are the same. This value can be determined both algebraically and experimentally. Solve the problem algebraically first and then write a program that determines if a solution exists by experimentation.

7

Functions

O B J E C T I V E S

- To be able to write and invoke a parameterless void function to implement a specified task.
- To be able to write and invoke a void function with value parameters to execute a specified task.
- To be able to write and invoke a void function with reference parameters to execute a specified task.
- To be able to debug a program with a function.

Chapter 7: Assignment Cover Sheet

Name _____   **Date** _____

Section _____

Fill in the following table showing which exercises have been assigned for each lesson and check what you are to submit: (1) lab sheets, (2) listings of output files, and/or (3) listings of programs. Your instructor or TA can use the Completed column for grading purposes.

Activities	Assigned: Check or list exercise numbers	Submit (1)	(2)	(3)	Completed
Prelab					
Review					
Prelab Assignment					
Inlab					
Lesson 7-1: Check Prelab Exercises					
Lesson 7-2: Functions without Parameters					
Lesson 7-3: Functions with Value Parameters					
Lesson 7-4: Functions with Reference Parameters					
Lesson 7-5: Debugging					
Postlab					

Prelab Activities

Review

Identifiers can name actions as well as data objects. There are two types of named actions in C++: value-returning functions and void functions. The name of a value-returning function is used in an expression; the action is executed and the returned value is substituted in the expression. **sqrt** and **pow** are named actions that are value-returning functions. The name of a void function is used as a statement in the executable part of a program. The action is executed and the program continues with the statement immediately following the action name. The **get** in **cin.get** and the **open** in **inData.open** are void-function identifiers that name actions or processes. Both value-returning and void functions can be used to implement modules in a top-down design. In this chapter, we focus on how to write void functions.

Using the name of a function in an expression or as a statement is called *invoking* or *calling* the function.

Defining Void Functions

A void function has a heading that names the function followed by a pair of parentheses. (The function identifier is preceded by the word **void**.) A list of the identifiers that the function needs can be inserted within the parentheses. This list of identifiers is called a *parameter list*.

The parameter list on the function heading is called the *formal parameter list*. Each identifier on the formal parameter list must have its type listed. These identifiers are used in the statements in the executable part of the function. When the function is invoked, there is a list of identifiers in parentheses after the function name. This list of identifiers is called the *actual parameter list*. The identifiers on the actual parameter list name the places that the function actually uses during execution. The formal parameter list and the actual parameter list must match up in number and type because each actual parameter is substituted for its corresponding formal parameter when the function is executed.

Let's examine the syntax in the context of an example. Before we look at a function with parameters, let's look at the case where the function does not need any information from the outside and therefore has no parameter list. The task is to write a box that looks as follows:

There are 20 periods on the first line, 2 periods on the second and third lines separated by 18 blanks each, and the fourth line is identical to the first line. Function **WriteBox** produces this output.

```
void WriteBox()                 // name of the action
// Post: A box (20 x 4) is printed using periods.
{                                               // begin action
   cout << "...................." << endl;
   cout << "." << setw(19)   << "."   << endl;
   cout << "." << setw(19)   << "."   << endl;
   cout << "...................." << endl;
}                                               // end action
```

The reserved word **void** precedes the name of the action. There is no parameter list, but the parentheses that enclose the parameter list must be present. The braces enclose the function body, the action part of the function. The four output statements write the box described above.

How does **WriteBox** get executed? The name of the action, **WriteBox**, is used as a statement in your program.

```
WriteBox();    // function invocation or 'call'
```

How does all this fit together? *Where* in the program? What *is* the program? A complete program containing function **WriteBox** is shown below. Notice that the function definition is set off with a row of asterisks before it. This design makes the parts of the program easier to distinguish for the human reader—the compiler doesn't care.

```
// Program Box writes a box using periods.

#include <iostream.h>
#include <iomanip.h>

void WriteBox();                    // function prototype
// Post: A (20 x 4) box of dots is written on the screen.

int main()
{
    cout << "A box: "  << endl;
    WriteBox();
    cout << "Box has been drawn."  << endl;
    return 0;
}

//*******************************************

void WriteBox()                 // name of the action
// Post: A box (20 x 4) is printed using periods.

{                                               // begin action
   cout << "...................." << endl;
   cout << "." << setw(19)   << "."   << endl;
   cout << "." << setw(19)   << "."   << endl;
   cout << "...................." << endl;
}                                               // end action
```

Physical Order and Logical Order

The text of the function definitions can be in any physical order. The logical order of executing the compiled program begins with the first statement in function **main**, which sends the characters "**A box:** " to the output stream. Function **WriteBox** is then executed. When function **WriteBox** is finished, control passes to the statement immediately following the call to **WriteBox**, and "**Box has been drawn.**" is sent to the output stream.

Most C++ programmers put function **main** first in the physical order of the program with the other function definitions following. Each function is separated by a row of some delimiter symbol. We use a row of asterisks. Because most C++ programs have function **main** listed first and each identifier must be declared before it is used, we have a problem. The functions invoked in function **main** are not known to the compiler because they have not been defined yet. We solve this dilemma by using a *function prototype*. A function prototype is the function heading without the body of the function. Look back at program **Box**; the comments identify the prototype for function **WriteBox**. Note that the function prototype ends with a semicolon, but the heading in the function definition does not.

Exiting a Function

We have seen with value-returning functions that the function is exited when a **return** statement is executed. That is, control is passed back to the place in the expression where the call occurred when a value is returned. How do you exit a void function? Control passes back to the statement immediately following the function call when the last statement in the function is executed or when a **return** that doesn't include an expression is executed. A **return** with no expression can occur only in a void function.

Functions with Parameters

Now, let's look at an example of a program with a function that has a parameter list.

```
// Program Demo prompts for and reads two integer
// values that represent the sides of a rectangle.
// The area of the rectangle is calculated and printed.

#include <iostream.h>

void GetData(int&, int&);                    // function prototype
// GetData gets two integer values.

int main()
{
    int   height;
    int   width;
    int   area;

    GetData(height, width);
    area = height * width;
```

```
        cout << "The area of the "  << height  << " by "
             << width  << " rectangle is "  << area  << endl;
        return 0;
}


//********************************************************

void GetData(int& firstValue, int& secondValue)
// Post: The user has been prompted to input two values
//        representing the length and width of a rectangle.
//        These values have been read and returned in
//        firstValue and secondValue.
{
        cout  << "Enter two integer values representing "
              << "a rectangle.  Press return."  << endl;
        cin  >> firstValue  >> secondValue;
}
```

The identifiers on the formal parameter list of function **GetData** are **firstValue** and **secondValue**, which are both of type **int**. The identifiers on the actual parameter list are **height** and **width**. When function **GetData** is executed, **height** (the actual parameter) is substituted for **firstValue** (the formal parameter) and **width** (the actual parameter) is substituted for **secondValue** (the formal parameter). The names used on the formal and actual parameter lists are immaterial; the individual items are matched solely by position.

The function prototype can have the names of the formal parameters listed, but the compiler only needs to know the number of parameters and their data types. Therefore, the function prototype for **GetData** has just the data types listed. (We explain the ampersands in the next section.)

Value and Reference Parameters

In C++, there are two types of parameters: *value parameters* and *reference parameters*. If the formal parameter is a value parameter, a *copy* of the value of the actual parameter is passed to the function. If the formal parameter is a reference parameter, the *address* of the actual parameter is passed to the function. This means that if a value parameter is changed within a function, only the copy is changed. However, if a reference parameter is changed within a function, the actual parameter is changed. How can you tell which parameters are value and which are reference? Reference parameters have the ampersand (**&**) following their type identifier in the function prototype and function heading. Value parameters are the default parameter type, so they have nothing following their type identifiers.

The parameters for function **GetData** are reference parameters because the ampersand follows their type identifiers.

Parameters that send back values to the calling function are called output parameters (or outgoing). Parameters that only give information to the function are called input parameters (incoming). Parameters that both give information to the function and transmit information back are called in/out parameters (or incoming/outgoing). Output parameters and in/out parameters *must be reference parameters*. Input parameters should be value parameters so that the function cannot inadvertently change the actual parameter. C++ requires that all files must be passed as reference parameters.

The task of function **GetData** is to prompt for and read two integer values from the standard input stream. Because these values are needed by the calling function, they are reference parameters. If we change program **Demo** so that the last output statement is put into a function, **PrintData**, with three parameters (**height, width,** and **area**), should the parameters be value parameters or reference parameters? Because these values are not changed, they should be value parameters.

If a function needs no information and returns no values to the calling routine, then the function doesn't need parameters. Function **main** is a function with no parameters. Notice, however, that function prototypes, function headings, and function calls always must have the parentheses even if there are no parameters.

Local Variables

Any user-defined function is a heading and a body, and the body is a block. Therefore, any function can include variable declarations. Declarations declared within a block are called *local variables*. Local variables are created when the function is called and disappear when the function finishes executing. Local variables are accessible only from within the block in which they are defined.

Documentation of Functions

There is a need-to-know principle in programming that says that the user of a function needs to know only *what* the function does, not *how* it does it. One way to implement this principle is to have the documentation on each function prototype state what the function does—just enough information for the program reader to understand the function's purpose. On the other hand, the documentation in the function heading and the body is for the person reading the details, usually the one responsible for maintaining the code. Therefore, the documentation in the function definition can state how the function is implemented.

As long as our programs are small enough to include all of the function definitions in the same file with function **main**, we use an informal style of documenting the function prototypes and definitions. In later chapters, when we separate the function prototypes and function definitions into different files, we use a more formal style in which preconditions describe the state of the parameters on input to the function and postconditions describe the state of the parameters on output from the function. Preconditions state what the function assumes is true on entry; postconditions state what the function guarantees to be true on exit from the function provided the preconditions are true. Preconditions and postconditions can be written in many different ways, ranging from simple English sentences to statements in formal logic.

In this formal documentation style, the function prototype becomes the *interface* to the function. It includes the formal description of the purpose of the function and a description of the parameters at the logical level. The implementation details are hidden within the definition of the function. The hiding of the implementation details within a separate block with a formally specified interface is called *encapsulation*. When our programs are large enough to warrant it, we use this style of documentation to emphasize encapsulation.

Data flow refers to information going into and out of a function. The direction of data flow can be documented by using one of the following statements as a comment beside each parameter in the prototype: 'in', 'out', 'in/out'. Note that 'out' and 'in/out' parameters must be designated as reference parameters.

Chapter 7: Prelab Assignment

Name _____   Date _____

Section _____

Examine program Stars carefully.

```cpp
// Program Stars prints NUM_STARS on the screen.

#include <iostream.h>

const int  NUM_STARS = 10;

void PrintStars();
// Prints NUM_STARS stars on the screen.

int main ()
{
    cout  << "The next line contains "  << NUM_STARS
          << " stars. "  << endl;
    PrintStars();
    PrintStars();
    return 0;
}
//*************************************************
void PrintStars ()
// Post: NUM_STARS asterisks are sent to cout.

{
    cout << "**********"  << endl;
    return;
}
```

Exercise 1:   Show below exactly what program **Stars** writes on the screen.

Exercise 2:   Trace the execution of program **Demo** on page 133. The data is keyed as follows:

10   23

What is printed?

Exercise 3:   If the values in the data line are entered in reverse order, what is printed?

Lesson 7-1: Check Prelab Exercises

Name _____   **Date** _____

Section _____

Exercise 1:   Run program **Stars** to check your answer to Exercise 1. Were you correct? If not, explain your error. (Did the output statement mislead you? What should the output statement say?)

Exercise 2:   Run program **Demo** to check your answers to Exercise 2. Discuss your results.

Exercise 3:   Run program **Demo** to check your answers to Exercise 3. Discuss your results.

Lesson 7-2: Functions without Parameters

Name _____   **Date** _____

Section _____

Lesson 1 uses program **Shell1**.

```
// Program Shell1 is a program shell with a function.

#include <iostream.h>

void  Print();
// FILL IN the documentation.

main ()
{
    Print();
    return 0;
}

//*************************************

void  Print()
// FILL IN the documentation.
{
    /* TO BE FILLED IN */
}
```

Exercise 1:   Fill in the code for function **Print** so that it prints your name and address (on two separate lines) enclosed or boxed in dollar signs on the screen. Don't forget to fill in the appropriate documentation for function **Print**. Run your program and show your documentation and your output.

Exercise 2:   Change function **Print** so that it reads the name and address from file **data.in**. Make your input file a reference parameter to function **Print**. Use '**\n**' to control your loops. You may assume that the name is on one line and the address is on the next line. Run your program and show your documentation and your output. (Did you remember to change the documentation for function **Print**?)

Lesson 7-3: Functions with Value Parameters

Name _____   **Date** _____

Section _____

Use program **Shell2** for Exercises 1 through 3.

Writing boxes on the screen is fun. Program **Shell2** is the shell of a program that prompts the user to enter an integer number. When completed this number is read and passed to function **Print** as parameter **numSigns**. The function prints a box of dollar signs on the screen that is **numSigns** by (**numSigns** / 2). For example, if **numSigns** is 10, the following box is printed on the screen.

```
$$$$$$$$$$
$        $
$        $
$        $
$$$$$$$$$$
```

Note the interior dimensions are (**numSigns**-2) x (**numSigns** / 2-2).

```cpp
// Program Shell2 prompts for the number of dollar signs for
// the top of the box.  That number / 2 - 2  lines are
// printed with dollar signs on the sides.

#include <iostream.h>

void  Print(int numSigns);
// FILL IN documentation.

int main ()
{
    int   number;

    cout  << "Enter the number of dollar signs for the top; "
          << "press return."
    cout  << "Enter end-of-file character to quit."  << endl;
    cin  >> number;
    while (cin)
    {
        /* FILL IN call to Print */
        cout  << "Enter the number of dollar signs for "
              << "the top; press return."
        cout  << "Enter end-of-file character to quit."
              << endl;
        cin >> number;
    }
    return 0;
}
```

```
//*************************************

void  Print(int numSigns)
// FILL IN documentation.
{
    /* FILL IN code to print numSigns $'s */

    /* FILL IN code to print (numSigns / 2)-2 lines with   */
    /* $'s lining up under the left-most and right-most     */
    /* $ ones on the top line.                              */

    /* FILL IN code to print numSigns $'s                   */

}
```

Exercise 1:   Fill in the missing code in function **Print** and the invoking statement in function **main** . Compile and run your program using 4, 10, and 7.

Exercise 2:   Change your program so that when the number of dollar signs is odd, it uses

```
(numSigns + 1) / 2 - 2
```

as the inside height dimension.

Exercise 3:   Rewrite your solution to Exercise 2 so that the symbol used as the border is also read as data and passed to function **Print** as a parameter. To make the symbol a parameter requires the following changes:

- Prompt for and read the symbol.
- Add the symbol and its type (or just the type) to the formal parameter list of the function prototype.
- Add the symbol and its type to the formal parameter list of the function prototype.
- Add the symbol to the actual parameter list.

Run the program three times using &, %, and A as symbols and 4, 10, and 7 as the number of symbols to use.

Lesson 7-4: Functions with Reference Parameters

Name _____   **Date** _____

Section _____

Exercise 1:   To do this exercise look at program **Shell3**. This program reads two real numbers, **miles** and **hours**, and prints **milesPerHour** on the screen. Function **GetData** prompts the user for the appropriate values, reads them, and returns them to function **main**.

```
// Program Shell3 reads miles and hours and prints miles
// per hour.

#include <iostream.h>
#include <iomanip.h>

/* FILL IN the function prototype for GetData */

int main ()
{
    float   miles;
    float   hours;
    float   milesPerHour;

    cout.setf(ios::fixed, ios::floatfield);
    cout.setf(ios::showpoint);

    /* FILL IN code to invoke function GetData */

    milesPerHour = miles / hours;
    cout  << setw(10)  << miles
          << setw(10)  << hours
          << setw(10)  << milesPerHour  << endl;
    return 0;
}

//****************************************************

/* FILL IN the function heading for GetData */
{
    /* FILL IN Code to prompt for miles and hours */
    /* FILL IN Code to read miles and hours */
}
```

Fill in the missing code, and compile and run your program three times using the values shown on the next page.

Miles	Hours	Miles per Hour
120.1	2.2	_____
332.0	5.5	_____
1250.0	20.0	_____

Exercise 2: Run program **Shell3** three more times, entering the hours first and the miles second. Fill in the answers below.

Miles	Hours	Miles per Hour
2.2	120.1	_____
5.5	332.0	_____
20.0	1250.0	_____

Exercise 3: Explain why the answers are different in Exercises 1 and 2.

Exercise 4: Complete program **Shell4**. When completed, the program reads, counts, and averages the numbers stored in a file.

```
// Program Shell4 averages the values on file dataFile.

#include <iostream.h>
#include <fstream.h>

void ReadAndSum(ifstream&, int&, float&);
// Reads two integer values from a file.

int main ()
{
    ifstream  dataFile;
    int   numberOfValues;
    float  average;

    cout.setf(ios::fixed, ios::floatfield);
    cout.setf(ios::showpoint);

    dataFile.open("Shell4.dat");

    /* FILL IN the invoking statement for ReadAndSum */

    cout  << "The average of "  << numberOfValues
          << " values is "  << average  << endl;
```

```
      return 0;
}
//*************************************
void  ReadAndSum /* TO BE FILLED IN */
// FILL IN documentation.
{
   /* TO BE FILLED IN */
}
```

Fill in function **ReadAndSum** to read, count, and average all the numbers in **dataFile**. Run the program using the data on **Shell4.dat**.

List the Parameters	*Reference or Value?*
_____	_____
_____	_____
_____	_____

The average of _____ values is _____.

Exercise 5:   Lesson 6-4, Exercise 1, contains a loop nested within a loop. The outer loop prompts for and inputs a digit. The inner loop sums the integers from zero through the digit. Rewrite your solution to this task so that the summing of the digits from zero through the input digit is done in void function **SumDigits**. The digit should be an input parameter and the sum of the digits should be an output parameter. Rerun your changed version with the same data: 0, 3, 7, and 9. The results should be the same.

Exercise 6:   Write a void function, **Count**, that takes a file name as input and returns the number of characters on the current line of the file. The function **main** should call the function within a loop that runs until the file stream fails (end of the file) and prints the answers on the screen. Test your program using **CharCt.dl**.

How many lines are there?

How many characters are there on each line?

Exercise 7:   Write a void function, **FindMinimum**, that takes as input a file of integers and returns as output the minimum value on the file. (Remember that all file parameters must be passed by reference.) Write a **main** function that calls **FindMinimum** and prints out the minimum value. Use file **Numbers.dat**. What is printed?

Lesson 7-5: Debugging

Name _____   **Date** _____

Section _____

Exercise 1:   Program **Triangle** inputs three values representing the three sides of a triangle. If the three sides represent an equilateral triangle, "Equilateral" is printed. If the three sides represent an isosceles triangle, "Isosceles" is printed. If the three sides are all different, "Scalene" is printed. There is one problem: the program doesn't work. Debug it.

What errors did you find?

Show the last three lines of output.

Exercise 2:   Look carefully at the last three answers. Did you notice that they are wrong? Yes, they have two equal sides—but they are not triangles at all! For the values to represent a triangle, the sum of any two must be greater than or equal to the third. Add this error checking to the program and print out a message stating that the sides do not represent a triangle. Show the last three lines of output.

Exercise 3:   Program **Triangle** has no documentation and non-problem-specific identifiers. Add appropriate documentation and make the identifiers more meaningful. How did the lack of documentation and the poor choice of identifiers make debugging more difficult?

Postlab Activities

Exercise 1:   The American Heart Association publishes brochures describing what it means to be "Heart Healthy."   We should watch our cholesterol and make sure that no more than 30 percent of our calorie intake comes from fat.   Write a program that reads all the food items eaten in a day along with the fat (in grams) and the calorie content. (Assume that each food item appears on a line by itself, with the fat and calories on the following line with a blank in between.) Echo-print your input on file **Diet.out**, followed by a statement that describes the day's food intake as heart healthy or not heart healthy.   Your program should be interactive.   Each module in your top-down design should be implemented as a function.

Exercise 2:   The following test plan is designed to test the program from Exercise 1. Execute this test plan.   Because of the amount of input required to test this program, we have used a different format for the test plan.

```
General Cases
  Input[1]
    food      : Egg McMuffin with orange juice and coffee.
    fat grams: 11
    calories : 360
    food      : Chunky chicken salad with iced tea.
    fat grams: 6
    calories : 198
    food      : Regular hamburger with small fries and diet
         coke.
    fat grams: 21
    calories : 476
Expected Output
    input echo printed
    'Warning!  You had too many fat calories today.'
Actual Output
```

```
Input
    food      : Whole-grain cereal with low-fat milk and orange
                juice.
```

---

[1]The nutritional information shown here came from a McDonald's placemat. Egg McMuffin, McLean Deluxe, and McDonald's are registered trademarks.

```
                fat grams: 3
                calories : 280
                food      : Chunky chicken salad with iced tea.
                fat grams: 6
                calories : 198
                food      : McLean deluxe, side salad, and diet coke.
                fat grams: 12
                calories : 375
```

    Expected Output
        input echo printed
        'Congratulations! You had a Heart Healthy day.'
    Actual Output

```
┌─────────────────────────────────────────────────────────────────┐
│                                                                   │
│                                                                   │
│                                                                   │
│                                                                   │
│                                                                   │
│                                                                   │
│                                                                   │
└─────────────────────────────────────────────────────────────────┘
```

End Cases
    Input
        food   : <eoln>
        fat grams: 0
        calories : 0
    Expected Output
        input echo printed with food taking up no characters
        'Congratulations! You had a Heart Healthy day.'
    Actual Output

```
┌─────────────────────────────────────────────────────────────────┐
│                                                                   │
│                                                                   │
│                                                                   │
│                                                                   │
│                                                                   │
│                                                                   │
│                                                                   │
└─────────────────────────────────────────────────────────────────┘
```

    Input
        food   : 47 A's
        fat grams: 0
        calories : 0
    Expected Output
        input echo printed with food taking up 46 characters
        'Congratulations! You had a Heart Healthy day.'
    Actual Output

```
┌─────────────────────────────────────────────────────────────────┐
│                                                                   │
│                                                                   │
│                                                                   │
│                                                                   │
│                                                                   │
│                                                                   │
│                                                                   │
└─────────────────────────────────────────────────────────────────┘
```

Exercise 3:   You are going on a round-the-world trip and wonder how many miles you must cover to go from one time zone to another. Write a program that writes out a table showing how many statute miles you must cover to go from one time zone to another when you are at the equator, 30° N and S, 60° N and S, and 180° N and S. You may ignore any local time differences. You must use at least one void function.

Exercise 4:   Alter the program you wrote in Exercise 3 so that it prints out both statute miles and nautical miles for the latitudes requested.

8

Scope, Lifetime, and More on Functions

OBJECTIVES

- To be able to determine which variables are global, which variables are local, and which variables are nonlocal.
- To be able to differentiate between declarations and definitions.
- To be able to differentiate between static and automatic variables.
- To be able to define and invoke a numeric value-returning function to implement a specified task.
- To be able to define and invoke a Boolean value-returning function to implement a specified task.

Chapter 8: Assignment Cover Sheet

Name _____ **Date** _____

Section _____

Fill in the following table showing which exercises have been assigned for each lesson and check what you are to submit: (1) lab sheets, (2) listings of output files, and/or (3) listings of programs. Your instructor or TA can use the Completed column for grading purposes.

Activities	Assigned: Check or list exercise numbers	Submit (1)	(2)	(3)	Completed
Prelab					
Review					
Prelab Assignment					
Inlab					
Lesson 8-1: Check Prelab Exercises					
Lesson 8-2: Static and Automatic Variables					
Lesson 8-3: Value-Returning and Void Functions					
Lesson 8-4: Test Plan					
Lesson 8-5: Debugging					
Postlab					

Prelab Activities

Review

In Chapter 7, we said that local variables are those declared within a block. The block does not have to be the body of a function—local identifiers can be declared within *any* block. In a large program, there may be several variables with the same identifier—*name*, for example. How do we know which variable is meant and where each variable is accessible? The answers to these questions are provided by scope rules.

Scope of an Identifier

There are three categories of scope for an identifier in C++: class scope, local scope, and global scope. Class scope is defined in Chapter 15. Local scope is the scope of an identifier defined within a block and extends from the point where the identifier is declared to the end of the block. Global scope is the scope of an identifier declared outside all functions and extends to the end of the file containing the program.

Function names in C++ have global scope. Once a function name has been declared, any subsequent function can call it. In C++ you cannot nest a function definition within another function. When a function defines a local identifier with the same name as a global identifier, the local identifier takes precedence. That is, the local identifier hides the existence of the global identifier. For obvious reasons this principle is called *name precedence* or *name hiding*.

The rules of C++ that govern who knows what, where, and when are called *scope rules*.

- A function name has global scope.
- The scope of a formal parameter is the same as the scope of a local variable declared in the outermost block of the function body.
- The scope of a local identifier includes all statements following the declaration of the identifier to the end of the block in which it is declared and includes any nested blocks unless a local identifier of the same name is declared in a nested block.
- The scope of an identifier begins with its most recent declaration.

The last two rules mean that if a local identifier in a block is the same as a global or nonlocal identifier to the block, the local identifier blocks access to the other identifier. That is, the block's reference is to its own local identifier.

To summarize, any variable or constant declared outside all functions is a *global identifier*. Any global identifier is known (and can be accessed directly) by any function that does not declare a variable or constant with the same name. Local identifiers of a function are *nonlocal* (but accessible) to any block nested within it.

If global identifiers are accessible to all functions, why don't we just make all identifiers global and do away with parameter lists? Good programming practice dictates that communication between the modules of our program should be explicitly stated. This practice limits the possibility of one module accidentally interfering with another. In other words, each function is given only what it needs to know. This is how we write "good" programs.

Declarations and Definitions

In Chapter 7, we used a function prototype to tell the compiler that a function with certain parameters would be defined later. The function prototype is a declaration that is not also a definition. The function definition includes a heading and a body. The need for a function prototype comes about because most C++ programmers put function **main** physically first in the file. **main** invokes other functions, so the names of the other functions and their parameter types must be known before function **main** is compiled. If we put the function definition physically before **main**, the prototype would not be necessary. The function definition would be both a declaration and a definition.

The distinction between a declaration and a definition is that memory space is reserved in a definition. In a function definition, the space for the compiled code of the function body is reserved. There are times when we want to declare a variable but not define it. That is, we want to let the compiler know about a global variable defined in another file. Look at the following two statements.

```
int  myValue;
extern int  anotherValue;
```

The first statement is both a declaration and a definition. Space is reserved for the variable **myValue** of data type **int**. The second statement is a declaration only. Your program can reference **anotherValue**, but the compiler does not reserve space for it. The reserved word **extern** tells the compiler that **anotherValue** is a global variable located in another file.

More about Variables

The *lifetime* of a variable is the time during program execution when the variable has storage assigned to it. The lifetime of a global variable is the entire execution of the program. The lifetime of a local variable is the execution of the block in which it is declared. There are times when we want to have the value of a local variable remain between calls to the same function. For example, if we want to know how many times a function is called during the execution of a program, we would like to use a local function variable as a counter and increment it each time the function is called. However, if space is allocated each time the function is called and deallocated when the function finishes executing, we can't guarantee that the space for the local variable is the same for each function invocation. In fact, it most likely would not be.

Therefore, C++ lets the user determine the lifetime of each local variable by assigning it a storage class: static or automatic. If you want the lifetime of a local variable to extend to the entire run of the program, you preface the data type identifier with the reserved word **static** when the variable is defined. The default storage class is automatic in which storage is allocated on entry and deallocated on exit from a block.

Any variable may be initialized when it is defined. This is the fourth way to assign a value to a place in memory. To initialize a variable, follow the variable identifier with an equal sign and an expression. The expression is called an *initializer*. The initializing process differs depending on whether the variable being initialized is static or automatic. For a static variable, the initializer must be a constant expression, and its value is stored only once. For an automatic variable, the initializer can be any expression, and its value is stored each time the variable is assigned storage.

User-Defined Value-Returning Functions

With void functions, we use the function name as a statement in our program to represent the action that the function performs. Value-returning functions are used when the action returns only one value and that value is used in an expression. For example, let's write a function that returns the smallest of its three input values.

```cpp
// Program PrintMin prints the smallest of three input values.

#include <iostream.h>

int  Minimum(int, int, int);     // function prototype
// Returns the minimum of three distinct values.

int main()
{
    int   one;
    int   two;
    int   three;
    cout  << "Input three integer values; press return." << endl;
    cin   >> one  >> two  >> three;
    cout  << "The minimum value of "  << one  << ", "  << two
          << ", and "  << three  << " is "
          << Minimum(one, two, three)  << "."  << endl;
    return 0;
}

//*******************************************************

int  Minimum(int first, int second, int third)
// Pre:  Input values are distinct.
// Post: Return minimum of three distinct int values.

{
    if (first < second && first < third)
        return first;
    else if (second < first && second < third)
        return second;
    else if (third < first && third < second)
        return third;
}
```

The function prototype declares a function of data type **int**. This means that the type of the value returned to the calling function is **int**. Because a value-returning function always sends back one value, we designate the type of the value before the function name. We call this data type the *function type*. However, *function value type, function return type*, or *function result type* is more accurate.

In this example, the function invocation occurs in the output statement in function **main**. Function **Minimum** is invoked and the value is returned and immediately sent to the output stream. There are three formal parameters: **first**, **second**, and **third**. The three actual parameters are **one**, **two**, and **three**. Notice that the documentation on the function prototype is different from the documentation on the function definition.

Chapter 8: Prelab Assignment

Name _____   Date _____

Section _____

Read program **Scope** carefully and answer Exercises 1 through 6.

```
// Program Scope demonstrates scope rules and lifetime
classes.

#include <iostream.h>
#include <fstream.h>

int   counter;
int   sum = 0;
int   number;

ifstream   inNums;

void   SumNumbers(ifstream&, int&);

int main ()
{
    inNums.open("Numeric.dat");
    {
        int   sum = 0;
        SumNumbers(inNums, sum);
        cout  << "Output from first call to SumNumbers"
              << endl;
        cout  << "Sum is "  << sum  << endl;

    }
    SumNumbers(inNums, sum);
    cout  << "Output from second call to SumNumbers"
           << endl;
    cout  << "Sum is "  << sum  << endl;
    return 0;
}
//***********************************

void   SumNumbers(ifstream& inFile, int& answer)
{
    static int  counter = 1;
    while (counter <= 4)
    {
        inFile  >> number;
        answer = answer + number;
        counter++;
    }
}
```

Exercise 1: File **Numeric.dat** contains the following values: 10 20 30 40 10 20 30 40. What is printed?

Exercise 2: List the global identifiers.

Exercise 3: Circle each of the blocks in program Scope and number them from top to bottom.

Exercise 4: List the local identifiers and state the block(s) in which each is accessible.

Exercise 5: List the automatic local variables.

Exercise 6: List the static local variables.

Lesson 8-1: Check Prelab Exercises

Name _____   **Date** _____

Section _____

Exercise 1:   Run program **Scope** to check your answers.   Were your answers correct? If not, explain what you did wrong.

Exercise 2:   **counter**, **sum**, **number**, **inNums**, and **SumNumbers**.

Exercise 3:

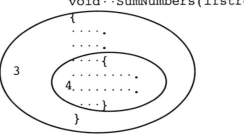

Exercise 4:   Block 1 has no local identifiers.   Block 2 has local identifier **sum**, which hides global identifier **sum**. Block 3 has three local identifiers: **inFile, answer,** and **counter.**

Exercise 5:   automatic local variable: **sum** (local to 2).   All parameters also are automatic variables.

Exercise 6:   static local variable: **counter** (local to 3).   All global variables also are static.

Lesson 8-2: Static and Automatic Variables

Name _____   **Date** _____

Section _____

Use program **Shell1** for Exercises 1 and 2.

```
// Program Shell1 is for investigating the differences between
// automatic and static variables.

#include <iostream.h>

void  TestLocals();

int main ()
{
    TestLocals ();
    TestLocals ();
    TestLocals ();
    return 0;
}

// **************************************

void  TestLocals()
{
    /* TO BE FILLED IN */
}
```

Exercise 1:   Function **TestLocals** defines an automatic variable, **count**, and initializes it to 1. The contents of **count** are incremented and sent to the output stream. Write this code and run program **Shell1**. Record your output. Was it what you expected?

Exercise 2:   Change function **TestLocals** so that variable **count** is a static variable. Rerun your program and show your output. Was it what you expected?

Exercise 3:   Explain the difference between automatic and static variables.

Lesson 8-3: Value-Returning and Void Functions

Name _____   **Date** _____

Section _____

Exercise 1:   Lesson 6-4, Exercise 1, contains a loop nested within a loop. The outer loop prompts for and inputs a digit. The inner loop sums the integers from zero through the digit. Rewrite your solution to this task so that the summing of the digits from zero through the input digit is done in an **int** function, **SumDigits**. The digit should be an input parameter. Rerun your changed version with the same data. The results should be the same.

Exercise 2:   Write an **int** function, **Minimum**, that finds the minimum value on a file. Write a **main** function that calls **Minimum** and prints out the minimum value. Use file **Numbers.dat**. What is printed?

Exercise 3:   In Exercise 2, did you access the file name globally or did you pass the file name as a parameter to function **Minimum**? If you passed the file name, you had a reference parameter to a value-returning function. Both accessing a variable globally and having a reference parameter to a value-returning function are bad style. Should this function have been a void function with two reference parameters? Justify your answer.

Exercise 4:   Program **Convert** is an old friend. This version uses an **int** function to convert temperatures from Fahrenheit to Celsius or from Celsius to Fahrenheit. Examine program **Convert** carefully. The next exercises ask you to modify it.

```
// Program Convert converts a temperature from Fahrenheit to
// Celsius or a temperature from Celsius to Fahrenheit
// depending on whether the user enters an F or a C.

#include <iostream.h>
int  ConvertedTemp(int, char);
```

```
int main ()
{
    char  letter;          // Place to store input letter
    int   tempIn;          // Temperature to be converted
    int   tempOut;         // Converted temperature
    cout  << "Input Menu"  << endl  << endl;
    cout  << "F:  Convert from Fahrenheit to Celsius"  << endl;
    cout  << "C:  Convert from Celsius to Fahrenheit"  << endl;
    cout  << "Q:  Quit"  << endl;
    cout  << "Type a C, F,  or Q; then press return."  << endl;

    cin  >> letter;
    while (letter != 'Q')
    {
        cout  << " Type an integer number, and press return."
              << endl;
        cin  >> tempIn;

        if (letter == 'F')
            cout << "Fahrenheit to Celsius"  << endl;
        else
            cout << "Celsius to Fahrenheit"  << endl;
        cout  << "Temperature to convert: "  << tempIn
              << endl;
        cout  << "Converted temperature:   "
              << ConvertedTemp(tempIn, letter)
              << endl  << endl;
        cout  << "Type a C, F,  or Q; then press return."
              << endl;

        cin  >> letter;
    }
    return 0;
}

// ******************************************

int  ConvertedTemp(int tempIn, char letter)
{
    if (letter == 'C')
        return (9 * tempIn / 5) + 32;
    else
        return 5 * (tempIn - 32) / 9;
}
```

Run program **Convert** using the following data.

Code	Temperature	Result
C	0	_____
C	100	_____
c (lowercase)	100	_____
C	57	_____
C	6	_____
F	42	_____
F	212	_____
F	134	_____
Q		(terminate run)

Exercise 5: Enclose the menu in a void function with no parameters. Rerun your program to check that the results are the same.

Exercise 6: Did you notice that the wrong answer was returned when a lowercase *c* was input? Programs **Convert** has no error checking. Incorrect input just produces an incorect answer. Write a **Boolean** function, **Error**, that takes **letter** and returns **TRUE** if **letter** is not an uppercase *C*, *F*, or *Q* and **FALSE** otherwise. Use **Error** to check for bad data immediately after **letter** is read. If **letter** is not correct, write an error message and prompt again for **letter**. Run the original program and your revised version using lowercase *c* and uppercase *X* as inputs.

Show output from the original version.

Show output from the revised version.

Exercise 7: Restricting the input to uppercase letters in program **Convert** is unreleasitic. Revise the program so that it accepts both uppercase and lowercase input. (Lesson 8-4, Exercise 1, asks you to write a test plan for the revised version of program **Convert**.)

Lesson 8-4: Test Plan

Name _____   **Date** _____

Section _____

Exercise 1:   Design a test plan for program **Convert** as revised in Lesson 8-3, Exercise 7.

Reason for Test Case	Input Values	Expected Output	Observed Output

Exercise 2:   Implement the test plan designed in Exercise 1. You may show the results in the chart in Exercise 1.

Lesson 8-5: Debugging

Name _____   **Date** _____

Section _____

Exercise 1:   Function **Swap** takes two values as input and returns them in reverse order. This little utility routine is very useful. However, it doesn't seem to work correctly. Can you fix it? Program **Driver** is written to test function **Swap**. A program whose only purpose is to test a subprogram is called a *driver*. The driver reads in two values, calls **Swap** with the two input values, and writes out the result. Run **Driver** using 10 and 15 as the input values. What is printed?

Exercise 2:   This answer looks correct but the program has a bug in it—take our word for it. Search until you find an error, correct it, and run the program again. What is printed?

Exercise 3: We bet there is still a problem with your program. Keep on trying. What error did you find this time?

Postlab Activities

Exercise 1: Along with eating a heart healthy diet, everyone should get regular exercise. You are attending an aqua jogging class. After you have been jogging for 15 minutes, the instructor stops the class and has everyone take his or her pulse for six seconds. (She times you.) She then asks if you are in your target zone. To help the class out, you decide to program a target-zone calculator. Each person's target zone is between 60 percent and 75 percent of his or her predicted maximal heart rate in beats per minute. A good approximation to this maximal heart rate is 220 less the person's age.

Write a function, **InTheZone**, that takes a person's age and the six-second pulse rate and returns **TRUE** if the person is within his or her zone and **FALSE** otherwise. Keep prompting for and reading an age and a pulse rate until the user enters end-of-file keystrokes. You must use at least one value-returning function in this assignment.

Exercise 2: Write a driver and a test plan for function **InTheZone**. Implement your test plan.

Exercise 3: In Postlab Exercise 6-6, you were asked to create a table comparing Celsius temperatures with the actual Fahrenheit equivalent and an approximated equivalent. Redesign that program and use **float** functions to calculate the actual value and the approximated value. Run your program with the same data.

Exercise 4: Add a column to the table in Exercise 3 that shows the difference between the actual Fahrenheit equivalent and the approximation. This change makes use of value-retruning functions as specified in Exercise 3 inappropriate. Rewrite the **float** functions as void functions and explain why value-returning functions are no longer appropriate.

9

Additional Control Structures

OBJECTIVES

- To be able to convert a series of If-Then-Else statements to a Switch statement.
- To be able to construct a Switch statement to implement a specified task.
- To be able to convert a While loop to Do-While loop.
- To be able to construct a Do-While loop to do a specified task.
- To be able to construct a For statement to do a specified task.

Chapter 9: Assignment Cover Sheet

Name _____   Date _____

Section _____

Fill in the following table showing which exercises have been assigned for each lesson and check what you are to submit: (1) lab sheets, (2) listings of output files, and/or (3) listings of programs. Your instructor or TA can use the Completed column for grading purposes.

Activities	Assigned: Check or list exercise numbers	Submit (1)	(2)	(3)	Completed
Prelab					
Review					
Prelab Assignment					
Inlab					
Lesson 9-1: Check Prelab Exercises					
Lesson 9-2: Multi-way Branching					
Lesson 9-3: Additional Control Structures					
Lesson 9-4: Test Plan					
Lesson 9-5: Debugging					
Postlab					

Prelab Activities

Review

In preceding chapters, we covered four control structures: the sequence, the If statement, the While statement, and void and value-returning functions. In this chapter, we introduce five additional control structures that make certain tasks easier. However, they are the icing on the cake. You cannot do anything with them that you cannot do with the control structures that you already know.

Break and Continue

Both **break** and **continue** are statements that alter the flow of execution within a control structure. **break** is used with the Switch statement, the While statement, the Do-While statement, and the For statement. (The Switch, Do-While, and For statements are defined below.) **break** interrupts the flow of control by immediately exiting these statements. In contrast, **continue** is used only with looping statements. It alters the flow of control by immediately terminating the current iteration. Note the difference between **continue** and **break** in a loop: **continue** skips to the next iteration of the loop, and **break** skips to the statement following the loop.

    break is extremely useful with the Switch statement but should be used with caution with looping statements. Good style dictates that loops have only one entry and one exit except under very unusual circumstances. **continue** is very seldom used; we only mention it for completeness.

Multi-Way Branching: Switch

The *Switch* statement is a selection statement that can be used in place of a series of If-Then-Else statements. Alternative statements are listed with a *switch label* in front of each. A switch label is either a *case label* or the word **default**. A case label is the word **case** followed by a constant expression. An integral expression called the *switch expression* is used to match one of the values on the case labels. The statement associated with the value that is matched is the statement that is executed. Execution then continues sequentially from the matched label until the end of the Switch statement is encountered or a **break** statement is encountered.

```
switch (grade)
{
    case 'A' : cout  << "Great work!";
               break;
    case 'B' : cout  << "Good work!";
               break;
    case 'C' : cout  << "Passing work!";
               break;
    case 'D' :
    case 'F' : cout  << "Unsatisfactory work.";
               cout  << "See your instructor.";
               break;
```

```
        default  : cout  << grade  << " is not a legal grade";
                   break;
}
```

grade is the switch expression; the letters beside the statements make up the case labels. The value in **grade** is compared with the value in each case label. When a match is found, the corresponding statement is executed. If the value of the switch expression does not match a value in any case label, the **defualt** label is matched by default. Because execution continues after a match until **break** is encountered, both '**D**' and '**F**' send the same message to the screen. What would happen if we forgot to put **break** after the statement associated with **case 'B'**? Every time **grade** contained a *B* both "Good work!" and "Passing work!" would be printed.

Looping: Do-While

The *Do-While* statement is a looping statement that tests the Boolean expression at the end of the loop. A statement (or sequence of statements) is executed *While* an expression is true. The Do-While statement differs from the While statement in one major respect: the body of the loop is always executed at least once in the Do-While statement. For example, the following loop reads and counts characters in stream **inFile** until a blank is found.

```
numberOfCharacters = 0;
inFile  >> character;

// assume first character is not a blank
do
{
    numberOfCharacters++;
    inFile >> character;
} (while character != ' ');
```

We may use the Do-While statement to construct both count-controlled loops and event-controlled loops.

Looping: For

In contrast, the *For* statement is a looping construct designed specifically to simplify the implementation of count-controlled loops. The loop-control variable, the beginning value, the ending value, and the incrementation are explicitly part of the For heading itself. The following For loop reads and sums 10 values.

```
sum = 0;
for (counter = 1; counter <= 10; counter++)
{
    cin  >> value;
    sum = sum + value;
}
```

counter, the loop-control variable, is initialized to 1. While **counter** is less than or equal to 10, the block of code is executed, and **counter** is incremented by 1. The loop is executed with **counter** equal to the initial value, the final value, and all the values in between. The second expression in the For heading is the assertion that controls the loop. If the assertion is false initially, the body of the loop is not executed. Here are a two For headings and what they mean.

for (counter = limit; counter != 0; counter - -): Initialize **counter** to the value stored in **limit**; if **counter** is not equal to 0, execute the body of the loop; decrement **counter** by 1 and go back to the test. If **limit** contains the value 10, this For loop is identical to the previous one: it executes 10 times.

for (int counter = 1; counter <= limit; counter++): Define an **int** variable **counter** and initialize it to 1. If **counter** is less than or equal to the value stored in **limit**, execute the body of the loop. Increment **counter** by 1. The scope of **counter** is not the body of the loop but the block in which the For statement is enclosed.

The For statement in C++ is very flexible. Although designed to simplify count-controlled loops, it can be used for event-controlled loops. The first statement in the For header can be any statement—even a stream extraction or the null statement. The second statement is a test that occurs at the beginning of the loop. The third statement is one that is executed at the end of the loop. So the For heading

```
for (cin >> character; character != '.'; cin >> character)
```

is legal. In fact, no loop body (except the null statement—a semicolon) is needed here because everything is done in the heading. However, we recommend that the For statement be used only for count-controlled loops. That is what For statements are designed for. Most other uses fall into the category of tricky code and should be avoided. (How long did it take you to determine what this loop is doing?)

Loops constructed with the While statement and the For statement are called pretest loops because the expression is tested at the beginning of the loop before the body of the loop is executed the first time. Loops constructed with the Do-While statement are called posttest loops because the expression is tested at the end of the loop.

Chapter 9: Prelab Assignment

Name _____   **Date** _____

Section _____

Read program **Loops** carefully and answer Exercises 1 and 2.

```
// Program Loops demonstrates various looping structures.
#include <iostream.h>
#include <fstream.h>

int main ()
{
    ifstream  inData;
    int  value;
    inData.open("Loop.dat");

    // while loop
    {
        int  counter = 1;
        int  sum = 0;
        while (counter <= 4)
        {
            inData  >> value;
            sum = sum + value;
            counter++;
        }
        cout  << sum  << endl;
    }

    // do-while loop
    {
        int  counter = 1;
        int  sum = 0;
        do
        {
            inData  >> value;
            sum = sum + value;
            counter++;
        } while (counter <= 4);
        cout  << sum  << endl;
    }

    // for loop
    {
        int  sum = 0;
        for (int counter = 1; counter <= 4; counter++)
        {
            inData  >> value;
            sum = sum + value;
        }
```

```
            cout  << sum  << endl;
    }
    return 0;
}
```

Exercise 1:   If file **Loop.dat** contains the following values, what is printed?

10 20 30 40 10 20 30 40 10 20 30 40

Exercise 2:   Which of these loops are pretest loops? Which are posttest?

Examine program Switches and answer Exercises 3 and 4.

```
// Program Switches demonstrates the use of the Switch
// statement.

#include <iostream.h>

int main ()
{
    char  letter;
    int   first;
    int   second;
    int   answer;

    cout  << "Enter an A for addition or an S for"
          << " subtraction, followed by two integer "  << endl
          << " numbers.  Press return.  Enter a Q to quit."
          << endl;
    cin  >> letter;
    while (letter != 'Q')
    {
        cin  >> first  >> second;

        switch (letter)
        {
            case 'A' : answer = (first + second);
                       cout << first  << " + "  << second
                            << " is "  << answer  << endl;
                       break;
            case 'S' : answer = (first - second);
                       cout << first  << " - "  << second
                            << " is "  << answer  << endl;
                       break;
        }
        cin  >> letter;
    }

    return 0;
}
```

```
A    5   -7
A   -5   -8
S    7    7
S    8   -8
Q
```

Exercise 4: What happens if the Q to quit is entered as a lowercase letter?

Lesson 9-1: Check Prelab Exercises

Name _____   **Date** _____

Section _____

Exercise 1:   Run program **Loops** and check your answers.   Were your answers correct?   If not, do you understand your mistakes?

Exercise 2:   While loops and For loops are pretest loops;   the loop body is not executed if the ending condition is true initially.   Do-While loops are posttest loops; their bodies are always executed at least once.

Exercise 3:   Run program **Switches** to check your answers.   Were your answers correct?   If not, do you understand your mistakes?

Exercise 4:   If a lowercase *Q* is entered, the body of the While   statement is executed again.   The screen freezes waiting for you to enter more values.

Lesson 9-2: Multi-Way Branching

Name _____ **Date** _____

Section _____

Exercise 1: As Prelab Exercise 4 demonstrated, program **Switches** is not very robust. Add the code necessary to allow the program to work properly with both lowercase and uppercase versions of the input letters. Run your program with the same data, but key the letters as lowercase.

Exercise 2: Program **Switches** is still not very robust. Add a default case that prints an error message and asks for the letter to be reentered. Test your program with the same data set, but add several letters that are not correct.

Exercise 3: Program **Shell1** is the shell of a program that counts all the punctuation marks in a file.

```
// Program Shell1 counts punctuation marks in a file.

#include <iostream.h>
#include <fstream.h>

int main ()
{
    ifstream  inData;
    char symbol;
    int   periodCt = 0;
    int   commaCt = 0;
    int   questionCt = 0;
    int   colonCt = 0;
    int   semicolonCt = 0;
    inData.open("switch.dat");
    /* FILL IN */
    return 0;
}
```

Fill in the missing code and run your program. Show the answers below.

Number of periods: _____   Number of commas: _____
Number of question marks: _____   Number of colons: _____
Number of semicolons: _____

Exercise 4: Add the code necessary for program **Shell1** to count blanks as well. How many blanks are there in file **switch.dat**? If you did not get 12, go back and check your program.

Lesson 9-3: Additional Control Structures

Name _____   **Date** _____

Section _____

Use program **Looping** for Exercises 1, 2, and 3. This program reads and sums
exactly 10 integers and then reads and sums integers until a negative value is read.

```
// Program Looping uses a count-controlled loop to read and
// sum 10 integer values and an event-controlled loop to
// read and sum values until a negative value is found.
// The data is on file Looping.dat.

#include <iostream.h>
#include <fstream.h>

int main ()
{
    ifstream  inData;
    int  value;
    int  counter;
    int  sum;
    inData.open("Looping.dat");

    counter = 1;
    sum = 0;
    while (counter <= 10)
    {// ten values read and summed
        inData  >> value;
        sum = sum + value;
        counter++;
    }
    cout  << "The first sum is "  << sum  << endl;

    inData  >> value;
    sum = 0;
    while (value >= 0)
    {// values are read and summed until a negative is read
        sum = sum + value;
        inData  >> value;
    }
    cout  << "The second sum is "  << sum  << endl;
    return 0;
}
```

Exercise 1:   Compile and run program **Looping**.

First sum is   _____ .

Second sum is   _____ .

Exercise 2:   Program **Looping** contains two loops implemented with While statements. Rewrite program **Looping**, replacing the While statements with Do-While statements.

First sum is   _____ .

Second sum is   _____ .

Exercise 3:   Can program **Looping** be rewritten using a For statement for each loop? Explain.

Rewrite program **Looping** using a For statement to implement the count-controlled loop.

First sum is   _____ .

Second sum is   _____ .

Exercise 4:   Rerun your program using data file **Looping.d2**. Describe what happens.

If an error condition was generated, correct your program and rerun the program.

First sum is   _____ .

Second sum is   _____ .

Exercise 5:   Yet another version of program **Convert** is shown on the next page. (Remember, this program converts Fahrenheit to Celsius or Celsius to Fahrenheit.)

```
// Program Convert converts a temperature from Fahrenheit to
// Celsius or a temperature from Celsius to Fahrenheit
// depending on whether the user enters an F or a C.

#include <iostream.h>

void  PrintMenu();
int   ConvertedTemp(int, char);

int main ()
{
    char letter;           // Place to store input letter
    int  tempIn;           // Temperature to be converted
    int  tempOut;          // Converted temperature

    PrintMenu();
    cin  >> letter;

    while (letter != 'Q')
    {
        if (letter == 'R')
            PrintMenu();
        else
        {
            cout  << "Type an integer number "
                  << "and press return."
                  << endl;
            cin  >> tempIn;
            if (letter == 'F')
               cout  << "Fahrenheit to Celsius"  << endl;
            else
                cout  << "Celsius to Fahrenheit"
                      << endl;
            cout  << "Temperature to convert: "
                  << tempIn  << endl;
            cout  << "Converted temperature:  "
                  << ConvertedTemp(tempIn, letter)
                  << endl  << endl;
            cout  << "Type a C, F, R, or Q;"
            cout  << " press return."
                  << endl;
        }
        cin  >> letter;
    }
     return 0;
}

// ******************************************
```

```
int  ConvertedTemp(int tempIn, char letter)
{
    if (letter == 'C')
        return (9 * tempIn / 5) + 32;
    else
        return 5 * (tempIn - 32) / 9;
}

//*********************************************

void  PrintMenu()
{
    cout  << "Input Menu"  << endl  << endl;
    cout  << "F:  Convert from Fahrenheit to Celsius"
          << endl;
    cout  << "C:  Convert from Celsius to Fahrenheit"
          << endl;
    cout  << "R:  Reprint the menu"  << endl;
    cout  << "Q:  Quit"  << endl;
    cout  << "Type a C, F, R or Q; then press return."
          << endl;
}
```

Rewrite program **Convert** replacing the If statements with Switch statements. Make your program as robust as possible. (Recall that robust is a descriptive term for a program that can recover from erroneous inputs and keep running.) Run your program using the following input data.

Code	Temperature	Result
C	0	_____
C	57	_____
R		menu printed
F	212	_____
R		menu printed
F	134	_____
Q		terminate run

Exercise 6: There is no error checking in program **Convert**, and only uppercase letters are accepted. Rewrite the solution to Exercise 5 with the following changes.

- The program accepts both uppercase and lowercase letters.
- If a letter that is not in the set of acceptable letters is entered, print an error message and ask for the letter to be reentered. (Hint: Use the **default** case.)

Lesson 9-4: Test Plan

Name _____   **Date** _____

Section _____

Exercise 1:   Design a test plan for program **Convert** as changed in Lesson 9-3, Exercise 6.

Reason for Test Case	Input Values	Expected Output	Observed Output

Lesson 9-5: Debugging

Name _____   **Date** _____

Section _____

Exercise 1:   Program **Bugs** is supposed to sum the first ten values on a file and the second ten values on a file. The second ten values are a duplicate of the first ten, so the answers should be the same. The program checks to be sure that the file has been found and halts execution if the file is not found. Program **Bugs** compiles, says that the file cannot be found, but then the screen freezes. Can you find the problem? Describe it.

Exercise 2:   Correct the problem and rerun the program. The file cannot be found, but now the program halts correctly. Correct the name of the file and rerun the program.

Exercise 3:   What—the screen freezes again? Back to the drawing board. Describe the next error you find. Correct the program and run it again.

Exercise 4:   Now you are getting output, but the answer is wrong for the second sum. When you find this last error, describe it, correct it, and rerun the program. What are the correct totals?

Postlab Activities

Exercise 1:   Write a top-down design and a program to analyze a sample of text. Collect statistics on the following categories of symbols:

- Uppercase letters
- Lowercase letters
- Digits
- End-of-sentence markers (periods, explanation points, and question marks)
- Intrasentence markers (commas, semicolons, and colons)
- Blanks
- All other symbols

Use a Switch statement in your processing. (If you are not using the ASCII character set, you need to use functions found in **<ctype.h>**.)

After collecting these statistics, use them to approximate the following statistics:

- Average word length
- Average sentence length

Exercise 2:   Design and implement a test plan for the program in Exercise 1.

Exercise 3:   Scoring a tennis game is different from scoring any other game. The following table shows how a tennis game is scored. The score is always given with the server's score first. In this table, Player 1 is the server.

Score	Player 1 Wins Point	Player 2 Wins Point
0/0	15/0	0/15
0/15	15/15	0/30
0/30	15/30	0/40
0/40	15/40	game
15/0	30/0	15/15
15/15	30/15	15/30
15/30	30/30	15/40
15/40	30/40	game
30/0	40/0	30/15
30/15	40/15	30/30
30/30	40/30	30/40
30/40	<u>30/30</u>	game
40/0	game	40/15
40/15	game	40/30
40/30	game	<u>30/30</u>

The two underlined scores (30/30) should actually be 40/40, but in tennis you have to win by 2 points, so 40/40 behaves like 30/30. (See what we mean about being strange?) Write a function that takes two scores and the player who won the point and returns the new scores. This function is more complex than any you have done so far. Treat it like a complete program. Begin with a top-down design that outlines your solution. There are 15 possibilities, but some can be combined. You must use at least one Switch statement in your program.

Exercise 4: Write a test plan for the function written for Exercise 3. Implement your test plan.

10

Simple Data Types: Built-In and User-Defined

OBJECTIVES

- To be able to determine the range of numeric types.
- To be able to work with character data.
- To examine the results of using floating point arithmetic.
- To be able to define and use enumeration data types.
- To be able to distinguish between widening and narrowing in type coercion.

Chapter 10: Assignment Cover Sheet

Name _____ **Date** _____

Section _____

Fill in the following table showing which exercises have been assigned for each lesson and check what you are to submit: (1) lab sheets, (2) listings of output files, and/or (3) listings of programs. Your instructor or TA can use the Completed column for grading purposes.

Activities	Assigned: Check or list exercise numbers	Submit (1)	(2)	(3)	Completed
Prelab					
Review					
Prelab Assignment					
Inlab					
Lesson 10-1: Check Prelab Exercise					
Lesson 10-2: Numeric Data Types					
Lesson 10-3: Char Data Types					
Lesson 10-4: Enumeration Data Types					
Lesson 10-5: Debugging					
Postlab					

Prelab Activities

Review

Simple Data Types

The built-in simple data types in C++ are integral types and floating types. The integral types are **char**, **short**, **int**, **long,** and **enum**. The floating types are **float**, **double**, and **long double**. You have seen all of these with the exception of the nonnumeric type **enum**, which we cover later in this chapter. All of these data types are called *simple* or *atomic* because they are composed of single, indivisible values.

The range of values that can be stored in a simple numeric data type depends on the number of bytes of storage assigned to the data type. C++ provides a unary operator, **sizeof**, that returns the number of bytes in its operand. C++ does not specify the number of bytes for any data type except **char**, which is defined to be one byte but guarantees that the following relationships are true.

```
 1= sizeof(char)
<= sizeof(short)
<= sizeof(int)
<= sizeof(long)
```

and

```
    sizeof(float)
<= sizeof(double)
<= sizeof(long  double)
```

Numeric Constants

C++ allows three types of integral constants: decimal, octal, and hexadecimal. All of the integral constants we have used so far have been decimal. An octal constant begins with an explicit 0 (zero) and contains only the digits 0 through 7. A hexadecimal constant begins with an explicit 0 followed by either x or X and the digits in the number chosen from the set of digits 0 through 9 and the letters A through F, which represent the digits 0 through 15. For the rest of this manual, we use only decimal constants. Octal and hexadecimal constants are used in more advanced programming.

Floating point constants are assumed to be of data type **double**. If you want the constant to be of data type **float**, append an f or F to the end of the number.

Numeric Processing

In a previous lesson, you wrote a program to convert temperatures from Fahrenheit to Celsius and from Celsius to Fahrenheit. Because the program uses integer values, some strange results occur. For example, the temperature 6 degrees Celsius is converted to 42 degrees Fahrenheit, but 42 degrees Fahrenheit is converted to 5 degrees Celsius. The temperature 57 degrees Celsius is converted to 134 degrees Fahrenheit, but 134 degrees Fahrenheit is converted to 56 degrees Celsius.

This strange behavior is caused by *truncation error*. The calculation is done using integer arithmetic. The / operator returns an integer quotient, and the remainder is thrown away. If the temperatures are stored in floating point variables, the results are more accurate.

There are also problems associated with floating point arithmetic. For example, we know that 1/3 + 1/3 + 1/3 should sum to 1. This is not true, however, when we are representing 1/3 in a computer. The real number 1/3 is a repeating fraction that never terminates. A repeating fraction represented in a computer must terminate, leading to inaccuracies. For example, if a particular computer can represent only five decimal places in a real number, look what happens with the following code segment:

```
oneThird = 1.0 / 3.0;
one = oneThird + oneThird + oneThird;
if one = 1.0;
        .
        .
        .
else
        .
        .
        .
```

Theoretically, the **else** branch is always taken because the value stored in **one** is 0.99999. If **one** is printed, however, it shows 1.0 because the displayed result is rounded unless the number of decimal places you request in the field specification is the exact number that can be represented in your machine.

Char Constants

Although data type **char** can be used to hold small integer values, its main purpose is to hold character data. Each character in a character set has two representations: an external and an internal. The external representation is what it looks like on an I/O device; the internal representation is the way in which it is encoded in memory. The external representation of the letter *B* is *B*; the internal representation is an integer value. The external representation of any character is the same in all character sets, but the internal representation is not. The internal representation of the letter *B* is 66 in ASCII and 194 in EBCDIC. When you send a variable to the output stream, how does it know whether to send the character or the number? If the variable is of data type **char**, the external representation is sent (printed). For any other integral type, a number is sent (printed).

There are two types of **char** constants: printable and nonprintable characters. The printable characters are listed in the text of a program enclosed in single quotes. The nonprintable characters, which are control characters used with hardware devices, are written in the program by their escape sequence. The escape sequence is one or more characters following a backslash (\). The most commonly used escape sequence is '\n' that forces a new line on an output device. In Chapter 6, an example of counting characters in lines of text used the expression (**character != '\n'**) to control a loop. That is, the loop executed as long as the character read was not the newline character '\n'.

Char Processing

Because data type **char** is considered a numeric data type, we can apply all the numeric operators to values of type **char**. Because we *can* does not mean we *should*. If you are using **char** variables to hold alphanumeric characters, adding two of them doesn't make sense. However, using them in relational expressions does make sense: we are making statements about the relationship between the two characters in terms of their relative positions in the collating sequence of the machine.

Compound conditions involving characters can be a problem depending on the character set of the machine. For example, if you want to test to see if a character is an uppercase letter, the following expression works correctly on an ASCII machine but not on an EBCDIC machine.

```
if (character >= 'A' && character <= 'Z')
```

In ASCII, the letters are sequential, but in EBCDIC there are several gaps between letters that are used to represent nonprintable characters. Therefore, **character** could contain a nonprintable character rather than an uppercase letter and the expression would still return true. To ensure that your programs are portable to any machine, you should use the collection of functions provided in **<ctype.h>** when working with character data. A few of the most useful functions are listed below:

isalpha(ch)	Returns true if **ch** is a letter; false otherwise.
isdigit(ch)	Returns true if **ch** is a digit; false otherwise.
iscntrl(ch)	Returns true if **ch** is a control character; false otherwise.
ispunct(ch)	Returns true if **ch** is a nonblank printable character (i.e., not a letter or a digit); false otherwise.
toupper(ch)	Returns **ch** in uppercase regardless of original case.
tolower(ch)	Returns **ch** in lowercase regardless of original case.

Enumeration Types

An *enumeration type* is a type in which the constant identifiers (called *enumerators*) are explicitly listed.

```
enum Birds {BLUEJAY, CARDINAL, ROBIN, SEAGULL, SWALLOW};
enum LetterGrade {A, B, C, D, F};

Birds    aBird;
LetterGrade   grade;
```

aBird can contain any of the enumerators (constants) listed in data type **Birds**. **grade** can contain any of the enumerators listed in data type **LetterGrade**. The enumerators of an enumeration type can be used in a program just like any other constant.

```
aBird = ROBIN;
grade = A;
if (grade == B)
```

Note that **grade** does not contain the character *A*. **grade** contains a value of the data type **LetterGrade**, the enumerator *A*. For obvious reasons, enumeration types are called *user-defined* data types.

Enumerators are ordered by the way in which they are listed. In a relational expression enumerators are evaluated exactly as characters would be: whether one enumerator comes before the other in the ordering of the enumerators.

Stream I/O is not defined for enumeration types. Printing out the values of an enumeration type must be done by converting the value from the enumeration type into a string that corresponds to the enumerator.

```
switch (aBird)
{
    case BLUEJAY : cout << "BlueJay";
                   break;
    case CARDINAL: cout << "Cardinal";
                   break;
    .
    .
}
```

Values of an enumeration type cannot be read; they must be set in the program. However, the name of the enumeration type can be used to convert, or type cast, a number representing the position of an enumerator in the listing of the data type into the enumerator in that position. For example,

```
aBird = Birds(0)
```

stores **BLUEJAY** into variable **aBird** because **BLUEJAY** is in the 0th position of the enumerators. You can use this technique to input values of enumeration types. The user can be given a menu showing the enumerators and asked to key in the number representing the enumerator they wish to input. The number is read and type cast into the enumerator.

If you create an enumeration type that you might want to use again, you can store the definition in a file with the **.h** extension and use **#include** to access the file. Rather than putting the file name in angled brackets, you put it in double quotes. This tells the preprocessor to look for the file in your current directory.

More on Type Coercion and Type Conversion

Recall that *type coercion* is the implicit changing of a data type by C++ and *type conversion* is explicit type changing by the programmer. Type coercion occurs whenever values of different data types are used in arithmetic and relational expressions, assignment operations, parameter passing, and as return values from value-returning functions.

In arithmetic and relational expressions, values of **char**, **short**, or **enum** data types are changed to values of type **int**. If all the data types involved are now type **int**, the expression is evaluated. If they are not all the same, the "lower" ones are promoted to the "highest" data type in the expression, and the expression is evaluated. The data types are ordered as follows from lowest (**int**) to highest (**long double**):

int, unsigned int, long, unsigned long, float, double, long double

Converting one data type to another that is higher is called *promotion* or *widening*. Notice that no information is lost.

When coercion occurs in assignment operations, parameter passing, and returning values from a value-returning function, a value is being stored into a variable. If the data type of the value and the variable are not the same, the value is coerced into the data type of the variable. If the data type of the variable is higher, then no information is lost, but it may be lost if the data type of the variable is lower. For example, if the function type is **int** and the value returned is **float**, the value is truncated. Converting a value from a higher to a lower data type is called *demotion* or *narrowing*.

Type coercion is defined from an **enum** type to an **int** type but not the other way around. You must use type conversion (type casting) to change an integer value into an enumerator. Look again at the following statement.

```
aBird = Birds(aBird + 1);
```

aBird is coerced to **int** and 1 is added. However, the result must be type cast back to the enumeration type to be stored.

Side Effects

C++ supplies a bewildering array of specialized operators that, like the control structures described in the last chapter, are nice to have but not necessary. We do not review them here, but we must take a few moments to review what we have called the basic *assignment operator*, a single equal sign, because all of the assignment operators behave in the same way.

A variable followed by an equal sign followed by an expression forms an *assignment expression*. Assignment expressions do two things: they calculate a value and (as a side effect) they store that value in the place named on the left of the equal sign. An assignment expression becomes an assignment statement when the expression is terminated by a semicolon. Because an assignment expression returns a value, it can be used within another expression. Thus,

```
if (value >= one = one + 1)
```

calculates the value of **one + 1** and compares **value** to the result. As a side effect, variable **one** has the incremented value stored back in it. We mentioned in Chapter 5 that an assignment is actually an expression in the context of explaining what happens when the equal sign is used when the double equal is meant.

We are not advocating that you use assignment expressions embedded within other expressions in your program. Quite the contrary. We just want you to be aware that this type of statement is legal and what it means if you encounter it. Because this feature is so complex, hard to understand, and unnecessary, we do not recommend its use.

Chapter 10: Prelab Assignment

Name _____   **Date** _____

Section _____

Exercise 1:   Program **Gauge** reads **int** values and converts them to the appropriate constant in an enumeration type. The constants in the enumeration type are used as the case labels in a Switch statement that controls which message is printed.

```
// Program Gauge inputs pressure readings from file Gauge.dat
// and writes appropriate messages.

#include <iostream.h>
#include <fstream.h>

enum DecisionType {ERROR, NORMAL, HIGH, EVACUATE};

void GetPressure(ifstream&, DecisionType&);
// Gets variable of DecisionType from a file.

int main ()
{
    ifstream  readings;
    DecisionType  pressure;
    readings.open("gauge.dat");
    do
    {
        GetPressure(readings, pressure);
        switch (pressure)
        {
            case ERROR    : cout  << "Error in input."
                                  << endl;
                            break;
            case NORMAL   : cout  << "Pressure in normal range."
                                  << endl;
                            break;
            case HIGH     : cout  << "Pressure on the high side."
                                  << endl;
                            break;
            case EVACUATE : cout  << "Evacuate plant!!!!"
                                  << endl;
                            break;
        }
    }  while (pressure != EVACUATE);
    return 0;
}

/****************************************************/
```

```
void GetPressure(ifstream& readings, DecisionType& pressure)
// Pre:   File readings has been opened.
// Post: An integer pressure has been read from file readings.
//        pressure is ERROR if a negative pressure was read.
//        pressure is NORMAL if the value was between 0 and 49.
//        pressure is HIGH if the value was between 50 and 99.
//        pressure is EVACUATE if the value was 100 or above.

{
    int  reading;

    readings  >> reading;
    if (reading < 0)
        pressure = ERROR;
    else if (reading < 50)
        pressure = NORMAL;
    else if (reading < 100)
        pressure = HIGH;
    else
        pressure = EVACUATE;
}
```

If file **Gauge.dat** has the following data values, what is printed?

10 1   49   50   99   -2   120

Lesson 10-1: Check Prelab Exercise

Name _____   **Date** _____

Section _____

Exercise 1:   Run program **Gauge** and check your answer.   Was your answer correct? If not, what did you calculate incorrectly?

Lesson 10-2: Numeric Data Types

Name _____   **Date** _____

Section _____

Exercise 1:   Write a program that prints out the followings values:

```
INT_MAX
1 + INT_MAX
1 + (- INT_MAX)
1 - INT_MAX
1 - (- INT_MAX))
```

In order to access **INT_MAX**, you must include file **<limits.h>**. Did you get what you expected? Explain.

Exercise 2:   Write a program that prints out the size in bytes of all of the numeric types, both integral and floating. Use the **sizeof** operator. Show your results.

Exercise 3:   Run program **Problems**.

```
// Program Problems demonstrates some problems associated
// with floating point arithmetic.

#include <iostream.h>
#include <iomanip.h>

int main ()
{
    float   oneThird;
    float   one;
    cout.setf(ios::fixed, ios::floatfield);
    cout.setf(ios::showpoint);

    oneThird = 1.0 / 3.0;
    cout  << " 1/3 "  << setprecision(5)  << setw(7)
          << oneThird  << endl;
    one = oneThird + oneThird + oneThird;
    cout  << " 1/3 + 1/3 + 1/3 "  << setw(7)
          << one  << endl;
    if (one == 1.0)
        cout  << "Result when used in test is 1.0."
              << endl;
    else
        cout  << "Result when used in test is NOT 1.0."
              << endl;
    return 0;
}
```

What was printed? What does this tell you about your C++ system?

Exercise 4:   Rewrite program **Problems**, substituting 1.0/10.0 for 1.0/3.0. In decimal arithmetic, 1/10 added to itself 10 times is exactly 1.0. Is this true when calculated on a computer? Run the program and record the results.

Exercise 5: Examine the following program:

```cpp
// Program FactTest is a driver program that tests function
// Factorial.

#include <iostream.h>

int  Factorial(int);
// Calculates factorial of an integer.

int main ()

{
    int  number;

    cout  << "Enter a nonnegative integer number. "
          << "Press return."  << endl;
    cin  >> number;
    while (number >= 0)
    {
        cout  << number  << " factorial is "
              << Factorial(number)  << endl;
        cout  << "To continue, enter another nonnegative "
              << "number; to quit, enter a negative number."
              << endl;
        cin  >> number;
    }
    return 0;
}

/*******************************************************/

int  Factorial(int  number)
// Pre:  number is positive.
// Post: Return value is the factorial of number, calculated
//       iteratively.
{
    int  tempFact = 1;

    while (number > 1)
    {
        tempFact = tempFact * number;
        number = number - 1;
    }
    return tempFact;
}
```

The factorial of 0 is 1; the factorial of a positive integer is the product of the numbers from 1 up to and including the integer. For example, the factorial of 4 is 4*3*2*1, or 24. Program **FactTest** is a driver for function **Factorial**, which computes the factorial of an input value. Compile and run this program using increasing integer values beginning with zero. Record the input values along with the associated factorials until something strange happens.

Value	Factorial	Value	Factorial
_____	_____	_____	_____
_____	_____	_____	_____
_____	_____	_____	_____
_____	_____	_____	_____
_____	_____	_____	_____

Factorials build up very quickly. When the value being calculated gets too large to be stored in a memory location in your particular computer (greater than **INT_MAX**), overflow occurs. Each system handles it differently. Describe what happens on your system. Relate the results to the answers to Exercise 1.

Exercise 6: Change function **Factorial** to be of type **long** and rerun your program. What is the largest factorial that can be computed using type **long**?

Lesson 10-3: Char Data Types

Name _____   **Date** _____

Section _____

Exercise 1:   **Shell** is the shell of a program designed to read characters and process them in the following way.

lowercase character   converts to uppercase and writes the character
uppercase character   writes the character
digit   writes the digit
blank   writes a blank
newline   writes newline
any other character   does nothing

```
// Program Shell reads characters from file DataIn and
// writes them to DataOut with the following changes:
//     all letters are converted to uppercase, digits are
//     unchanged, and all other characters except blanks and
//     newline markers are removed.

#include <iostream.h>
#include <ctype.h>
#include <fstream.h>

int main ()
{
    ifstream  dataIn;
    ofstream  dataOut;
    char  character;

    dataIn.open("ReFormat.dat");
    dataOut.open("DataOut.dat");

    dataIn.get(character);      // priming read
    while (dataIn)
    {
        /* FILL IN THE Code to output the correct character */
        dataIn.get(character);
    }
    return 0;
}
```

You are to fill in the code to make the required conversions and create the output file. Run your program. List below the last three lines of output written on file **DataOut**.

Exercise 2: Write a program that prints out all of the characters in the character set that your C++ compiler uses. Describe what happens.

Exercise 3: If you are using a machine that has the ASCII character set, change the program in Exercise 2 to print the characters between ' ' and '~'. Describe what happens. Why are the outputs from Exercises 2 and 3 so different?

Exercise 4: If you are using a machine that has the EBCDIC character set, explain why Exercise 3 is not appropriate for you.

Lesson 10-4: Enumeration Data Types

Name _____ Date _____

Section _____

Exercise 1: **Shell2** is the shell of a program that solves the problem in Lesson 10-3, Exercise 1, using an enumeration data type.

```cpp
// Program Shell2 reads characters from file DataIn and
// writes them to DataOut with the following changes:
//    all letters are converted to uppercase, digits are
//    unchanged, and all other characters except blanks and
//    newline markers are removed.

#include <iostream.h>
#include <ctype.h>
#include <fstream.h>

enum CharType {LO_CASE, UP_CASE, DIGIT, BLANK_NEWLINE, OTHER};

CharType  KindOfChar(char);
// Gets the enumerator equivalent to its character input.

int main ()
{
    ifstream  dataIn;
    ofstream  dataOut;
    char  character;

    dataIn.open("ReFormat.dat");
    dataOut.open("DataOut.dat");

    dataIn.get(character);     // priming read
    while (dataIn)
    {
        switch (KindOfChar(character))
        {

        // FILL IN THE Code to output the correct character

        }
        dataIn.get(character);
    }
    return 0;
}


/*************************************************/

CharType  KindOfChar(char  character)
// Post: character has been converted to the corresponding
//       constant in the enumeration type CharType.
```

```
{
    if (isupper(character))
        return  // TO BE FILLED IN
    else if (islower(character))
        return  // TO BE FILLED IN
    else if (isdigit(character))
        return  // TO BE FILLED IN
    else if (character == ' ' || character == '\n')
        return  // TO BE FILLED IN
    else
        return  // TO BE FILLED IN
}
```

You are to fill in the code of function **KindOfChar** and the Switch statement in the body of function **main**. Run your program. List below the last three lines of output written on file **DataOut**.

Lesson 10-5: Debugging

Name _____   **Date** _____

Section _____

Exercise 1:   Program **EnumIO** compiles correctly, but the answers are wrong. Read the documentation carefully and correct the program. Describe the error.

Exercise 2:   Program **Time** takes an Eastern standard time in hours, minutes, and seconds and prints it out in Eastern time, Central time, Mountain time, or Pacific time. Again, the program compiles, but the answer is wrong. Correct the program. Describe the error. (Hint: This bug is very subtle—you need a good test plan in order to find it.)

Postlab Activities

Exercise 1:   Postlab Exercise 1 in Chapter 9 asked you to collect statistics on a sample of text. Rewrite your solution using an enumeration type to represent all of the items that you wish to count.

Exercise 2:   Postlab Exercise 2 in Chapter 9 asked you to design and implement a test plan for the program in Exercise 1. Can you use the same test plan for your revised program? Explain.

Exercise 3:   Postlab Exercise 3 in Chapter 9 asked you to score a tennis match. Recall that scoring a tennis game is different from scoring any other game. The following table shows how a tennis game is scored. The score is always given with the server's score first. In this table, Player 1 is the server.

Score	Player 1 Wins Point	Player 2 Wins Point
0/0	15/0	0/15
0/15	15/15	0/30
0/30	15/30	0/40
0/40	15/40	game
15/0	30/0	15/15
15/15	30/15	15/30
15/30	30/30	15/40
15/40	30/40	game
30/0	40/0	30/15
30/15	40/15	30/30
30/30	40/30	30/40
30/40	<u>30/30</u>	game
40/0	game	40/15
40/15	game	40/30
40/30	game	<u>30/30</u>

The two underlined scores (30/30) should actually be 40/40, but in tennis you have to win by 2 points, so 40/40 behaves like 30/30. (See what we mean about being strange?)

You were asked to write a function that takes two scores and the player who won the point and returns the new scores. Rewrite your solution making the players an enumeration type.

11

One-Dimensional Arrays

OBJECTIVES

- To be able to define a one-dimensional array data type with integer indexes.
- To be able to declare a one-dimensional array variable with integer indexes.
- To be able to use a one-dimensional array variable with integer indexes.
- To be able to define a one-dimensional array data type with enumeration indexes.
- To be able to declare a one-dimensional array variable with enumeration indexes.
- To be able to use a one-dimensional array variable with enumeration indexes.
- To be able to pass arrays as parameters.
- To be able to apply subarray processing.
- To be able to use an array where the indexes have semantic content.

Chapter 11:   Assignment Cover Sheet

Name _____   **Date** _____

Section _____

Fill in the following table showing which exercises have been assigned for each lesson and check what you are to submit: (1) lab sheets, (2) listings of output files, and/or (3) listings of programs. Your instructor or TA can use the Completed column for grading purposes.

Activities	Assigned: Check or list exercise numbers	Submit (1)	(2)	(3)	Completed
Prelab					
Review					
Prelab Assignment					
Inlab					
Lesson 11-1: Check Prelab Exercises					
Lesson 11-2: One-Dimensional Array Data Types with Integer Indexes					
Lesson 11-3: One-Dimensional Array Data Types with Enumeration Indexes					
Lesson 11-4: Test Plan					
Postlab					

Prelab Activities

Review

In addition to naming places and processes, an identifier can name a *collection of places*. When a collection of places is given a name, it is called a *structured data type* and is characterized by how the individual places within variables of the data type can be accessed.

One-Dimensional Array Data Type

A *one-dimensional array* is a structured data type in which a collection of places is given a name and the individual places are accessed by their position within the collection. There are two types associated with the array data type: the type of the items to be stored in the individual places in the structure and the type of the index used to specify the individual places within the structure. In C++, the type of the index must be an integral type.

```
const int MAX_ITEMS = 100;

int   numberList[MAX_ITEMS];
int   index;
```

numberList is an array variable that contains 100 **int** variables. An individual **int** variable within the array is accessed by giving the name of the array variable followed by its position (index). For example, **numberList[0]** accesses the first variable in the collection; **numberList[1]** accesses the second variable in the collection; and **numberList[MAX_ITEMS-1]** accesses the last variable in the collection. Notice that the items in the collection are indexed from zero through the number in the collection minus one. The following code segment would set all of the variables in the array variable **numberList** to zero.

```
for (index = 0; index < MAX_ITEMS; index++)
    numberList[index] = 0;
```

The index type can be any integral type. For example, we can define an array where the indexes are of an enumeration type **Birds** and the contents of the array are of type **int**.

```
const int MAX_BIRDS = 5;
enum  Birds {BLUEJAY, CARDINAL, ROBIN, SEAGULL, SWALLOW};

int   birdsSighted[MAX_BIRDS];
Birds  aBird;
int   index;
```

The following code segment sets all places in the array to zero.

```
for (aBird=BLUEJAY; aBird<MAX_BIRDS; aBird = Birds(aBird + 1))
    birdsSighted[aBird] =  0;
```

If the individual **int** values have all been set to zero, the following code segment reads and counts different types of birds until **cin** goes into the fail state (no more data).

```
cout  << "Enter a number between 0 and 4 representing a bird."
    << endl;
cin  >> index;
while (cin)
{
    aBird = Birds(index);
    birdsSighted[aBird] = birdsSighted[aBird] + 1;
    cout  << "Enter a number between 0 and 4"
        << " representing a bird."
        << endl;
    cin  >> index;
}
```

Notice that we read the value entered in the input stream as an **int** value and used the name of the enumeration type to convert it to an enumerator in that type. What would happen if the person at the keyboard accidentally keyed in the number 5? Unfortunately, the contents of what would be **birdsSighted[5]** (if it existed) probably would be accessed and incremented. The address of the first element in an array is called the *base address* of the array. To access a place in an array, the compiler generates the code to add the value of the index to the base address. If this calculation gives an out-of-bounds array index, the program does not notice and continues as if the reference were correct.

This type of error is hard to detect because it usually surfaces later in the program when a variable unrelated to an array reference has a wrong value. The moral here is to be very careful with array indexing expressions. The type of an index may be any integral type, but its value at run time must be between zero and the number of elements in the array minus one. If the index type is an enumeration type, the value must be a legitimate enumerator of the type.

There are no aggregate operations defined on arrays, but any operation that is defined on the component data type may be applied to items stored in an array.

Arrays as Parameters

Simple variables can be passed by value or by reference. Arrays are *always* passed by reference, so the ampersand indicating pass-by-reference is never used. The programmer passes the base address and the number of elements to the function. Let's define a void function, **PrintBirds**, which takes array variable **birdsSighted** and prints out the number of each type sighted.

```
void PrintBirds(/* in */ int  birdsSighted[],
                /* in */ int  numOfTypes)
{
    int  i;
```

```
    for (i = 0; i < numOfTypes; i++)

        switch (Birds(i))
        {
            case BLUEJAY : cout << "Blue jays seen: "
                              << birdsSighted[BLUEJAY]  << endl;
                              break;
            case CARDINAL: cout << "Cardinals seen: "
                              << birdsSighted[CARDINAL]  << endl;
                              break;
            .
            .
            .
        }
}
```

The call to function **PrintBirds** would be

```
PrintBirds(birdsSighted, MAX_BIRDS);
```

The brackets on the formal parameter list alert the compiler that the actual parameter in that slot is to be the base address of an array variable. The processing within function **PrintBirds** uses the second parameter to determine how many items in the array are to be processed. It is up the caller of the function to be sure that the actual parameters are consistent—that is, that the actual parameter for **numOfTypes** is the number of items in the actual parameter for **birdsSighted**.

For simple variables, we use value parameters when the actual parameter is not to be changed. How can we protect incoming-only arrays from inadvertent changes if they are always reference parameters? If we insert the word **const** before the data type on the formal parameter list, the compiler does not let the code of the function change the array parameter.

```
void PrintBirds(/* in */ const int birdsSighted[],
                /* in */ int numOfTypes)
```

Because the processing is controlled by the second parameter, it can be the size of the array if all the elements are used or the number of data values that are actually stored if fewer values are stored than the size calls for. The latter type of processing is called *subarray* processing.

Initialization of Arrays

Just as we can initialize values within the definition of a simple variable, we can initialize array variables. The following declarations initialize each item in the array **birdsSighted** to zero.

```
const int MAX_BIRDS = 5;
enum  Birds {BLUEJAY, CARDINAL, ROBIN, SEAGULL, SWALLOW};

int  birdsSighted[MAX_BIRDS] = {0, 0, 0, 0, 0};
```

If this declaration is within a function other than **main**, **birdsSighted** is initialized each time the function is called. If **birdsSighted** is declared within a function and has the reserved word **static** before the **int**, it is initialized only once.

Chapter 11: Prelab Assignment

Name _____ **Date** _____

Section _____

Exercise 1: Read program **Arrays** carefully.

```
// Program Arrays manipulates values in an array.

#include <iostream.h>

int main ()
{
    const int MAX_ARRAY = 5;
    int   numbers[MAX_ARRAY];
    int   index;
    int   sum;

    // Stored values in the array.
    for (index = 0; index < MAX_ARRAY; index++)
        numbers[index] = index * index;

    // The values in the array are summed.
    sum = 0;
    for (index = 0; index < MAX_ARRAY; index++)
        sum = sum + numbers[index];
    cout << "Sum is "  << sum  << endl;
    return 0;
}
```

Describe what is written on the screen.

Exercise 2: What would happen if the For loop headings were changed as follows?

```
for (index = 0; index <= MAX_ARRAY; index++)
```

Lesson 11-1: Check Prelab Exercises

Name _____   **Date** _____

Section _____

Exercise 1:   Run program **Arrays**   to check your answer. Was your answer correct? If not, do you understand what you did wrong?

Exercise 2:   C++ doesn't define what happens if you store more values than there are places in the array. Each system handles this differently. For example, on one system, the program may work correctly while on another system the program may crash. The moral is: don't do it.

Lesson 11-2: One-Dimensional Array Data Types with Integer Indexes

Name _____   Date _____

Section _____

This lesson uses the following program shell.

```
// Program Reverse reads numbers into an array
// and prints them out in reverse order.

#include <iostream.h>
#include <fstream.h>

const int MAX = 10;

int main ()
{
    int   numbers[MAX];
    ifstream  inData;
    int   value;
    int   index;

    inData.open("reverse.dat");
    for (index = 0; index < MAX; index++)
    {
        // FILL IN Code to read value
        // FILL IN Code to store value into numbers
    }

    for (index = MAX - 1; index >= 0; index--)
        // FILL IN Code to write numbers on the screen
    return 0;
}
```

Exercise 1:   Complete the missing code in program **Reverse** and run it. What is printed on the screen?

Exercise 2:   Exercise 1 asked you to fill in the body of the first For loop with two statements. Replace these two statements with a single statement and rerun your program; your answer should be the same. If it is not, correct your code and rerun the program. Describe any problems that you had.

Exercise 3:   Extend the program in Exercise 2 to print the sum of the values stored in **numbers**. What is the sum?

Lesson 11-3: *One-Dimensional Array DataTypes with Enumeration Indexes*

Name _____   **Date** _____

Section _____

This lesson uses program **Favorit.**

```
// Program Favorit determines the favorite soft drink.

#include <iostream.h>

enum  DrinksType {COKE, PEPSI, SPRITE, DR_PEPPER};
void Prompt();

int main ()
{
    int   sums[4];
    int   number;
    DrinksType  index;

    for (index = COKE; index <= DR_PEPPER; index =  DrinksType(index+1))
      // FILL IN Code to set sums to zero

    Prompt();
    cin  >> number;
    while (number != 4)
    {
        // FILL IN Code to increment the proper drink
      Prompt();
      cin  >> number;
    }

    // FILL IN THE Code to write out the totals
    return 0;
}

/*******************************************************/

void Prompt()
{
    cout  << "Enter a 0 if your favorite drink is a Coke."
          << endl;
    cout  << "Enter a 1 if your favorite drink is a Pepsi."
          << endl;
    cout  << "Enter a 2 if your favorite drink is a Sprite."
          << endl;
    cout  << "Enter a 3 if your favorite drink is a DrPepper."
          << endl;
    cout  <<"Enter a 4 if you wish to quit the survey."
          << endl;
}
```

Exercise 1:   Complete program **Favorit** and run it. What data did you use? What did the program write?

Exercise 2:   Add a function to program **Favorit** that sums the number of responses to the survey. Pass the array **sums** as a parameter. Print the number of responses on the screen. Run the program with the same data you used in Exercise 1. How many responses were there?

Exercise 3:   Add a function that takes the array **sums** as a parameter and prints the percentage of responses each drink received. Run your program on the same data. Show the results.

Lesson 11-4: Test Plan

Name _____   **Date** _____

Section _____

Exercise 1:   Design and implement a test plan for program **Favorit** as modified in Lesson 11-3, Exercise 2.

Reason for Test Case	Input Values	Expected Output	Observed Output

Postlab Activities

Exercise 1:   Write a program to grade a set of true/false tests. There are 15 true/false questions. True is represented by *T*, and false is represented by *F*. The key to the quiz is on file **Quiz.dat** followed by the student responses. Each student's name (maximum of 15 characters) immediately follows the student's last answer. For each student write out the name followed by the number answered correctly and the number missed. Use stream failure to terminate processing.

Exercise 2:   An organization that your little cousin belongs to is selling low-fat cookies. If your cousin's class sells more cookies than any other class, the teacher has promised to take the whole class on a picnic.   Of course, your cousin volunteered you to keep track of all the sales and determine the winner.

Each class has an identification number.   Each sales slip has the class identification number and the number of boxes sold. You decide to create two arrays: one to hold the identification numbers and one to record the number of boxes sold. The identification numbers range from 1 through 10. Here is a sample of the data.

Id. Number	Boxes Sold
3	23
4	1
2	13
2	7
4	5
1	6
10	16
.	
.	

The first time an identification number is read, store it in the next free slot in the array of identification numbers and initialize the corresponding position in the array of boxes sold to the number sold on the sales slip. Each subsequent time an identification number is read, add the number of boxes sold to the corresponding position in the array of boxes sold.

When there are no more sales slips, scan the array of boxes sold for the largest value. The identification number in the corresponding position in the array of identification numbers is the class that wins.

Write your program and run it using data file **Boxes.dat**. Which class won and how many boxes of cookies did they sell?

Exercise 3:   In Exercise 2, the class identification numbers range from 1 through 10. If they ranged from 0 through 9, the identification number could be used as an index into the array of boxes sold. Using this scheme, you need only one array to hold the boxes sold. Rewrite your program implementing this scheme. You can use the same data file by always subtracting one from the identification number on input and adding one to the identification number on output. Run your program using **Boxes.dat**. You should get the same results as in Exercise 2. Did you?

Exercise 4:   Write test plans for Exercises 2 and 3. Can these test plans be the same, or must they be different? Explain.

Exercise 5:   If an index has meaning beyond simply indicating the place in the collection, we say that it has *semantic content*. Exercise 3 is an example of processing in which the array indexes have semantic content. Explain.

12

Applied Arrays: Lists and Strings

OBJECTIVES

- To be able to define the data type list.
- To be able to implement the operations on the data type *unsorted* list.
- To be able to implement the operations on the data type *sorted* list.
- To be able to declare and use character strings.

Chapter 12: Assignment Cover Sheet

Name _____   **Date** _____

Section _____

Fill in the following table showing which exercises have been assigned for each lesson and check what you are to submit: (1) lab sheets, (2) listings of output files, and/or (3) listings of programs. Your instructor or TA can use the Completed column for grading purposes.

Activities	Assigned: Check or list exercise numbers	Submit (1)	(2)	(3)	Completed
Prelab					
Review					
Prelab Assignment					
Inlab					
Lesson 12-1: Check Prelab Exercises					
Lesson 12-2: Linear (Unsorted) List Operations					
Lesson 12-3: Sorted List Operations					
Lesson 12-4: Strings					
Lesson 12-5: Debugging					
Postlab					

Prelab Activities

Review

An array data type gives a name to a collection of data values and lets us access individual items by their position within the collection. Arrays are ideal structures to represent *lists* of items.

Lists

Lists occur as naturally in programming as they do in real life. We manipulate guest lists, grocery lists, class lists, things-to-do lists. . . . The list of lists is endless. Three properties characterize lists: the items are homogeneous, the items are linear, and lists have varying length. By linear we mean that each item except the first has a unique component that comes before it and each item except the last has a unique component that comes after it. For example, if there are at least three items in a list, the second item comes after the first and before the third.

   A set of operations that manipulate lists must include at least initializing the list, putting an item on the list, removing an item from the list, searching for an item in a list, determining if the list is empty, and displaying the items in the list.

Array-Based Lists

An array data type is the structure that is often used to represent items in a list. The first item in the list is stored in the first place in the array, the second item in the list is stored in the second place in the array, and so on. The number of positions in an array is fixed at compile time, but the number of items in a list varies as a program executes. Therefore, when an array is used to implement a list, there must be a length parameter associated with the list. Let's examine a declaration that defines a general list of items. (The comments must be replaced with actual values before the declarations can be used.)

```
const int MAX_LENGTH = /* some value */;
typedef /* type of item on the list */ ItemType;
typedef ItemType List[MAX_LENGTH];

List  list;
int   length;
```

   The first statement defines a **int** constant, **MAX_LENGTH**, that is the maximum number of elements that might be in the list. The next statement defines data type **ItemType**. Whenever **ItemType** appears in the program, the actual type filled in when the declaration is used is substituted for **ItemType**. The next statement defines a data type **List** that is an array of **MAX_LENGTH** items of type **ItemType**. The next two statements define an array variable **list** of data type **List** and an **int** variable **length**. Notice that there are

MAX_LENGTH places in the array variable **list**, but **length** is used to tell us how many of these places contain actual list items.

Distinction between the Array and the List

If **/* some value */** is replaced with 100, and **/* type of item on the list */** is replaced with **char**, the array variable **list** has 100 slots each of which can contain one character. At the logical level, the length of an empty list is zero. As each successive item is entered into the list, the item is stored into the array variable at the position indexed by **length**, and **length** is incremented. All processing of the logical list is done from the zeroth position in the array variable **list** through the **length-1** position.

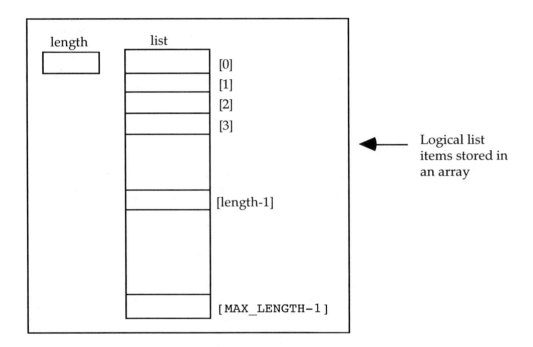

Sorted and Unsorted Lists

Lists can be categorized into two classes: sorted and unsorted. In an unsorted list, the component that comes before or after an item has no semantic relationship with it. In a sorted list, the items are arranged in such a way that the component that comes before or after an item has a semantic relationship with that item. For example, a grade list can be a random list of numbers or sorted by value. The following diagrams show an unsorted list of grades and a sorted list of grades.

Unsorted List

Sorted List

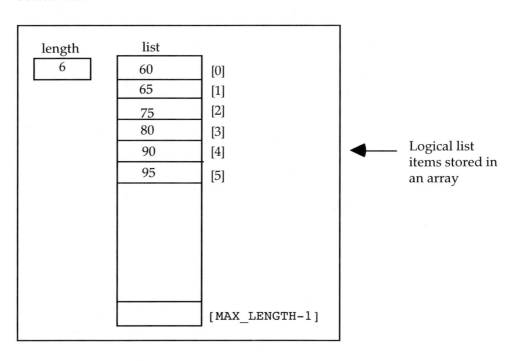

List Algorithms

In the following algorithms, we use *list* and *length* in their logical meaning. That is, they are not program variables but logical entities.

Storing an item in an unsorted list: The item is stored in the length position and length is incremented.

Inserting an item in a sorted list: Find the position where the item should be inserted (use one of the sorted searches below), move the items in the array from that point to the end down one position, store the item, and increment the length.

Linear search in an unsorted list: To search for an item in an unsorted list, loop through the items in the list examining each one until you find the item you are searching for or you run out of items to examine.

Linear search in a sorted list: If the list items are sorted, the loop can terminate when the item is found or when the place where the item would be if it were in the list is passed. For example if you are searching for the grade 70, you can terminate the search when the value 75 is encountered.

Binary search: A binary search is only possible if the list is sorted. Rather than looking for the item starting at the beginning of the list and moving forward, you begin at the middle in a binary search. If the item for which you are searching is less than the item in the middle, continue searching between the beginning of the list and the middle. If the item for which you are searching is greater than the item in the middle, continue searching between the middle and the end of the list. If the middle item is equal to the one for which you are searching, the search stops. The process continues with each comparison cutting in half the portion of the list left to be searched. The process stops when the item is found or when the portion of the list left to be searched is empty.

Sorting: Sorting a list converts it from unsorted to sorted. One algorithm for doing so is as follows. Define the current item to be the first in the list (the value in the zeroth position). Find the minimum value in the rest of the list and exchange it with the value in the current position. Increment the current position and repeat the process. When the current position is equal to the length minus two, the process stops and the list is sorted.

Strings

Strings are one-dimensional arrays where the component type is **char**. A special character is appended following the last character in the array to signal the end of the string. In other words, strings are lists of characters. But rather than having a separate variable that contains the number of items in the list, a special symbol, the *null character*, is used to signal the end of the list. The null character is the escape sequence **\0** (backslash zero). When declaring an array for a string, the array size must be one more than the number of characters in the string in order for there to be a slot for the null character.

Like other arrays, strings can be initialized in their declaration statement. For example, the following statement declares a string and initializes it.

```
char greeting[7] = "Hello!";
```

greeting is stored in memory as follows.

```
            greeting
          ┌──────────┐
          │   'H'    │
          ├──────────┤
          │   'e'    │
          ├──────────┤
          │   'l'    │
          ├──────────┤
          │   'l'    │
          ├──────────┤
          │   'o'    │
          ├──────────┤
          │   '!'    │
          ├──────────┤
          │   '\0'   │
          └──────────┘
```

Like other arrays, strings cannot be assigned to one another; they must be copied character by character.

Strings have certain properties that arrays do not have. For example, we can declare string constants and strings can be sent to the output stream as a whole rather than having to send them character by character. Both the extraction operator (**>>**) and the function **get** from **<iostream.h>** can be used with strings. If **title** is defined as a **char** array of 21 characters, then

```
cin  >>  title;
```

extracts characters from **cin** one at a time and stores them in **title** until whitespace is encountered. The null character is stored in the position immediately following the last character stored. Therefore, an array size of 21 provides room for 20 input characters plus the null character. The extraction operation terminates when whitespace is encountered, and the next extraction operation is positioned at the whitespace.

When function **get** is used to input a string, it requires two parameters: first, the name of the string variable and second, an **int** expression that is one more than the number of characters to be read. Characters are stored one at a time, including whitespace characters, until the proper number have been stored or the newline character ('**\n**') is encountered. The next extraction operation is positioned to read the newline character if it is what stopped the previous operation.

The parameter to function **open** in file **<fstream.h>** is a string. In previous chapters we used a literal string as a parameter, but a string variable also can be used. Being able to use a string variable means that you can read in the file name, thus changing the data file without having to change the program.

Because strings are such useful structures, C++ provides a set of string-handling functions in file **<string.h>**. Two useful ones are shown below.

strlen(s)	Returns the number of characters in **s** (excluding '**\0**').
strcmp(s1, s2)	Returns a negative integer if **s1** comes before **s2**; returns zero if **s1** is equal to **s2**; and returns a positive integer if **s2** comes before **s1**.
strcpy(s1, s2)	Copies **s2** into **s1**; the previous contents of **s1** are destroyed.

Chapter 12: Prelab Assignment

Name _____   **Date** _____

Section _____

Read program **FloatLst** carefully.

```cpp
#include <iostream.h>
#include <fstream.h>

const int MAX_LENGTH = 50;
typedef float ItemType;
typedef ItemType ListType[MAX_LENGTH];

void  CreateList(ListType, int&);

void  GetList(ifstream&, ListType, int&);

void  PrintList(const ListType, int);

int  main ()
{
    ifstream  tempData;
    ListType  list;
    int  length;

    cout.setf(ios::fixed, ios::floatfield);
    cout.setf(ios::showpoint);

    tempData.open("real.dat");

    // Create, input, and print a list

    CreateList(list, length);
    GetList(tempData, list, length);
    PrintList(list, length);
    return 0;
}

//*****************************************

void  CreateList(ListType  list, int&  length)
{
    length = 0;
}

//*****************************************

void  GetList(ifstream&  data, ListType  list, int& length)
{
    ItemType  item;
    data  >> item;
```

```
        data  >> item;
        while (data)

        {
            list[length] = item;
            length++;
            data  >> item;
        }
}

//****************************************************

void  PrintList(ListType  list, int  length)
{
    int  index;

    for (index = 0; index < length; index++)
        cout  << list[index]  << endl;
}
```

Exercise 1:   Document the program heading.

Exercise 2:   Document function **CreateList**.

Function prototype:

Function definition:

Exercise 3:   Document function **GetList**.

Function prototype:

Function definition:

Exercise 4: Document function **PrintList**.

Function prototype:

Function definition:

Lesson 12-1: Check Prelab Exercises

Name _____   **Date** _____

Section _____

In order to be able to write documentation, you must thoroughly understand the code. Run program **FloatLst**. What were the last four values printed?

The version of program FloatLst on the disk is documented.

Exercise 1:   Check the documentation for the program heading.   Did you understand what the program was doing?   If not, describe what you did not understand.

Exercise 2:   Check the documentation for function **CreateList**.   Did you understand what the function was doing?   If not, describe what you did not understand.

Exercise 3:   Check the documentation for function **GetList**.   Did you understand what the function was doing?   If not, describe what you did not understand.

Exercise 4:   Check the documentation for function **PrintList**.   Did you understand what the function was doing?   If not, describe what you did not understand.

Lesson 12-2: Linear (Unsorted) List Operations

Name _____   **Date** _____

Section _____

Use the declaration for **ListType** in program **FloatLst** for this lesson.

Exercise 1:   Write a function, **Create**, that initializes an unsorted list to empty. Pass the list and the length as parameters.

Exercise 2:   Write a function, **StoreItem**, that stores a value in the next available slot in the list. Pass the list, the length and the value to be stored as parameters.

Exercise 3:   Write a **Boolean** function, **IsThere**, that searches a list for a specified value. Pass the list, the length, and the value as parameters.

Exercise 4:   Write a function, **RemoveItem**, that removes a value from a list. Pass the list, the length, and the value to be removed as parameters. The value is in the list.

Exercise 5:   Write a function, **WriteList**, that writes the values in a list to a file. Pass the file name, the list, and the length as parameters.

Exercise 6:   Write a test driver that tests the functions in Exercises 1 through 5 using the data on file **Int.dat**. **ItemType** is **int**. Have your driver complete the following activities:

- Read and store the values into the list.
- Print the values to a file.
- Search for a value that is there (10) and print the results.
- Search for a value that is not there (5) and print the results.
- Delete a value (10) and print the list with the value removed.

Write your driver so that it prompts for and reads the names of the input and output files.

Lesson 12-3: Sorted List Operations

Name _____   **Date** _____

Section _____

Use the declaration for **ListType** in program **FloatLst** for this lesson.

Exercise 1:   Write a function, **Create**, that initializes a sorted list to empty. Pass the list and the length as parameters.

Exercise 2:   Write a function, **InsertItem**, that stores a value into its proper slot in the list. Pass the list, the length, and the value to be stored as parameters.

Exercise 3:   Write a **Boolean** function, **IsThere**, that searches a list for a specified value using the binary search algorithm. Pass the list, the length, and the value as parameters.

Exercise 4:   Write a function, **RemoveItem** that removes a value from a list. Pass the list, the length, and the value to be removed as parameters. The value is in the list.

Exercise 5:   Write a function **WriteList**, that writes the values in a list to a file. Pass the file name, the list, and the length as parameters.

Exercise 6:   Write a test driver that tests the functions in Exercises 1 through 5 using the data on file **Int.dat**. **ItemType** is **int**. Have your driver complete the following activities:

- Read and insert the values into the list.
- Print the values to a file.
- Search for a value that is there (10) and print the results.
- Search for a value that is not there (5) and print the results.
- Delete a value (10) and print the list with the value removed.

Write your driver so that it prompts for and reads the names of the input and output files.

Exercise 7:   Were you able to use any of the operations you wrote in Lesson 12-2 for Exercises 1 through 6? Explain.

Lesson 12-4: Strings

Name _____   Date _____

Section _____

Exercise 1:   Write a function, **GetFileName**, that prompts for and reads a file name from **cin**. Did you encapsulate the code to do this task in Lessons 2 and 3 into a function? If so, this exercise is already completed.

Exercise 2:   Program **Shell1** is a driver for function **Compare** that compares two strings. The return value type of function **Compare** is **CompareType** (**LESS, EQUAL, GREATER**). Complete this program.

```
// Program Shell1 is a driver for function Compare.
#include <iostream.h>
#include <string.h>

typedef  char String20[21];
enum  CompareType {LESS, EQUAL, GREATER};
CompareType  Compare(const String20, const String20);

int  main ()
{
    String20  str1;
    String20  str2;

    cout  << "Enter a string of up to 20 characters."
          << " Do not include whitespace."  << endl;
    cin  >> str1;
    cout  << "Enter a string of up to 20 characters."
          << " Do not include whitespace."  << endl;
    cin  >> str2;
    switch (Compare(str1, str2))
    {
        // FILL IN Code to write out which string
        // comes first alphabetically
    }
    return 0;
}

//************************************************

CompareType Compare(const String20 str1, const String20  str2)
{
    int  result;
    result = strcmp(str1, str2);

    // FILL IN Code to return the appropriate enumerator

}
```

Test this program as many times as it takes to test function **Compare**. Show your data and your results.

Exercise 3:   Enclose the body of function **main** in program **Shell** in a loop that continues until **Quit** is entered for **str1**. Test your program. Show your data and your results.

Exercise 4:   Rewrite the solution to Exercise 3 so that the data are on file **StringPr.dat** as pairs of strings separated by whitespace. Run your program and list the results of the last three pairs of strings.

Exercise 5:   Function **Compare** used the built-in string function **strcmp**. Outline the algorithm you would have to use if **strcmp** were not available.

Lesson 12-5: Debugging

Name _____   **Date** _____

Section _____

Exercise 1: Program **ListEr** is a slight variation on program **FloatLst**. Note, however, that **MAX_LENGTH** has been changed in **ListEr**. Run program **ListEr** and check the results against the output from program **FloatLst**. Describe what happens.

Exercise 2: In Lesson 11-1, Exercise 2, we said that C++ does not define what happens when you store more values into an array than there are places defined. Because an error of this type happens so frequently, we want you to see what happens on at least one system. If you have an opportunity to use another C++ system, try the same experiment and record what happens.

There are two important lessons to be learned here. The first is that you should be very careful about storing values in an array. The second is that a program with an error might run correctly on one system but not on another.

Exercise 3: Rewrite program **ListEr** so that the reading stops when either the stream fails or the array is full.

Postlab Activities

Exercise 1: In Postlab Exercise 2 in Chapter 11, you wrote a program to keep track of low-fat cookie sales for your cousin. Rewrite that program using the sorted list operations you wrote for this chapter. Can you keep both lists sorted? Can you keep one or the other sorted but not both? Write a justification for the data structures you chose to use.

Exercise 2: Write and implement a test plan for your program in Exercise 1.

Exercise 3: A clothing manufacturer wants to keep track of how many copies of each item are sold over a period of a week. The information on the sales slip includes the item identification number, the number of copies sold, the unit price, and the total amount of the sale. How is the problem similar to judging a cookie contest (Postlab Exercise 2, Chapter 11)? How is the problem different? What changes would be necessary if the manufacturer asked you to include a total sales figure at the end of the week?

Exercise 4: Write a program to implement the problem described in Exercise 3, including the total sales figure.

Exercise 5: Postlab Exercises 4 and 5 in Chapter 6 were simulations of a children's game to determine who would be "it." Rewrite your solution to Exercise 4 using a list of childrens' names. Print out the name of the child who is it rather than the position that the child occupies in the original grouping.

Exercise 6: Rewrite your solution to Exercise 5 using the altered form described in Postlab Exercise 5 in Chapter 6.

13

Multidimensional Arrays

OBJECTIVES

- To be able to define a two-dimensional array data type.
- To be able to read, store, and print values in a table (two-dimensional array variable).
- To be able to find the minimum value and the maximum value in a table.
- To be able to sum the individual rows of a table.

Chapter 13: Assignment Cover Sheet

Name _____   **Date** _____

Section _____

Fill in the following table showing which exercises have been assigned for each lesson and check what you are to submit: (1) lab sheets, (2) listings of output files, and/or (3) listings of programs. Your instructor or TA can use the Completed column for grading purposes.

Activities	Assigned: Check or list exercise numbers	Submit (1)	(2)	(3)	Completed
Prelab					
Review					
Prelab Assignment					
Inlab					
Lesson 13-1: Check Prelab Exercises					
Lesson 13-2: Two-Dimensional Tables					
Lesson 13-3: Multidimensional Tables					
Lesson 13-4: Debugging					
Postlab					

Prelab Activities

Review

A *two-dimensional array* is a collection of components of the same type that is structured in two dimensions. Individual components are accessed by their position within each dimension. Three types are associated with a two-dimensional array data type: the type of the items to be stored in the individual places in the structure, the type of the index for the first dimension, and the type of the index for the second dimension. In C++ the type of both dimensions must be integral.

```
const int MAX_ROWS = 10;
const int MAX_COLUMNS = 5;

typedef float ItemType;

ItemType  twoDimAry[MAX_ROWS][MAX_COLUMNS];
```

twoDimAry is an array variable that has 10 rows and 5 columns. Each row and column entry is of type **float**. The following code fragment sets all the entries in **twoDimAry** to zero.

```
for (int column = 0; column < MAX_COLUMNS; column++)
    for(int row = 0; row < MAX_ROWS; row++)
        twoDimAry[row][column] = 0.0;
```

Table Processing

Just as a one-dimensional array data type is the structure used to represent items in a list, a two-dimensional array data type is the structure that is often used to represent items in a *table*. The number of rows and columns in the two-dimensional array variable is fixed at compile time. The number of rows and columns in the table can vary as the program executes. Therefore, each dimension should have a length parameter associated with it that contains the number of rows or columns actually used.

Processing a table requires two loops: one for the rows and one for the columns. If the outer loop is the index for the column, the table is processed by column. If the outer loop is the index for the row, the table is processed by row. The loop above processes **twoDimAry** by columns.

Multidimensional Arrays

You have seen one-dimensional and two-dimensional arrays. In C++, arrays may have any number of dimensions. To process every item in a one-dimensional array, you need one loop. To process every item in a two-dimensional array, you need two loops. The pattern continues to any number of dimensions. To process every item in an *n*-dimensional array, you need *n* loops.

Passing Arrays as Parameters

In Chapter 11, we said that the programmer passes the base address of an array and the number of elements in the array as parameters. The function does not need to know the actual size of the array. For arrays of more than one dimension, the function must know the sizes of all of the dimensions except the first. For example, if a function is defined to set the first **num** values of each row in **twoDimAry** to a specific value, the prototype might look like this:

```
void SetSomeVals(/* out */ ItemType twoDimAry[][MAX_COLUMNS],
                 /* in */  int rowsUsed,
                 /* in */  int num,
                 /* in */  ItemType initialValue);
```

Any actual parameter must have exactly the same number of elements specified for the second dimension. If it does not, the program continues but does not initialize the correct locations. It is safer to define a type using a Typedef statement, put the type name on the formal parameter list, and define the actual array to be of that type. Here is an example of how this could be done.

```
const int MAX_ROWS = 10;
const int MAX_COLUMNS = 5;
typedef char ItemType;

typedef ItemType TableType[MAX_ROWS][MAX_COLUMNS];

void SetSomeVals(/* out */ TableType twoDimAry,
                 /* in */  int rowsUsed,
                 /* in */  int num,
                 /* in */  ItemType initialValue);
```

Any array to be passed to **SetSomeVals** should be defined to be of type **TableType**. Althoughthis example is of a two-dimensional array, this pattern of defining a type and using the type name can be used for arrays of any number of dimensions.

Chapter 13: Prelab Assignment

Name _____ **Date** _____

Section _____

Exercise 1: What does the following code segment print if **MAX_ROWS** is 10 and **MAX_COLS** is 10? Fill in the table shown below the code.

```
rowsUsed = 5;
colsUsed = 5;

for (int column = 0; column < MAX_COLS; column++)
    for (int row = 0; row < MAX_ROWS; row++)
        table[row][column] = '*';

for (row = rowsUsed; row < MAX_ROWS; row++)
    for (column = colsUsed; column < MAX_COLS; column++)
        table[row][column] = '+';

for (column = 0; column < colsUsed; column++)
    for (row = 0; row < rowsUsed; row++)
        table[row][column] = '-';
```

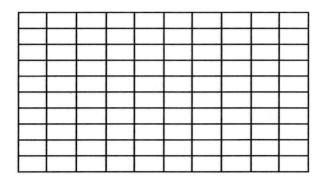

Exercise 2: Is the first nested For loop in Prelab Exercise 1 processing the table by row or by column?

Is the second nested For loop processing the table by row or by column?

Is the third nested For loop processing the table by row or by column?

Lesson 13-1: Check Prelab Exercises

Name _____   **Date** _____

Section _____

Exercise 1:   Run program **Tables** to see the output. Was your diagram correct? If not, do you understand what you did wrong?

Exercise 2:   The first loop is processing by column; the second by row; the third by column.

Lesson 13-2: Two-Dimensional Tables

Name _____   **Date** _____

Section _____

This lesson uses program **TwoDim**.

```cpp
// Program TwoDim manipulates a two-dimensional array
// variable.

#include <iostream.h>
#include <fstream.h>

const int ROW_MAX = 8;
const int COL_MAX = 10;

typedef int ItemType;

typedef ItemType TableType[ROW_MAX][COL_MAX];

void  GetTable(ifstream&, TableType, int&, int&);
// Reads values and stores them in the table.

void  PrintTable(ofstream&, const TableType, int, int);
// Writes values in the table to a file.

int  main ()
{
    TableType  table;
    int  rowsUsed;
    int  colsUsed;
    ifstream  dataIn;
    ofstream  dataOut;

    dataIn.open("twod.dat");
    dataOut.open("twod.out");
    GetTable(dataIn, table, rowsUsed, colsUsed);
    PrintTable(dataOut, table, rowsUsed, colsUsed);
    return 0;
}

//************************************************

void  GetTable(ifstream&  data, TableType  table,
               int&  rowsUsed, int&  colsUsed)
// Pre:  rowsUsed and colsUsed are on the first line of
//       file data; values are one row per line
//       beginning with the second line.
// Post: Values have been read and stored in the table.

{

ItemType  item;
```

```
        data  >> rowsUsed >> colsUsed;

    for (int row = 0; row < rowsUsed; row++)
        for (int col = 0; col < colsUsed; col++)

            // FILL IN Code to read and store the next value.
}

//*****************************************************

void  PrintTable(ofstream&  data, const TableType  table,
                 int  rowsUsed, int  colsUsed)
// Pre:  The table contains valid data.
// Post: Values in the table have been sent to a file by row,
//       one row per line.
{

    // FILL IN Code to print table by row.

}
```

Exercise 1: Read the documentation carefully and complete program **TwoDim.** Show what is printed.

____ ____ ____ ____ ____

____ ____ ____ ____ ____

____ ____ ____ ____ ____

____ ____ ____ ____ ____

Exercise 2: Add a function that prints the largest value in **table**. Rerun the program.

Largest value _____.

Exercise 3: Add a function that prints the smallest value in **table**. Rerun the program.

Smallest value _____.

Exercise 4: Add a function that sums the values in a column of **table**. Pass the column you want to sum as a parameter. Call your function to print the sum of each column appropriately labeled.

Sum of Column 1 _____.   Sum of Column 2 _____.

Sum of Column 3 _____.   Sum of Column 4 _____.

Sum of Column 5 _____.

Exercise 5:   The specifications on the data have been changed. The data is to be entered one column per line instead of one row per line. In addition, the order of **rowsUsed** and **colsUsed** has been reversed; that is, **colsUsed** is the first value on the first line and **rowsUsed** is the second value. Rewrite function **GetTable** to input **table** using the new specifications. Run your program using **twodalt.dat**.

Smallest value   _____ .

Largest value   _____ .

Sum of Column 1   _____ .

Sum of Column 2   _____ .

Sum of Column 3   _____ .

Sum of Column 4   _____ .

Sum of Column 5   _____ .

Lesson 13-3: Multidimensional Tables

Name _____   **Date** _____

Section _____

> **Exercise 1:** Write a void function, **SetThreeDi**, that sets all the cells in a three-dimensional table to a value that is passed as a parameter. You may access the dimension sizes nonlocally.

> **Exercise 2:** Write a void function, **PrintThreeD**, that prints the values in the three-dimensional table.

> **Exercise 3:** Write a driver that defines a three-dimensional table, declares a variable of that kind, passes it to function **ThreeDi** to set the table to all zeros, and passes it to **PrintThreeDi** to print the values.

Lesson 13-4: Debugging

Name _____　　**Date** _____

Section _____

Exercise 1:　Program **ReadData** reads data into a two-dimensional array.　The data is input as described in Lesson 13-2, Exercise 1.　The data file is shown below:

```
3   4
1   2   3   4
5   6   7   8
9   8   7   6
```

Unfortunately, program **ReadData** contains an error.　Can you find and fix it? Describe the error.

Exercise 2:　Unless you found two errors at once in Exercise 1, there is still an error lurking in program **ReadData**.　Correct the error and rerun the program.　Describe the error.

Postlab Activities

Exercise 1: Two-dimensional arrays are good structures to represent boards in games. Write a function that takes a two-dimensional array as input and marks the array as a checkerboard. Put an asterisk in the black squares and a blank in the white squares. Write a second function that prints the checkerboard on the screen. Because a checkerboard is a fixed size, the dimensions of the board may be set as constants and accessed nonlocally.

Exercise 2: Write a program that keeps track of stock prices for five stocks for one week. Choose any five stocks on the New York Stock Exchange. Use actual stock prices for one week as your data. Include the clippings from the paper with your program.

Your program should be interactive. Prompt the user to enter the names of the five stocks. Then prompt the user to enter a week's worth of prices for each stock. The program should print the table showing the stock values for a week, the average daily value of the stocks, and the average price for each stock for the week.

Exercise 3: A two-dimensional array is the ideal structure to represent a matrix. Write the following functions, which implement the matrix operations add and subtract. In order to test your operations, you need a function to read values from a file and store them in a matrix and a function to write the values in a matrix on a file. Let your matrices be 5 by 4.

Add	Takes two matrices (**A** and **B**) as input and returns a matrix (**Result**) in which each position is the sum of the corresponding positions in **A** and **B**.
Sub	Takes two matrices (**A** and **B**) as input and returns a matrix (**Result**) in which each position is the corresponding position in **A** minus the corresponding position in **B**.
Write	Takes a file name and a matrix as input and writes the matrix by row, one row per line on the file.
GetMat	Takes a file name and a matrix as input and reads values from the file and stores them into the matrix.

Exercise 4: Write and implement a test plan for the matrix operations you wrote in Exercise 3.

14

Records (C++ Structs)

OBJECTIVES

- To be able to define a record data type.
- To be able to declare and use a record variable.
- To be able to declare and use a hierarchical record.
- To be able to declare and use an array of records.

Chapter 14: Assignment Cover Sheet

Name _____   **Date** _____

Section _____

Fill in the following table showing which exercises have been assigned for each lesson and check what you are to submit: (1) lab sheets, (2) listings of output files, and/or (3) listings of programs. Your instructor or TA can use the Completed column for grading purposes.

Activities	Assigned: Check or list exercise numbers	Submit (1)	(2)	(3)	Completed
Prelab					
Review					
Prelab Assignment					
Inlab					
Lesson 14-1: Check Prelab Exercise					
Lesson 14-2: Record Data Type					
Lesson 14-3: Lists as Records					
Lesson 14-4:Hierarchical Records					
Lesson 14-5: Arrays of Records					
Lesson 14-6: Test Plans					
Postlab					

Prelab Activities

Review

The *record* is a very versatile data type. It is a collection of components of any data type in which the components are given names. The components of a record are called *fields*. Each field has its own *field identifier* and data type. Hence, a record often contains variables of different types.

Structs

C++ has its own vocabulary in relation to the general concept of a record. Records are called *structures* (abbreviated to **struct**), fields are called *members*, and field identifiers are called *member names*. We use *record* when we are referring to the general concept and **struct** when we are referring to a specific C++ type or variable.

```
typedef char String15[16];

enum MediaType  {CD, TAPE, RECORD};

struct  Recording
{
    String15  title;
    String15  artist;
    MediaType medium;
    float     cost;
    int       quantity;
};

Recording   song;
```

Recording is a pattern for a group of five variables. **song** is a **struct** variable with five members: **title**, **artist**, **medium**, **cost**, and **quantity** are the member names. The accessing expression for members of a **struct** variable is the **struct** variable identifier followed by the member name with a period in between. This accessing expression is called the *member selector*.

song.title is a string variable.
song.artist is a string variable.
song.medium is a variable of type **MediaType**.
song.cost is a **float** variable.
song.quantity is an **int** variable.

The only aggregate operation defined on structures is assignment, but structures may be passed as parameters and they may be the return value type of a function.

Hierarchical Structs

A member of a record can be another record. For example, we can define an additional member, **date**, of type **DateType** that is a **struct** containing members **month**, **day**, and **year** .

```
struct  Date Type
{
    int  month;
    int  day;
    int  year;
};

struct  Recording
{
    String15  title;
    String15  artist;
    MediaType medium;
    float     cost;
    int       quantity;
    Date Type  date;
};

Recording  song;
```

song.date.month accesses the **month** member of the **date** member of **song**.
song.date.day accesses the **day** member of the **date** member of **song**.

Arrays of Structs

The components of an array can be of any data type, including a record. This means that we can, for example, keep a list of songs.

```
const int MAX_SONGS = 200;

// include previous declarations

Recording  songList[MAX_SONGS];
int  length;
```

songList[0] accesses the first **struct** of type **Recording** in the array variable **songList**.
songList[0].title[0] accesses the first letter in the **title** member of the first **struct** of type **Recording** in the array variable **songList**.
songList[length-1].cost accesses the **cost** member of the last **struct** of type **Recording** in the array variable **songList**.
songList[length-1].date.month accesses the **month** member of the **struct** of type **Date Type** of the last **struct** of type **Recording** in the array variable **songList**.

Initialization of Structs

You can initialize records just as you do arrays by listing the values for the members. The following definition creates **struct** variable **myFavorite**, of type **Recording** (defined earlier), and initializes the members.

```
Recording  myFavorite =
{
    "La Vie En Rose",
    "Edith Piaf",
    TAPE,
    5.00,
    1,
    {
        10, 11, 1935
    }
};
```

Lists Revisited

Now that we have a way of incorporating items of different data types into a structure, we should combine the length of a list and the array containing the list items into a record (**struct**).

list

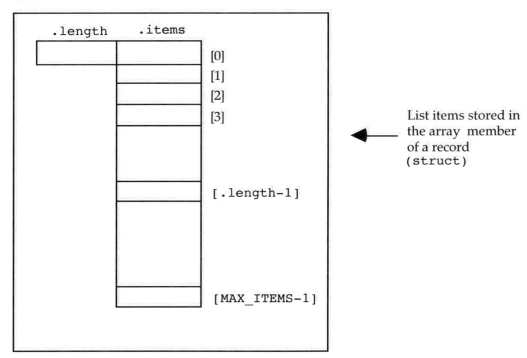

List items stored in the array member of a record (struct)

The following declarations create this structure.

```
const int MAX_ITEMS = /* some value */;

typedef /* type of item on the list */ ItemType;
typedef ItemType Items[MAX_ITEMS];

struct ListType
{
    int    length;
    Items  items;
};
```

Chapter 14: Prelab Assignment

Name _____ **Date** _____

Section _____

Read program **Cars** carefully.

```
// Program Cars reads a record from a file and writes
// its contents back to another file with the price member
// increased by 10%.
#include <iostream.h>
#include <fstream.h>

typedef  char String15[16];
struct  Date Type
{
    int  month;
    int  day;
    int  year;
};
struct  CarType
{
    float     price;
    Date Type purchased;
    String15 customer;
};

void  GetCar(ifstream&, CarType&);
// Reads a variable of CarType from a file.

void  WriteCar(ofstream&, CarType);
// Writes a variable of CarType on a file.

int main ()
{
    CarType  car;
    ifstream dataIn;
    ofstream dataOut;

    dataIn.open("cars.dat");
    dataOut.open("cars.out");
    dataOut.setf(ios::fixed, ios::floatfield);
    dataOut.setf(ios::showpoint);

    GetCar(dataIn, car);
    while (dataIn)
    {
        car.price = car.price * 1.10;
        WriteCar(dataOut, car);
        GetCar(dataIn, car);
    }
```

```
return 0;
}

//****************************************************

void  GetCar(ifstream&  dataIn, CarType&  car)
// Pre:  File dataIn has been opened.
// Post: The fields of car are read from file dataIn.
{
    dataIn.get(car.customer, 15);
    dataIn >> car.price  >> car.purchased.day
         >> car.purchased.month  >> car.purchased.year;
    dataIn.ignore(2,  '\n');
}

//****************************************************

void  WriteCar(ofstream&  dataOut, CarType  car)
// Pre:  File dataOut has been opened.
// Post: The fields of car are written on file dataOut,
//        appropriately labeled.
{
    dataOut  << "Customer: "  << car.customer  << endl
        << "Price:     "  << car.price  << endl
        << "Purchased:"  << car.purchased.day  << "/"
        << car.purchased.month  << "/"
        << car.purchased.year  << endl;
}
```

Exercise 1: If file **Cars.dat** is as follows, what is written on file **Cars.out**?

```
Tiny Tim            35000   1 1 1985
Mary Murphay        12500   2 7 1995
Bear Bare           44444   9 6 1990
Sally Sale           7500   6 3 1970
Betty Bye           18888   4 8 1988
Alice Alas          23005   6 6 1992
```

Lesson 14-1: Check Prelab Exercise

Name _____   **Date** _____

Section _____

Exercise 1:   Run program **Cars** to check your answers. Were they correct? If not, describe your error.

Lesson 14-2: Record Data Type

Name _____   **Date** _____

Section _____

Exercises 1, 2, and 3 use the declarations in file **Shell.cpp**.

DistanceType is defined as a record type with three fields: **feet**, **yards**, and **miles**. The following four operations (functions) are defined on variables of **DistanceType**:

- **AddDistance**: Adds two variables of type **DistanceType** and leaves the result in a third variable of type **DistanceType**. For example, 2 feet, 1750 yards, 2 miles + 2 feet, 10 yards, 0 miles = 1 foot, 1 yard, 3 miles.
- **ConvertFeet**: Converts feet into a variable of type **DistanceType**. For example, 6002 feet is converted to 2 feet, 240 yards, 1 mile.
- **ConvertYards**: Converts yards into a variable of type **DistanceType**. For example, 5230 yards is converted to 0 feet, 1710 yards, 2 miles.
- **PrintDistance**: Prints a variable of type **DistanceType**.

```
const int FEET_IN_YARDS = 3;
const int YARDS_IN_MILES = 1760;

struct  DistanceType
{
    long  feet;
    long  yards;
    long  miles;
};

DistanceType  AddDistance(DistanceType, DistanceType);
DistanceType  ConvertYards(long);
DistanceType  ConvertFeet(long);
void  PrintDistance(DistanceType);

//********  DistanceType Operations *******************

DistanceType  AddDistance
    (DistanceType  distance1, DistanceType  distance2)
// Pre:  distance1 and distance2 contain valid data.
// Post: Returns distance1 + distance2.
{
    // FILL IN Code to add two variables of DistanceType.
}

//***********************************************************

DistanceType  ConvertYards(long  yards)
// Post: yards has been converted into a variable of
//       DistanceType.
{
```

```
        // FILL IN Code to convert yards to a variable of
        // DistanceType.
}
//******************************************************

DistanceType  ConvertFeet(long  feet)
// Post:  feet has been converted into a variable of
//        DistanceType.
{
        // FILL IN Code to convert feet to a variable of
        // DistanceType.
}

//******************************************************

void  PrintDistance(DistanceType  Distance)
// Post:  A vriable of DistanceType is printed as as feet,
//        yards, and miles.
{
        // FILL IN Code to print a variable of DistanceType.
}
```

Exercise 1:   Fill in the missing code in these operations.

Exercise 2:   Write a driver (function **main**) that tests the operations with the data used in the description of the operations. Describe any bugs in your implementation and correct them. (Lesson 14-6 asks you to write and implement a complete test plan for these operations.)

Exercise 3:   Write a function that takes a variable of type **DistanceType** and a time (in minutes) and calculates miles per hour. Convert the variable of type **DistanceType** to **miles** (a **float** variable) before performing the calculation. The result should be a **float** value representing miles per hour rather than a value of **DistanceType**. Your function heading should be as shown below.

```
float  MilesPerHour
          (DistanceType  distance,   // distance traveled
           long  time)               // time in minutes
```

Use your function to calculate miles per hour where the distance is (15,000 feet + 12,000 yards + 37 miles) and the time is 45 minutes.

Miles Per Hour Traveled _____ .

Lesson 14-3: Lists as Records

Name _____   **Date** _____

Section _____

This lesson uses program **List** shown below.

```
// Program List reads and stores strings from file
// list.dat until the stream fails.

#include <iostream.h>
#include <fstream.h>
#include <string.h>

const int MAX_LENGTH = 50;
typedef char ItemType[16];
typedef ItemType ItemsType[MAX_LENGTH];

struct  ListType            // declare list structure
{
    int        length;
    ItemsType items;
};

void  CreateList(ListType&);
// Sets list to the empty list.

void  GetList(ifstream&, ListType&);
// Reads values from a file and stores them in a list.

void  PrintList(ListType&);
// Prints values in the list on the screen.

int  main ()
{
    ifstream   tempData;
    ListType   list;          // define list variable

    tempData.open("list.dat");
    CreateList(list);
    GetList(tempData, list);
    PrintList(list);
    return 0;
}

//*******************************************

void  CreateList(ListType&  list)
// Post: length has been set to zero.
{
    // FILL IN Code to initialize list.
}
```

```
//*******************************************

void GetList(ifstream&  data, ListType&  list)
// Pre:  length has been set to zero.
// Post: Values have been read from file data and stored into
//       list and length contains the number of values read.
{
  // FILL IN Code to input values into the list.
  // Be careful with newline character.
}

//*********************************************************

void PrintList(ListType&  list)
// Pre:  list has valid data.
// Post: list items have been written on cout one per line.
{
    // FILL IN Code to print the items in the list.
}
```

Exercise 1:   Fill in the missing code in program **List** and run it. Show the last three lines of output.

Lesson 14-4: Hierarchical Records

Name _____   **Date** _____

Section _____

This lesson works with program **Cars** defined in the Prelab assignment.

Exercise 1:   Augment **CarType** in program **Cars** with the following two members:

```
sold        Boolean
soldDate    if (sold), then soldDate contains the date of sale;
            otherwise soldDate is undefined.
```

Function **GetCar** should initialize **sold** to **FALSE**. Write a function, **CarSold**, that takes variables of **Date Type** and **CarType** and records that the car has been sold and the date. Before invoking **PrintCar**, write the car owner's name on the screen and ask if it has been resold. If it has, call function **CarSold** and then write the car to file **dataSold** rather than file **dataOut**. Run your program using file **cars.dat**. Let Betty's and Alice's cars be resold.

Exercise 2:   Rewrite **CarType** so that **soldDate** and the new owner's name are encapsulated into a **struct** member **soldTo**. If the car has been resold, prompt for and read the new owner's name. Run your program again using **cars.dat**. Let Betty's car be sold to John and Alice's car be sold to Cliff.

Lesson 14-5: Arrays of Records

Name _____ **Date** _____

Section _____

This lesson uses program **Parts**.

```
// Program Parts reads in stock numbers, prices, and
// quantities from file inventory, stores them in a list,
// and prints the list.

#include <iostream.h>
#include <fstream.h>

const int MAX_LENGTH = 50;

struct  ItemType          // declare record of items
{
    int    stockNumber;
    float price;
    int    quantity;
};
struct  ListType          // declare list structure
{
    int        length;
    ItemType   items[MAX_LENGTH];
};

void  CreateList(ListType&);
// Sets list to the empty list.

void  GetList(ifstream&, ListType&);
// Reads values from a file and stores them in a list.

void  PrintList(ListType&);
// Prints values in a list on the screen.

int  main ()
{
    ListType  list;           // define list variable
    ifstream  inventory;
    cout.setf(ios::fixed, ios::floatfield);
    cout.setf(ios::showpoing);
    inventory.open("parts.dat");
    CreateList(list);
    GetList(inventory, list);
    PrintList(list);
    return 0;
}

//*******************************************
```

```
void  CreateList(ListType&  list)
// Post: length has been set to zero.
{
     // FILL IN Code to initialize list.
}


//*******************************************

void  GetList(ifstream&  data, ListType&  list)
// Pre:  length has been set to zero.
// Post: Values have been read from file data and stored into
//       list; length contains the number of values read.
{
    int  stockNumber;
    data  >> stockNumber;
    while (data)
    {
        // FILL IN Code to store stockNumber.
        // FILL IN Code to input the rest of the record.
    }
}


//*****************************************************

void  PrintList(ListType&  list)
// Pre:  list has valid data.
// Post: Items in the list have been written on cout one
//       per line.
{
    // FILL IN Code to print the items in the list.
}
```

Exercise 1: Read the internal documentation of program **Parts**. Fill in the missing code and run the program using the data in file **parts.dat**. Show the last two lines printed.

Exercise 2: Write a function that calculates and prints the value of the entire inventory—that is, sum **quantity** times **price** for all the items in **list**.

The value of the inventory is _____.

Exercise 3: Did you notice how much of program **Parts** came directly from program **List**? Why was this possible?

Lesson 14-6: Test Plans

Name _____   **Date** _____

Section _____

Exercise 1:   Write and implement a test plan for function **AddDistance**.

Reason for Test Case	Input Values	Expected Output	Observed Output

Exercise 2:   Write and implement a test plan for function **ConvertFeet**.

Reason for Test Case	Input Values	Expected Output	Observed Output

Exercise 3: Write and implement a test plan for function **ConvertYards**.

Reason for Test Case	Input Values	Expected Output	Observed Output

Exercise 4: Write and implement a test plan for function **PrintDistance**.

Reason for Test Case	Input Values	Expected Output	Observed Output

Exercise 5:   Write and implement a test plan for function **MilesPerHour**.

Reason for Test Case	Input Values	Expected Output	Observed Output

Postlab Activities

Exercise 1:   You have an extensive music collection.   You decide to write a program to create a file containing information on each individual recording.   Use the **Recording** data type described in the Review.   Write an interactive program that prompts the user to enter the data for each recording. Run your program entering at least five recordings.

Exercise 2:   Add error checking to your program (if you did not include i t originally) from Exercise 1. After an entry has been entered, print it back to the screen and ask the user if the entry should be saved or discarded.

Exercise 3:   Write a program that takes the data file created in Exercise 1 and calculates the value of your record collection.

15

Classes and Data Abstraction

OBJECTIVES

- To be able to declare a class data type.
- To be able to implement class member functions.
- To be able to define and use an instance of a class data type (a class object) in a client program.
- To be able to write class constructors.

Chapter 15: Assignment Cover Sheet

Name _____   Date _____

Section _____

Fill in the following table showing which exercises have been assigned for each lesson and check what you are to submit: (1) lab sheets, (2) listings of output files, and/or (3) listings of programs. Your instructor or TA can use the Completed column for grading purposes.

Activities	Assigned: Check or list exercise numbers	Submit (1)	(2)	(3)	Completed
Prelab					
Review					
Prelab Assignment					
Inlab					
Lesson 15-1: Check Prelab Exercises					
Lesson 15-2: Class Data Type					
Lesson 15-3: Header and Implementation Files					
Lesson 15-4: Class Constructors					
Lesson 15-5: Debugging					
Postlab					

Prelab Activities

Review

Abstract Data Type

When you combine a variable or a collection of variables with the operations that create and manipulate them, you have an *abstract data type*. An abstract data type, often abbreviated ADT, is more than just a user-defined data type. An ADT has a specified set of properties, and the operations that create and manipulate the ADT must maintain these properties.

The operations for an ADT fall into one of the following four classes:

- *Constructors:* Operations that build or create new instances of an ADT.
- *Transformers:* Operations that build new values of an ADT based on one or more previous values of the ADT.
- *Observers:* Operations that report on the state of an instance of an ADT—for example, operations that tell how many values there are in an instance of an ADT or that tell if the structure is empty or full.
- *Iterators:* Operations that allow us to process all of the components sequentially.

Class Data Type

The **class** data type is a C++ language feature that encourages good programming style by allowing the user to encapsulate both data and actions into a single object.[1]

```
class MoneyType
{
public:
    void  Initialize(long, long);
    // Initializes dollars and cents.
    long  DollarsAre() const;
    // Returns dollars.
    long  CentsAre() const;
    // Returns cents.
private:
    long   dollars;
    long   cents;
};
MoneyType   money;
```

MoneyType is a **class** data type. Like any type, it is a pattern for a structure. This pattern has two data items (member variables): **dollars** and

---

[1]We put class in monospaced bold when we are referring to the C++ language construct (data type **class**), but leave it in regular type when we are referring to the general concept of an encapsulation of data and actions into one structure.

cents; and three actions (member functions): **Initialize, DollarsAre,** and **CentsAre**. The word **public** means that the members defined in this section are accessible to anyone using the class (defining a variable of the class). The members defined following the word **private** are accessible only to the class's member functions. Member variables and functions defined between **public** and **private** form the interface between the class and its *clients*. A client is any software that declares variables of the class. Notice that member function prototypes, not definitions, are used in the class definition. This interface provides no information on how the member functions are implemented.

money is an instance of the **class** data type **MoneyType;** it is called a *class instance* or a *class object*. **money** has two member variables and three member functions. To apply a class instance's member functions, you append the function name to the instance of the data type separated by a period. For example,

```
money.Initialize(56, 23);
cout  << money.DollarsAre();
cout  << money.CentsAre();
```

instruct **money** to apply its member functions **Initialize, DollarsAre,** and **CentsAre** to itself.

Member Function Definitions

A member function is defined like any function with one exception: the name of the class type within which the member is declared precedes the member function name with a double colon in between (**::**). The double colon operator is called the *scope resolution operator*.

```
void  MoneyType::Initialize(long newDollars, long newCents)
// Post: dollars is set to newDollars; cents is set to
//       newCents.
{
    dollars = newDollars;
    cents = newCents;
}

long  MoneyType::DollarsAre()
// Post: Class member dollars is returned.
{
    return dollars;
}

long  MoneyType::CentsAre()
// Post: Class member cents is returned.
{
    return cents;
}
```

When the statement

```
money.Initialize(56, 23);
```

is executed, 56 is stored in **money.dollars** and 23 is stored in **money.cents**. Because **Initialize** is an action defined within class **MoneyType**, any invocation of **Initialize** is applied to a specific instance of **MoneyType**, in this case the variable **money**. The variable identifiers used in the body of the definition of function **Initialize** refer to those of the instance to which it is applied.

The following statement prints the data fields of **money**.

```
cout << "$"  << money.DollarsAre()
     << "."  << money.CentsAre();
```

Binary Operations

When a binary operation is defined within a class type, one of the operands is passed as a parameter and the other is the class instance to which the member function is applied. For example, let's assume that a binary operation, **Add**, has been added as a member in **MoneyType**. Here is its definition.

```
MoneyType   MoneyType::Add(MoneyType   value)
// Pre:  Both operands have been initialized.
// Post: value + self is returned.
{
    MoneyType   result;
    result.cents = cents + value.cents;
    result.dollars := dollars + value.dollars;
    return result;
}
```

Given the following statement,

```
result = money.Add(value);
```

cents and **dollars** in the code of member function **Add** refer those members in the class object to which **Add** has been applied—that is, to **money.cents** and **money.dollars**. The class object to which a member function is applied is often called *self*. Thus we say that **cents** and **dollars** without a variable appended refer to self.

Class Constructors

Because we use classes to encapsulate abstract data types, it is essential that the ADTs be initialized properly. We defined a member function, **Initialize**, to initialize the values of the member variables. What if the client forgets to call **Initialize**? This can be such a serious problem that C++ provides a mechanism to guarantee that all class instances are properly initialized, called the *class constructor*. A class constructor is a member function with the same name as that of the class data type.

```
class MoneyType
{
public:
    void   Initialize(long, long);
    long   DollarsAre();
    long   CentsAre();
    MoneyType  Add(MoneyType  value) const;
    MoneyType(long, long);              // class constructor
    MoneyType();                        // class constructor
private:
    long   dollars;
    long   cents;
};

MoneyType   money;
MoneyType   myMoney(5000, 98);
```

There are two constructors: one with two parameters and one with none. They look a little strange because there is no type identifier or **void** before them. They are invoked differently as well. A class constructor is invoked when a class instance is declared. In this example, **money** is initialized by the default class constructor (the one with no parameters), and **myMoney** is initialized with 5000 in member **dollars** and 98 in member **cents**. These constructors are defined as follows.

```
MoneyType::MoneyType(long initDollars, long initCents)
{
    dollars = initDollars;
    cents   = initCents;
}

MoneyType::MoneyType()
{
    dollars = 0;
    cents   = 0;
}
```

Notice that the class constructors do not make member function **Initialize** unnecessary. If you want to reinitialize a class object during run time, you must use member function **Initialize**. Class constructors are invoked only when a class object is declared.

In C++, if you declare an array of some **class** type and there is at least one constructor for the type, then you must provide a parameterless constructor for the type. You must have a parameterless constructor because you cannot pass parameters to a constructor when creating an array of the class type.

Packaging

Because classes are used to encapsulate abstract data types and because the separation of the logical properties of an ADT from the implementation details is so important, you should package the class declaration and the implementation of the member functions in different files. The class declaration should be in a file with a ".**h**" extension (called the specification file), and the implementation should be in a file with the same name but with a ".**cpp**" extension (called the implementation file). The implementation file must use the **#include** directive to access the specification file. Any client program must use the **#include** directive for the specification file (.**h** extension) to include your files in their source code.

In the next chapter, we assume that the definitions for class **MoneyType** are on file **money.h**, and that the member function implementations are on file **money.cpp**.

Chapter 15: Prelab Assignment

Name _____   **Date** _____

Section _____

Examine program **Money** carefully.

```cpp
// Program Money manipulates instances of class MoneyType.

#include <iostream.h>

class MoneyType
{
public:
    void    Initialize(long, long);
    long    DollarsAre() const;
    long    CentsAre() const;
    MoneyType  Add(MoneyType) const;
private:
    long   dollars;
    long   cents;
};

//********************************************************

int main ()
{
    MoneyType   money1;
    MoneyType   money2;
    MoneyType   money3;
    money1.Initialize(10, 59);
    money2.Initialize(20, 70);
    money3 = money1.Add(money2);
    cout << "$"  << money3.DollarsAre() << "."
         << money3.CentsAre()  << endl;
    return 0;
}

//********************************************************

void  MoneyType::Initialize(long newDollars, long newCents)
// Post: dollars is set to newDollars; cents is set to
//       newCents.
{
    dollars = newDollars;
    cents = newCents;
}

//********************************************************
```

```
long  MoneyType::DollarsAre()
// Post: Class member dollars is returned.
{
    return dollars;
}

//********************************************************

long  MoneyType::CentsAre()
// Post: Class member cents is returned.
{
    return cents;
}

//********************************************************

MoneyType MoneyType::Add(MoneyType  value)
// Pre:  Both operands have been initialized.
// Post: value + self is returned.
{
    MoneyType  result;
    result.cents = cents + value.cents;
    result.dollars = dollars + value.dollars;
    return result;
}
```

Exercise 1: What is printed by program **Money**?

Exercise 2: Why does member function **Add** have only one parameter?

Exercise 3: The declaration and definition of class **MoneyType** are included in program **Money**. Circle and label the part of the program that should be in file **money.h** (the specification file), circle and label the part that should be in file **money.cpp** (the implementation file), and label the parts that should be in the client program **Money**.

Exercise 4: What is missing from the definition of class **MoneyType**?

Lesson 15-1: Check Prelab Exercises

Name _____   **Date** _____

Section _____

Exercise 1:   Run program **Money** to check your answer to Exercise 1. Was your answer correct? If not, do you understand where you made your mistake?

Exercise 2:   The second parameter for the **Add** operation is the object to which the member function is being applied. It is often referred to as "self"—in this example, **money1**.

Exercise 3:   Program **Money** on the disk is documented to show what should be in the **money.h** file, what should be in the **money.cpp** file, and what is the client code.

Exercise 4:   No constructors have been supplied with class **MoneyType**.

Lesson 15-2: Class Data Type

Name _____   **Date** _____

Section _____

Exercise 1:   Add a member function, **Normalize**, to class **MoneyType** that normalizes the cents to between 0 and 99 and adjusts the dollar amount accordingly. Apply function **Normalize** to **money3** before printing it. Run the revised program **Money**. What is printed?

Exercises 2, 3, and 4 use the declarations in file Shell.h and the definitions in Shell.cpp.

DistanceType is defined as a class with three data members: **feet**, **yards**, and **miles**.

Seven member functions are defined within class **DistanceType**:

- **FeetAre**: Returns the **feet** data member.
- **YardsAre**: Returns the **yards** data member.
- **MilesAre**: Returns the **miles** data member.
- **AddDistance**:   Returns the result of adding two variables of type **DistanceType**. For example, 2 feet, 1,750 yards, 2 miles + 2 feet, 10 yards, 0 miles = 1 foot, 1 yard, 3 miles.
- **ConvertFeet**: Returns the result of converting feet into a variable of type **DistanceType**. For example, 6002 feet is converted to 2 feet, 240 yards, 1 mile. Returns a variable of **DistanceType**.
- **ConvertYards**: Returns the result of converting yards into a variable of type **DistanceType**. For example, 5230 yards is converted to 0 feet, 1710 yards, 2 miles.
- **PrintDistance**: Prints a variable of type **DistanceType**.

```
// File Shell.h

const int FEET_IN_YARDS = 3;
const int YARDS_IN_MILES = 1760;

class DistanceType
{

    // TO BE FILLED IN.
}

// File Shell.cpp
```

```
//************ Member functions for DistanceType ********

long  DistanceType::FeetAre() const
// Post: Member feet is returned.
{
    // TO BE FILLED IN.
}

long  DistanceType::YardsAre() const
// Post: Member yards is returned.
{
  // TO BE FILLED IN.
}

long  DistanceType::MilesAre()
// Post: Member miles is returned.
{
    // TO BE FILLED IN.
}

DistanceType  DistanceType::AddDistance
    (DistanceType  distance1) const
// Post: Result of adding two instances of DistanceType
//       is returned.
{
    // FILL IN Code to add two variables of DistanceType.

}

DistanceType  DistanceType::ConvertYards (int  conYards)
// Post: Yards has been converted into a distance in feet,
//       yards, and miles.
{
    // FILL IN Code to convert from yards to variable
    // of type DistanceType.

}

DistanceType  DistanceType::ConvertFeet (int  conFeet)
// Post: feet has been converted into a distance in feet,
//       yards, and miles.
{
    // FILL IN Code to convert from feet to variable
    // of type DistanceType.

}

void  DistanceType::PrintDistance()
// Post: Distance has been printed on the screen as feet,
//       yards, and miles.

{

    // FILL IN Code to print a variable of DistanceType.

}
```

Exercise 2:   Fill in the missing code in these operations.

Exercise 3:   Write a driver that tests the operations with the data used in the description of the operations. Describe any bugs in your implementation and correct them.

Exercise 4:   Write a function that takes a variable of type **DistanceType** and a time (in minutes) and calculates miles per hour. Convert the variable of type **DistanceType** to **miles** (a **float** variable) before performing the calculation. The result should be a **float** value representing miles per hour rather than a value of **DistanceType**. Your function heading should be as shown below.

```
float   MilesPerHour
          (DistanceType  distance,      // distance traveled
           long  time) const;           // time in minutes
```

   Use your function to calculate miles per hour where the distance is (15,000 feet + 12,000 yards + 37 miles) and the time is 45 minutes.

Miles Per Hour Traveled   _____.

Lesson 15-3: Header and Implementation Files

Name _____   **Date** _____

Section _____

Exercise 1: Take program **Money** and reorganize it into three files: **money.h**, **money.cpp**, and **UseMoney.cpp**. **UseMoney.cpp** is the client program that uses class **MoneyType**. Run program **UseMoney**. The results should be the same.

Exercise 2: Exercises 2 and 3 use the following **FracType.h** and **FracType.cpp**.

```
// Header file FracType declares class FracType.

class FracType
{
public:
    FracType  Add(FracType  frac1) const;
    // Pre:  frac1 and self have been initialized.
    // Post: self + frac1 is returned.

    FracType  Sub(FracType  frac1) const;
    // Pre:  frac1 and self have been initialized.
    // Post: self - frac1 is returned.

    FracType  Mult(FracType  frac1) const;
    // Pre:  frac1 and self have been initialized.
    // Post: self * frac1 is returned.

    FracType  Div(FracType  frac1) const;
    // Pre:  frac1 and self have been initialized.
    // Post: self / frac1 is returned.

    int  NumIs() const;
    // Pre:  self has been initialized.
    // Post: Numerator of frac1 is returned.

    int  DenomIs() const;
    // Pre:  self has been initialized.
    // Post: Denominator of frac1 is returned.

    void  Set(int  num, int  denom);
    // Post:  self has been set to num / denom.

private:
    int  numerator;
    int  denominator;
};
```

```
// Implementation file FracType implements the member
// functions of class FracType.

#include "FracType.h"

FracType  FracType::Add(FracType  frac1) const
// Pre:  frac1 and self have been initialized.
// Post: frac1 + self is returned in reduced form.
{
    // FILL IN Code.
}

FracType  FracType::Sub(FracType  frac1) const
// Pre:  frac1 and self have been initialized.
// Post: self - frac1 is returned in reduced form.are
{
    // FILL IN Code.
}

FracType  FracType::Mult(FracType  frac1) const
// Pre:  frac1 and self have been initialized.
// Post: frac1 * self is returned in reduced form.
{
    // FILL IN Code.
}

FracType  FracType::Div(FracType  frac1) const
// Pre:  frac1 and self have been initialized.
// Post: frac1 is inverted and Mult is called.
{
    // FILL IN Code.
}

int  FracType::NumIs() const
// Pre:  self has been initialized.
// Post: numerator member of self is returned.
{
    // FILL IN Code.
}

int  FracType::DenomIs() const
// Pre:  self has been initialized.
// Post: denominator member of self is returned.
{
    // FILL IN Code.
}
```

Exercise 2:   Read the documentation of the header file and the implementation file carefully. Compare the documentation in the two files. How are they alike? How are they different?

Exercise 3:   Fill in the missing code in the implementation file, and compile **FracType.cpp**. Were there many bugs in your file? Describe any problems that you had.

Lesson 15-4: Class Constructors

Name _____   **Date** _____

Section _____

Exercise 1:   Add class constructors to **class MoneyType**. One should have parameters, and one should be parameterless setting **dollars** and **cents** to zero. Initialize **money1** and **money2** using the parameterized class constructor. Initialize **money3** using the default constructor. Write out the value of **money3** before the call to member function **Add**. Show your results.

Exercise 2:   Add class constructors to class **DistanceType**. Describe your constructors. Run a test case and show the results.

Exercise 3:   Add class constructors to class **FracType**.   Describe your constructors. Run a test case and show the results.

Exercise 4:   We have chosen to make the writing of class constructors a separate activity to emphasize its importance. From now own, you should always include class constructors in every class that you define. Explain why.

Lesson 15-5: Debugging

Name _____   **Date** _____

Section _____

Exercise 1:   Program **Mystery** (file **Mys.cpp**) is a version of one of the programs that you have been working with in this lesson. Unfortunately, it is buggy. Debug and run the program. Describe the bugs you found.

Exercise 2:   **MysteryType** is an alias for which type?

Postlab Activities

Exercise 1: Write a test plan for class **FracType**.

Exercise 2: Write a command-driven driver to implement the test plan written for Exercise 1. A command-driven program is one in which the user enters the operation to be tested followed by the values to use in the test. For example, to test if the **Add** member function correctly adds 1/2and 3/4, the user might input

 + 1 2 3 4

The operation is invoked with the appropriate data, and the result is written on the screen. The user is prompted to enter another operation or quit.

Exercise 3: Generating test data is a time-consuming process, as you probably noticed. Write a program that uses a random number generator to generate a file of integers. The program should be interactive. The user enters the number of integers to generate, the range of the numbers, and the file to which they should be written. **int** function **rand** returns a random integer ranging from zero up to **RAND_MAX**. **rand** should be initialized by a call to **srand(seed)** where **seed** is a nonnegative integer. **rand**, **srand**, and **RAND_MAX** are available in **<stdlib.h>**.

Exercise 4: Program **Parts** in Chapter 14 creates and prints a list of parts. Rewrite this program, making **ItemType** a class rather than a record. Be sure to put the definition of **ItemType** in a header file and the implementation of the member functions in an implementation file. All accesses to objects of **ItemType** should be through member functions defined within the class.

16

Object-Oriented Software Development

OBJECTIVES

- To be able to define a descendant class from an existing class data type.
- To be able to declare and use descendant-class objects.
- To be able to define a class data type in which a private member is of an existing class data type.
- To be able to define a class type with a dynamically bound (virtual) member function.
- To be able to declare and use a class object with a dynamically bound member function.
- To be able to relate object-oriented terminology to C++ constructs.

Chapter 16: Assignment Cover Sheet

Name _____   **Date** _____

Section _____

Fill in the following table showing which exercises have been assigned for each lesson and check what you are to submit: (1) lab sheets, (2) listings of output files, and/or (3) listings of programs. Your instructor or TA can use the Completed column for grading purposes.

Activities	Assigned: Check or list exercise numbers	Submit (1)	(2)	(3)	Completed
Prelab					
Review					
Prelab Assignment					
Inlab					
Lesson 16-1: Check Prelab Exercises					
Lesson 16-2: Classes					
Lesson 16-3: Classes with Inheritance					
Lesson 16-4: Virtual Methods					
Lesson 16-5: Debugging					
Postlab					

Prelab Activities

Review

Object-Oriented Terminology

The vocabulary of object-oriented programming (OOP) has its roots in the programming languages Simula and Smalltalk and can be very bewildering. Such phrases as "sending a message to," "methods," and "instance variables" are sprinkled throughout the OOP literature. Don't panic! These are just synonyms for C++ constructs you already know. First of all, an object is a class object or class instance. A method is a public member function, and an instance variable is a private data member. Sending a message is a call to a public member function. In order for you to become more comfortable with object-oriented terminology, we mix these terms with their C++ counterparts in the rest of this Review.

Objects may be related to one another in one of two ways. An object may be a descendant of another object and inherit the ancestor's properties, or it may include another object as a member. The first is called *inheritance*, and the second is called *composition* or *containment*.

Inheritance

In C++, class data types can inherit data and actions from another class data type. For example, to extend our **MoneyType** to include a currency name, we define a data type that inherits from **MoneyType**.

```
class MoneyType
{
public:
    void    Initialize(long, long);
    long    DollarsAre() const;
    long    CentsAre() const;
    void    Print() const;
    MoneyType  Add(MoneyType  value) const;
    MoneyType(long, long);
    MoneyType();
private:
    long    dollars;
    long    cents;
};

typedef char String10[11];
class ExtMoneyType : public MoneyType
{
public:
    void    CurrencyIs(String10);
    void    Initialize(long, long, const String10);
    void    Print() const;
    ExtMoneyType();
    ExtMoneyType(long, long, const String10);
```

```
private:
    String10  currency;
};

ExtMoneyType  extMoney;
```

The colon followed by the words **public** and **MoneyType** (a class identifier) says that the new class being defined (**ExtMoneyType**) is inheriting the members of class **MoneyType**. **MoneyType** is called the *base* class or *superclass* and **ExtMoneyType** is called the *derived* class or *subclass*.

extMoney has three member variables: one of its own (**currency**) and two that it inherits from **MoneyType** (**dollars** and **cents**). **extMoney** has five member functions: two of its own (**Initialize** and **CurrencyIs**) and three that it inherits from **MoneyType** (**Initialize**, **DollarsAre**, and **CentsAre**). Notice that **CurrencyIs** must be a void function that sends back its answer in a reference parameter, because an array cannot be a function return value. **ExtMoneyType** also has two constructors, and **extMoney** is defined using the default constructor.

Although **extMoney** inherits the private member variables from its base class, it does not have direct access to them. **extMoney** must use the public member functions of **MoneyType** to access its inherited member variables.

```
void  ExtMoneyType::Initialize
   (long newDollars, long newCents, String10 newCurrency)
{
    strcpy(currency, newCurrency);
    MoneyType::Initialize(newDollars, newCents);
}

void ExtMoneyType::CurrencyIs(String10 theCurrency) const
{
    strcpy(theCurrency, currrency);
}

void ExtMoneyType::Print() const
{
    MoneyType::Print();
    cout  << currency;
}

ExtMoneyType::ExtMoneyType()
{
    strcpy(currency, "dollars");
}

ExtMoneyType::ExtMoneyType
   (long newDollars, long newCents, const String10 newCurrency)
   : MoneyType(newDollars, newCents)
{
    strcpy(currency, newCurrency);
}
```

There are several points to notice about the syntax of these constructor and member function definitions. The first is that the scope resolution operator (**::**) is used between the type **MoneyType** and the member functions **Initialize** and

Print in the definition of these member functions. Because there are now two member functions named **Initialize** and two named **Print**, you must indicate the **class** in which the one you mean is defined. (That's why it's called the scope resolution operator.) If you do not, the compiler assumes you mean the most recently defined one.

There are two constructors. The parameterless constructor sets the member **currency** to a default value of **"dollars"**. What about the inherited member variables? They are automatically set by the default constructor for the base class. The other constructor takes three values, one for its own member and two for its inherited members. But note that the inherited member variables are not set in the body of the function but by a call to the base class's parameterized constructor. A colon separates the function heading and the call to the constructor before the body of the function.

Virtual Methods

In the previous section we defined two methods with the same name, **Initialize**. The statements

```
money.Initialize(20, 66);
extMoney.Initialize(20, 66, "francs");
```

are not ambiguous, because the compiler can determine which **Initialize** to use by examining the type of the object to which it is applied. There are times, however, when the compiler cannot make the determination of which member function is intended, and the decision must be made at run time. If the decision is to be left until run time, the word *virtual* must precede the member function heading in the base class definition and a class object passed as a parameter to a virtual function must be a reference parameter.

Class Objects as Parameters

If the formal parameter for a function is of the base class, you may pass an actual parameter of the base class or any class derived from it. If the formal parameter is a reference parameter, all is fine. If the formal parameter is a value parameter, only those members defined in the base class are actually passed to the function.

Chapter 16: Prelab Assignment

Name _____   Date _____

Section _____

Read the following header files and driver carefully. The implementation files are not shown.

```
// Money.h is the header file for class MoneyType with
// constructors.

class MoneyType
{
public:
    void   Initialize(long, long);
    long   DollarsAre() const;
    long   CentsAre() const;
    void   Print() const;
    MoneyType Add(MoneyType) const;
    MoneyType(long, long);              // constructor
    MoneyType();                        // constructor
private:
    long   dollars;
    long   cents;
};

// This is the header file for class ExtMoneyType
// (file ExtMoney.h)

#include "money.h"
typedef char String10[11];

class ExtMoneyType : public MoneyType
{
public:
    void   Print() const;
    void   CurrencyIs(String10) const;
    void   Initialize(long, long, String10);
    ExtMoneyType();
    ExtMoneyType(long, long,String10);
private:
    String10  currency;
};

// Program UseMny manipulates objects of class ExtMoneyType.

#include <iostream.h>

#include "extMoney.h"
```

```
int main ()
{
    MoneyType   money;
    cout  << "initialized by default constructors"  << endl;
    money.Print();
    ExtMoneyType   extMoney1;
    extMoney1.Print();
    cout  << "initialized by parameterized constructors"
          << endl;
    ExtMoneyType   extMoney2(3000, 88, "forints");
    extMoney2.Print();
    cout  << "initialized at run time"  << endl;
    extMoney1.Initialize(5000, 99, "pounds");
    extMoney1.Print();
    return  0;
}
```

Exercise 1: What is printed?

Exercise 2: Why did we not show the implementation files?

Exercise 3: Fill in the C++ names or constructs for the following object-oriented concepts.

Object-Oriented	C++
Object	
Instance variable	
Method	
Message Passing	

Lesson 16-1: Check Prelab Exercises

Name _____   **Date** _____

Section _____

Exercise 1:   Run program **UseMny.cpp** to check your answers.   Were they correct? Explain.

Exercise 2:   You do not need to see the implementation files to understand what a program is doing.   The information for the user (the client program) is in the header files.

Exercise 3:

Object-Oriented	C++
Object	Class object or class instance
Instance variable	Private data member
Method	Public member function
Message Passing	Invoking a public member function

Lesson 16-2: Classes

Name _____   **Date** _____

Section _____

Exercise 1:   Define a class made up of one **int** data member called **value**. There should be an observer function for **value**, a print function, an initializer, a parameterized constructor, and a default constructor. Place this definition in a header file.

Exercise 2:   Write the implementation file for the header file in Exercise 1. Let the default constructor set the value to 0.

Exercise 3:   Write a driver program that tests the files in Exercises 1 and 2. Show your input data and the results.

Exercise 4:   Write a program that reads items of the type defined above, stores them in a list, and then prints out the list. Run your program using file **int.dat**. List the last three values. Be sure to encapsulate the items in the list and the length in a **struct**. (See Lesson 14-3.)

Exercise 5:   Convert the list type from a record to a **class**. Make the operations on the list member functions. Name your type **ListType** and the print function **PrintList**. Be sure to include a member function, **Length**, that returns the number of items in the list. Write a driver to read in the values, store them in the list, and print the list using file **int.dat**. The results should be the same as in Exercise 3, Lesson 16-2. Describe any errors that you made in this conversion and what you did to correct them.

Exercise 6:   Now that the list is encapsulated in a **class** data type, client programs cannot access the elements in the list. This protection is both good news and bad news. The items in the list cannot be changed by the client program except through the member functions provided: that is good news. However, each time a client program needs to access each individual item to process it in some way, a new member function must be added to **ListType**: this is bad news because it contradicts the whole idea of encapsulation.

There are two solutions. We can make the items in the list public, or we can add an iterator to **ListType**. This exercise asks you to provide an iterator for **ListType**. The iterator requires a new instance variable, **nextItem**, and two member functions, **Reset** and **GetNext**. **Reset** sets **nextItem** to 0, and **GetNext** returns the item at the **nextItem** position in the list and increments **nextItem**. The client program can then use member functions **Length**, **Reset**, and **GetNext** to iterate through the items in the list.

Use file **int.dat** to test your program by having the driver iterate through the items in the list and print each one.

Lesson 16-3: Classes with Inheritance

Name _____   **Date** _____

Section _____

Exercise 1:   Derive a new class from the one you defined in Exercise 1 in the last lesson. This new class has a binary member function, **Compare**, with one parameter that returns {**LESS**, **EQUAL**, **GREATER**} depending on whether **value** is less than, equal to, or greater than the parameter. Change the declaration of **ListType** so that **ItemType** is your new derived class. Derive a new class from **ListType** that has a member function that goes through the items in the list and prints out how many values in it are greater than a given value, equal to a given value, and less than a given value. Pass the value to be tested against as a parameter. Test your function using value 678. Show the results.

Exercise 2:   Define type **HiPriorityType** that inherits from **ListType** and has the member function **Priority** that returns the maximum value in the list. Run your program using file **int.dat**.

Priority item is _____ .

Exercise 3:   Define type **LoPriorityType** that inherits from **ListType** and has the member function **Priority** that returns the minimum value in the list. Run your program using file **int.dat**.

Priority item is _____ .

Lesson 16-4: Virtual Methods

Name _____   **Date** _____

Section _____

Exercise 1:   To both **LoPriorityType** and **HiPriorityType** from Lesson 16-3 add a member function, **PrintList**, that prints the priority item (appropriately labeled) and then prints the entire list using the member function **PrintList** defined in **ListType**. Test these functions using file **int.dat**.

You are going to add the following function to a client program that uses **ListType**, **HiPriorityType**, and **LoPriorityType**.

```
void  Print(ListType&  list)
{
    cout << "The list is: "  << endl;
    list.PrintList();
}
```

Exercise 2:   Can the compiler tell which member function **PrintList** to use in the following statements?

```
ListType  list;

HiPriorityType  list1;

LoPriorityType  list2;

int main ()
{
    Print(list);
    Print(list1);
    Print(list2);
    return 0;
}
```

Explain.

Exercise 3:   No, the compiler cannot determine.   Therefore, member function `PrintList` must be a virtual method. Describe the changes to the following definitions:

`ListType`:

`HiPriorityType`:

`LoPriorityType`:

Exercise 4:   Implement these changes and run your program applying function `Print` to an instance of `ListType`, an instance of `HiPriorityType`, and an instance of `LoPriorityType`. Run your program using `int.dat`. Show your output.

Lesson 16-5: Debugging

Name _____   **Date** _____

Section _____

Exercise 1:   Program **UsePart** is a client program that uses **PartsType** (file **Parts.h**) and **ExtPartsType** (file **ExtParts.h**). The **.cpp** files for these classes don't even compile! There is one syntax error in file **Parts.h** and two syntax errors in **ExtParts.h**. Find these errors and correct them. Describe the errors.

Exercise 2:   Look at your output carefully. You are missing some values! Correct the logic, recompile, and rerun your program. Describe the error.

Exercise 3:   Some of the missing output is now showing but not all! Keep looking. When you find this error, correct it and rerun the program. The output should now be correct. Describe the error.

Postlab Activities

Your music collection is getting quite a reputation. Friends are always calling you and asking if you have such and such recording. Create an ADT MusicCollection. The set of operations must include at least the following functionality.

- List the song titles alphabetically within **MediaType**.
- Given a song title as input, determine if you have a recording of the song.
- Add new recordings to your list.
- Delete recordings.

Design your classes carefully. Make your function **main** just a driver that uses the classes that you have defined.

Exercise 1:   Write a design document showing your classes and how they interact.

Exercise 2:   Write the header files for your classes.

Exercise 3:   Write the implementation files for your classes.

Exercise 4:   Write test plans for each class and implement them.

Exercise 5:   Write a command-driven driver that lets the user determine the operations to apply. Write a test plan for integrating all the classes. Use the command-driven driver to implement your integration test plan. (An integration test is one that tests the interactions among different classes.)

17

Pointers Dynamic Data, and Reference Types

OBJECTIVES

- To be able to define pointer types.
- To be able to create dynamic variables, read values into them, and print them.
- To be able to manipulate dynamic variables.
- To be able to distinguish between shallow copying and deep copying.

Chapter 17: Assignment Cover Sheet

Name _____   **Date** _____

Section _____

Fill in the following table showing which exercises have been assigned for each lesson and check what you are to submit: (1) lab sheets, (2) listings of output files, and/or (3) listings of programs. Your instructor or TA can use the Completed column for grading purposes.

Activities	Assigned: Check or list exercise numbers	Submit (1)	(2)	(3)	Completed
Prelab					
Review					
Prelab Assignment					
Inlab					
Lesson 17-1: Check Prelab Exercises					
Lesson 17-2: Pointer Variables					
Lesson 17-3: Dynamic Data					
Lesson 17-4: Classes and Dynamic Data					
Lesson 17-5: Debugging					
Postlab					

Prelab Activities

Review

Pointer Types

The *pointer* type is a simple data type that contains the address (or otherwise indicates the location) of a variable of a given type.

```
#include <iostream.h>

char*  charPtr;
int    *intPtr;
char*  aString;

char   letter = 'B';
int    value = 1066;
char   myName[10] = "Nell";
```

charPtr is a pointer that can point to a location in memory that can contain an alphanumeric character. **intPtr** is a pointer that can point to a location in memory that can contain an integer. Note that the asterisk (*) that indicates a pointer can go either to the right of the type or to the left of the variable. If it is appended to the type, and more than one variable is being defined, the * only applies to the first variable in the list. We consistently use the asterisk as a postfix operator on the type and define only one variable at a time. **aString** is a pointer that can point to a location in memory that can contain a character. **letter**, **value**, and **myName** are variables of types **char**, **int**, and **char[10]**, respectively.

Now look at the following three assignment statements.

```
charPtr = &letter;
intPtr  = &value;
aString = myName;
```

The prefix operator ampersand (**&**) means "address of." So **&letter** means the address in memory assigned to the variable **letter**; **&value** means the address of the variable **value**; and **myName** without a subscript means the base address of the string variable **myName**. These three assignments are legal, because the identifiers on the left of the assignment operator are pointers to the appropriate type.

To access the location that the pointer points to, you use the dereferencing operator: a prefix asterisk (*). For example, the following three lines write what is shown on the next page.

```
cout  << aString;
cout  << " "  << *charPtr  << ". ";
```

```
cout  <<  *intPtr  <<  endl;
Nell B. 1066
```

If we send ***aString** to the output stream rather than **aString,** the first letter is sent to the output stream rather than the entire string.

Pointers to Structures

In the last chapter we defined a class **MoneyType**. Let's use it to define a pointer to an instance of **MoneyType**.

```
#include "money.h"
MoneyType*  moneyPtr;
```

moneyPtr is a pointer to an instance of class **MoneyType**, and ***moneyPtr** is the class variable pointed to by **moneyPtr**. We access the member functions of the class with **(*moneyPtr).DollarsAre()** and **(*moneyPtr).CentsAre()**. The parentheses are necessary in each case because the dot operator has higher precedence than the dereferencing operator (the asterisk). For this reason, C++ supplies the arrow operator made up of a hyphen and a greater-than sympol (**->**). This operator both dereferences the pointer and accesses the member field. That is, the following pairs of expressions are equivalent.

(*moneyPtr).CentsAre() and **moneyPtr->CentsAre()**

(*moneyPtr).DollarsAre() and **moneyPtr->DollarsAre()**

Dynamic Variables

In the previous discussion, we created a variable and stored its address in a pointer variable. By now, you should be asking, *but why?* Why would you go to this much trouble if it is only an alternative way to do something you can already do? Just be patient. The ability to store and manipulate the addresses of variables allows us to create a new kind a variable: *dynamic*. In Chapter 8, we described two kinds of data: static and automatic. Static variables exist for the lifetime of the program. Automatic variables are created when control reaches their declaration and deleted when control exits the block in which they are declared. Dynamic variables, in contrast, are created and destroyed as needed by the program itself. **new** is an operator that allocates a dynamic variable; **delete** is an operator that deallocates it.

```
#include <iostream.h>
#include <string.h>

char*  charPtr;
int*   intPtr;
char*  aString;

charPtr = new char;
intPtr  = new int;
aString = new char[10];
```

```
*charPtr = 'B';
*intPtr  = 1066;
strcpy(aString, "Nell");

cout << aString ;
cout << " "  << *charPtr  << "." ;
cout << *intPtr   << endl;

delete  charPtr;
delete  intPtr;
delete  aString;
```

This code segment produces the same output as the previous example, but there is one major difference. In the first example, the variables **letter**, **value**, and **myName** exist for as long as the program that includes the code segment is running. In the second example, the variables created by **new** to hold the same data exist only from the execution of **new** to the execution of **delete**. The locations that were allocated for them can now be allocated for some other variables. Here, we are talking about three variables, so space is not important. However, when you graduate to writing very large programs, this technique of using space only during the time that you need it becomes important.

The variables generated by **new** are called dynamic variables because they are created at run time. Dynamic variables are used just like any other variables of the same type, but pointer variables only should be assigned to one another, tested for equality, and dereferenced. Other operators are defined on pointer variables, but their application is outside the scope of this manual.

Pointer Constants

There is only one literal pointer constant in C++: the value zero. Zero is called the *null* pointer and points to nothing. Because C++ does not now have the Boolean data type, we have used a Typedef statement to simulate logical variables by defining the constants **TRUE** and **FALSE**. We use the same technique here to define a constant **NULL**. Logically, a pointer that points to memory address zero does point to something, so we define a constant **NULL** and use it in our programs to make this logical distinction clear. The definition can be found in file **<stddef.h>**.

An array variable without index brackets is a constant pointer expression whose value is the base address of the array.

Reference Types

Reference variables, like pointer variables, can contain the address of another variable. Reference variables are defined in the same way that pointer variables are defined, but the operator ampersand (**&**) is used rather than the asterisk (*****). That is, the operator may be a postfix operator on the type identifier or a prefix operator on the variable being defined. If more than one variable is being defined, the ampersand operator on the type only applies to the first in the list. There is no dereferencing operator for reference variables because the compiler dereferences them automatically.

You used reference variables before when you declared a formal parameter to be a reference parameter. The address of the actual parameter is sent to a function if the formal parameter is a reference parameter. The code within the function uses the name of the formal parameter, and the compiler automatically accesses the place pointed to.

Copying Structures with Pointer Variables

It is very important to make the distinction between a pointer and what the pointer points to. If you assign a **struct** variable or **class** variable to another **struct** or **class** variable and the structure contains a pointer variable, the pointers themselves are copied, not what the pointers point to. Let's redefine class **ExtMoneyType** slightly and show what we mean.

```
class MoneyType
{
public:
    void   Initialize(long, long);
    long   DollarsAre() const;
    long   CentsAre() const;
    MoneyType  Add(MoneyType  value) const;
    MoneyType(long, long);
    MoneyType();
private:
    long   dollars;
    long   cents;
};

typedef char String10[11];

class ExtMoneyType : public MoneyType
{
public:
    char*  CurrencyIs();
    Initialize(long, long, const String10);
    ExtMoneyType();
    ExtMoneyType(long, long, const String10);
private:
    char*  currency;
};
```

We have made **currency** a pointer to an array of **char** rather than include the entire string within the class. This change allows us to make member function **CurrencyIs** a pointer-returning function. Of course, the corresponding appropriate changes must be made to the definition of the member functions themselves. Now look what happens after the following statements.

```
ExtMoneyType  extMoney1;
ExtMoneyType  extMoney2 = (5000, 99, "pounds");
extMoney1 = extMoney2;
extMoney2.Initialize(300, 77, "francs");
cout << "extMoney1 "  << extMoney1.CurrencyIs()  << endl;
cout << "extMoney2 "  << extMoney2.CurrencyIs()  << endl;
```

What do you think is printed? We would expect the **currency** member of **extMoney1** to be "**pounds**" and the **currency** member of **extMoney2** to be "**francs**." But it isn't; here is the output.

```
extMoney1 francs
extMoney2 francs
```

How can this be? The assignment statement **extMoney1 = extMoney2** copies **extMoney2** into **extMoney1**, so **extMoney1.currency** points to **"pounds."** When **extMoney2** is reinitialized in the next statement, what **extMoney2.currency** points to is changed. **extMoney1.currency** is still the same pointer, so it now points to **"francs"** as well.

When copying occurs and one or more of the member data variables are pointers, we need a *deep copy* operation. A deep copy copies what a pointer points to, not the pointer itself. The copying that occurred in the assignment statement above is called *shallow copying*; the pointer was copied, not what the pointer pointed to.

When working with classes in which one or more of the member variables is a pointer, the class should provide a class destructor, a deep copy operation, and a class copy-constructor.

Recall that when an automatic object goes out of scope, its memory locations automatically go back to be used again. However, if a member is a pointer, its location is returned, but what it points to is not. A destructor is a function that is called automatically when an object goes out of scope. The function prototype for the destructor for **ExtMoneyType** would be

```
~ExtMoneyType();
```

and the following code would be in the body of the destructor.

```
delete [] currency;
```

A class copy-constructor has the following pattern:

```
TypeName(const TypeName& newData);
```

If a class copy-constructor is present, it overrides the default method of initialization and is used implicitly when a class object is initialized by another in its declaration, is passed by value to a function, or is the result of a value-returning function.

Summary of New Operators

Operator	Where placed	Meaning
*	postfix on a type or prefix on a variable in a pointer variable declaration	declare a variable that is a *pointer to* a place that can contain a variable of the type; must be dereferenced to access the place pointed to
*	prefix on a pointer variable in an expression	dereferencing operator; accesses *place pointed to*
&	postfix on a type or prefix on a variable in a reference variable declaration	declare a variable that is a *pointer to* a place that can contain a variable of the type; is dereferenced automatically by the compiler
&	prefix on a variable	*address of* variable
->	infix between a pointer variable to **struct** or **class** and member name	dereferences a pointer variable and accesses a member

Chapter 17: Prelab Assignment

Name _____ **Date** _____

Section _____

Read program Pointer carefully.

```cpp
// Program Pointer reads in three variables, assigns
// pointers to them, adds them, and prints the result.

#include <iostream.h>

int  main ()
{
    int   one;
    int   two;
    int   three;
    int   result;
    int*  ptrOne;
    int*  ptrTwo;
    int*  ptrThree;

    cout  << "Enter three integer numbers separated"
          << " by blanks; press return."  << endl;
    cin  >> one  >> two  >> three;
    ptrOne = &one;
    ptrTwo = &two;
    ptrThree = &three;
    cout  << endl  << *ptrOne  << " + "  << *ptrTwo
          << " + "  << *ptrThree  << " = ";
    result = *ptrOne + *ptrTwo + *ptrThree;
    cout  << result  << endl;
    return 0;
}
```

Exercise 1:   If the three input values are 20, 10, and 30, what is printed by the first output statement?

Exercise 2:   What is printed by the second output statement?

Exercise 3:   What is the lifetime of the variables in this program?

Lesson 17-1: Check Prelab Exercises

Name _____   **Date** _____

Section _____

Exercise 1:   Run program **Pointer** to check your answer to Exercise 1. Was your answer correct? If not, explain where you made your error.

Exercise 2:   Was your answer correct? If not, explain where you made your error.

Exercise 3:   The variables in program **Pointer** exist as long as the program is running.

Lesson 17-2: Pointer Variables

Name _____   **Date** _____

Section _____

Exercise 1:   Extend program **Pointer** by adding the code to print the three input values in ascending order using the pointers to them. Show your output.

Exercise 2:   Write a program that is the mirror image of program **Pointer** but the values that are read in are strings of length ten rather than integer values. That is, read in three strings, write them out, concatenate them (the string equivalent of addition), and print the result. Show your input data and your output.

Lesson 17-3: Dynamic Data

Name _____   **Date** _____

Section _____

Exercise 1:   File **AltPtr.cpp** contains a shell of a program that does exactly what program **Pointer** does (Exercise 1, Lesson 17-2), but it uses dynamic variables. Fill in the code and run the progam.

```
// Program AltPtr reads in three variables, assigns
// pointers to them, adds them, and prints the result.
#include <iostream.h>

int  main ()
{
    int*  one;
    int*  two;
    int*  three;
    int   result;

    // FILL IN THE Code to create dynamic variables
    // *one, *two, *three.

    cout  << "Enter three integer numbers separated"
          << " by blanks; press return."  << endl;

    // FILL IN THE Code to read the values into the
    // dynamic variables.

    // FILL IN THE Code to print the values that are to
    // be summed.

    // FILL IN THE Code to add the three values and store
    // the answer in result.

    cout  << result  << endl;

    // FILL IN THE Code to deallocate the dynamic data.
    return 0;
}
```

Show the output. It should be the same as Exercise 1, Lesson 17-2.

Exercise 2:   Alter the program in Exercise 1 so that it reads strings of length ten rather than integers. That is, read in three strings, write them out, concatenate them, and print the result. Show your input data and your output.

Exercise 3:   The outputs from Exercises 1 and 2 in this lesson are identical to the outputs from Exercises 1 and 2 in the previous lesson. The lifetime of the variables involved, however, is different. Explain.

Lesson 17-4: Classes and Dynamic Data

Name _____   **Date** _____

Section _____

Exercise 1: The header file for **MoneyType** is shown below.

```
// Header file for class MoneyType with constructors.

#include <iostream.h>

class MoneyType
{
public:
    void  Initialize(long, long);
    long  DollarsAre() const;
    long  CentsAre() const;
    void  Print() const;
    MoneyType  Add(MoneyType) const;
    MoneyType(long, long);
    MoneyType();
private:
    long  dollars;
    long  cents;
};
```

Does class **MoneyType** need either a copy-constructor or deep-copy operation? Explain.

Exercise 2: The header file for class **ExtMoneyClass** is shown below.

```
// Header file for class ExtMoneyType

#include "money.h"
typedef char String10[11];

class ExtMoneyType : public MoneyType
{
public:
    void  Print() const;
    void  CurrencyIs(String10) const;
    void  Initialize(long, long, String10);
    ExtMoneyType();
    ExtMoneyType(long, long, String10);
```

```
private:
    String10   currency;
};
```

Does class **ExtMoneyType** need either a copy-constructor or deep-copy operation? Explain.

Exercise 3: How is the version of **ExtMoneyType** shown in the Prelab Review different from the one shown above? Discuss the impact of the difference on the concept of determining if either a copy-constructor or deep-copy operation is necessary.

Lesson 17-5: Debugging

Name _____   **Date** _____

Section _____

Exercise 1:   Program **UseParts** from the last chapter has been altered to add a part name to class **ExtPartsType**. It seems to compile but gives the wrong answer. Can you find the bug? Describe it.

Exercise 2:   The output is still wrong! Keep looking until you find another bug. Describe it, correct it, and rerun the program.

Postlab Activities

Exercise 1:   In Exercise 5, Lesson 16-2, you wrote a program that read in class objects and stored them in a list class object and then printed them out again. Rewrite that program so that the items in the list are pointers to the class objects rather than the class objects themselves. Test your program using the same data.

Exercise 2:   The algorithm for *insertion sort* is given below. Add a member function to your list class object in Exercise 1 that implements this algorithm. That is, the sort function transforms an unordered list into an ordered list. Note that the algorithm sorts values in an array, and your function should sort pointers to values in an array.

```
FOR Index  ← 0 TO List.Length-1 DO
   Item ← List.Items[Index ]
   Index2← Index - 1
   PlaceFound ← False
   WHILE NOT PlaceFound AND Index2 >= 0
      IF Item < List.Items[Index2]
         THEN
               List.Items[Index2 + 1] ← List.Items[Index2]
               Index2 ← Index2 - 1
         ELSE
               PlaceFound ← True
      List.Items[Index2 + 1] ← Item
```

Exercise 3:   The algorithm for *selection sort* is given below. Write a member function that implements this algorithm. Again, the algorithm sorts values not pointers to values.

```
FOR Index ←  0 TO List.Length - 2 DO
   FOR Index2 ←   Index  TO Length-1 DO
      Find Minimum Value
   Swap Minimum Value with List.Items[Index]
```

Exercise 4:   The algorithm for *bubble sort* is given below. Write a member function that implements this algorithm.

```
FOR Index ←  0 TO List.Length - 2 DO
   FOR Index2 ←  List.Length-1 DOWNTO Index + 1
      IF List.Items[Index2] < List.Items[Index2 - 1]
         THEN
               Swap (List.Items[Index2], List.Items[Index2 - 1])
```

Exercise 5: Bubble sort is unique among sorting algorithms because it has the capability of knowing when the list is already sorted. If no swap occurs for one iteration of the outer loop, the list is already sorted and the algorithm can stop. Add a member function that implements this improved version of bubble sort.

Exercise 6: Compare the performance of the four sorting algorithms. Postlab Exercise 4 in Chapter 15 asked you to write a program to generate test data. Use that program to generate data. If your system has built-in routines for timing the execution of a program, use them in your experiment. Otherwise, use a watch and time the execution yourself. Fill in the following chart. Notice that the chart calls for the data to be in random order, in sorted order, and sorted in reverse order.

Number of Items	Insertion	Selection	Bubble	Modified Bubble
10				
random				
in order				
in reverse				
100				
random				
in order				
in reverse				
1000				
random				
in order				
in reverse				
10000				
random				
in order				
in reverse				

Exercise 7: Write a report comparing the four sorting algorithms based on your test results.

18

Linked Structures

Chapter 18: Assignment Cover Sheet

Name _____   **Date** _____

Section _____

Fill in the following table showing which exercises have been assigned for each lesson and check what you are to submit: (1) lab sheets, (2) listings of output files, and/or (3) listings of programs. Your instructor or TA can use the Completed column for grading purposes.

Activities	Assigned: Check or list exercise numbers	Submit (1)	(2)	(3)	Completed
Prelab					
Review					
Prelab Assignment					
Inlab					
Lesson 18-1: Check Prelab Exercises					
Lesson 18-2: Unordered Linked Lists					
Lesson 18-3: Linked Lists of Objects					
Lesson 18-4: Sorted Lists of Objects					
Lesson 18-5: Debugging					
Postlab					

Prelab Activities

Review

Linked Structures

Dynamic variables can be linked together to form dynamic lists. We define a record (called a *node*) that has two members: **next** (a pointer to the next node in the list) and **component** (the type of the items on the list). For example, let's assume that our list is a list of integers.

```
typedef int ComponentType;
struct NodeType;                    // forward declaration
typedef NodeType* NodePtr;
struct NodeType
{
    ComponentType   component;
    NodePtr   next;
};

NodePtr   listPtr;                  // external pointer
NodePtr   newNodePtr;               // extra pointer
NodePtr   currentNodePtr;           // extra pointer
```

Because an identifier must be declared before it can be used, we have to tell the compiler that **NodeType** is going to be a **struct**. We do this with a forward declaration that has the type name following the word **struct**. The forward declaration is similiar in use to a function prototype.

To form dynamic lists, we link variables of **NodeType** together to form a chain using the **next** member. We get the first dynamic list node and save its address in an *external pointer*. The external pointer is the name of the pointer to the first node in the list. We then get another node and store its address in the **next** member of the first node.

```
listPtr = new NodeType;             // external pointer
newNodePtr = new NodeType;
listPtr->next = newNodePtr;
```

We get a third node and store its address in the **next** member of the second node. This process continues until the list is complete. The pointer constant **NULL** (defined in **<stddef.h>**) is a pointer that indicates the end of a list. The following code fragment reads and stores integer numbers into a list until the input stream fails.

```
#include <iostream.h>
#include <stddef.h>          // to access NULL
```

```
ComponentType  tempValue;
listPtr = new NodeType;;
cin  >> listPtr->component;        // assumes at least one value
currentNodePtr = listPtr;
cin  >> tempValue;
while (cin)
{
    newNodePtr = new NodeType;
    newNodePtr->component = tempValue;
    currentNodePtr->next = newNodePtr;
    currentNodePtr = newNodePtr;
    cin >> tempValue;
}

currentNodePtr->next = NULL;
```

We read the first value outside the loop so that we can store it in the node pointed to by **listPtr**, the external pointer to the list. **currentNodePtr** is then set to point to **listPtr**. Within the loop we continue to get a node (**newNodePtr**), store a value in it, put the node's address in the **next** member of **currentNodePtr**, make **currentNodePtr** point to **newNodePtr**, and lastly read a new value. When all the values have been read and stored, **NULL** is placed in the **next** member of the last node in the list (the node pointed to by **currentNodePtr**).

Lists of dynamic variables are traversed (nodes accessed one by one) by beginning with the first node (the one pointed to by the external pointer) and accessing each node until the **next** member of a node is **NULL**. The following code fragment prints out the values in the list whose external pointer is **listPtr**.

```
currentNodePtr = listPtr;
while (currentNodePtr != NULL)
{
    cout  << currentNodePtr->component  << endl;
    currentNodePtr = currentNodePtr->next;
}
```

currentNodePtr is initialized to **listPtr**, the first node. If **listPtr** is **NULL**, the list is empty and the loop is not entered. If there is at least one node in the list, we enter the loop, print the member **component** of **currentNodePtr**, and update **currentNodePtr** to point to the next node in the list. **currentNodePtr** is **NULL** when the last component has been printed, and we exit the loop.

Because the component type of a list node can be any data type, we can create an infinite variety of lists. Pointers also can be used to create very complex data structures such as stacks, queues, and trees that are the subject of more advanced computer science courses.

Chapter 18: Prelab Assignment

Name _____   **Date** _____

Section _____

Read program **RealList** carefully and answer Exercises 1 through 4.

```
// Program RealList creates a linked listPtr of values from a
// file and prints the listPtr.

#include <iostream.h>
#include <stddef.h>          // to access NULL
#include <fstream.h>

typedef float ComponentType;

struct NodeType;                   // forward declaration
typedef NodeType* NodePtr;
struct NodeType
{
    ComponentType  component;
    NodePtr  next;
};

int main ()
{
    NodePtr   listPtr;                  // external pointer
    NodePtr   newNodePtr;                   // extra pointer
    NodePtr   currentNodePtr                 // extra pointer
    ComponentType  tempValue;
    ifstream  data;

    data.open("real.dat");
    listPtr = new NodeType;
    data  >> listPtr->component;
    if (data)
    {   // read in values
        currentNodePtr = listPtr;
        data >> tempValue;
        while (data)
        {
            newNodePtr = new NodeType;
            newNodePtr->component = tempValue;
            currentNodePtr->next = newNodePtr;
            currentNodePtr = newNodePtr;
            data  >> tempValue;
        }
        currentNodePtr->next = NULL;
    }
    else
        listPtr = NULL;
```

```
// print out values
    currentNodePtr = listPtr;
    while (currentNodePtr != NULL)
    {
        cout << currentNodePtr->component  << endl;
        currentNodePtr = currentNodePtr->next;
    }
    return 0;
}
```

Exercise 1:   Draw a picture of the structure when the data file contains the values 11.1, 22.2, 33.3, and 44.4. Use a slash (/) to represent **NULL**.

Exercise 2:   What is printed?

Exercise 3:   Draw a picture of the structure when the data file is empty.

Exercise 4:   What is printed?

Lesson 18-1: Check Prelab Exercises

Name _____   **Date** _____

Section _____

Exercise 1:

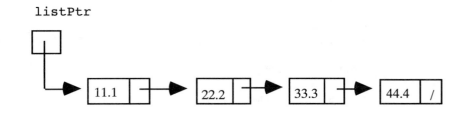

Exercise 2:   Run program **RealList** to check your answer. Were you answers correct? If not, can you explain the difference?

Exercise 3:

listPtr

/

Exercise 4:   Nothing is printed.

Lesson 18-2: Unordered Linked Lists

Name _____ **Date** _____

Section _____

This lesson uses class **ListType**.

```
// Header file for class ListType

#include "Boolean.h"
#include "DataDefn.h"            // to access ItemType

struct  NodeType;               // forward declaration

class  ListType
{
public:
    ListType();
    // Post: List is the empty list.

    ListType(const ListType& otherList);
    // Copy-constructor for ListType.

    Boolean  IsThere(ItemType  item) const;
    // Post: If item is in the list IsThere is
    //       True; False, otherwise.

    void  Insert(ItemType  item);
    // Pre:  item is not already in the list.
    // Post: item is in the list.

    void  Delete(ItemType  item);
    // Pre:  item is in the list.
    // Post: item is no longer in the list.

    void  Print() const;
    // Post: Items on the list are printed on the screen.

    int  Length() const;
    // Post: Length is equal to the number of items in the
    //       list.

    ~ListType();
    // Post: List has been destroyed.

private:
    NodeType* listPtr;
};


// This is the implementation file for class ListType
```

```
#include <iostream.h>
#include <stddef.h>        // to access NULL
#include "ListType.h"

typedef NodeType* NodePtr;

struct NodeType;
{
    ItemType item;
    NodePtr  next;
};

ListType::ListType()
// Post:  listPtr is set to NULL.
{
    // FILL IN Code.
}

//***********************************************************

ListType::ListType(const ListType&  otherList)
// Copy-constructor for ListType.
{
    // FILL IN Code.
}

//***********************************************************


Boolean  ListType::IsThere(ItemType  item) const
// Post: If item is in the list IsThere is
//       True; False, otherwise.
{
    // FILL IN Code.
}

//***********************************************************

void  ListType::Insert(ItemType  item)
// Pre:  item is not already in the list.
// Post: item is the first item in the list.
{
    // FILL IN Code.
}

//***********************************************************

void  ListType::Delete(ItemType  item)
// Pre:  item is in the list.
// Post: item is no longer in the list.
{
    // FILL IN Code.
}

//***********************************************************

void  ListType::Print() const
// Post: Items on the list are printed on the screen.
```

```
{
    // FILL IN Code.
}

//***********************************************************

int  ListType::Length() const
// Post: Number of items have been counted; result returned.
{
    // FILL IN Code.
}

//***********************************************************

ListType::~ListType()
// Post: All the components are deleted.
{
    // FILL IN Code.
}
```

Exercise 1:   Read the internal documentation for class **ListType** carefully. Fill in the missing code in the implementation file, taking advantage of the preconditions. (**ItemType** is defined to be **int** in file **DataDefn.h**.) Compile your program.

Exercise 2:   Write a simple driver that reads values from file **int.dat**, inserts them into the list, prints the length of the final list, and prints the items. Be sure that your driver checks for the preconditions on the member functions of class **ListType** before calling them. How many items are in the list? If your answer is not 11, your driver did not adhere to the preconditions. Correct your driver and rerun your program.

Exercise 3:   Add code to your driver to test the remaining member functions. Delete -47, 1926, and 2000 and print the list to be sure they are gone. How do you test the copy-constructor and the destructor?

Exercise 4:   Add member functions to class **ListType** that find the minimum and maximum values in the list. Rerun your program.

Minimum value is _____.

Maximum value is _____.

Lesson 18-3: Linked Lists of Objects

Name _____   **Date** _____

Section _____

Exercise 1:   Define a **class** data type, **StringType**, that contains one data field, a string of 10 characters.   There should be four member functions: **Initialize**, **GetString**, **PrintString**, and **CompareString**. **Initialize** stores a value in an instance of **StringType**; **GetString** returns as a parameter the value stored in an instance of **StringType**; and **PrintString** prints the value in an instance of **StringType** on the screen. Do you need a copy-constructor, a destructor, and a deep copy function? Explain.

Exercise 2:   What changes are necessary to class **ListType** (in Lesson 18-2) to convert **ItemType** into **StringType**—that is, to make the list a list of strings rather than a list of integers?

Describe the changes necessary in the specification file.

Fill in the chart on the next page showing which member function implementations must be changed and which could be changed.

Member Function	Not Changed	Must Be Changed	Could Be Changed
`IsThere`			
`Insert`			
`Delete`			
`Print`			
`Length`			
`MinValue`			
`MaxValue`			
Constructor			
Destructor			

Describe the changes necessary in the driver program.

Exercise 3: Make the changes necessary and run your complete test program, deleting *Dove* and *sandpiper*.

Minimum value is _____.

Maximum value is _____.

Exercise 4: Examine your output from Exercise 3 carefully. Notice that *sandpiper* is printed as the maximum although *Wren* is logically the maximum. We tend to ignore the difference between uppercase and lowercase letters when we are looking for the one closest to the beginning of the alphabet (minimum) or closest to the end of the alphabet (maximum). Unfortunately, the computer does not. Add the code to your program to convert the strings to all uppercase before you store them in the list. Rerun your program.

Minimum value is _____.

Maximum value is _____.

Lesson 18-4: Sorted List of Objects

Name _____   **Date** _____

Section _____

Exercise 1:   Class **ListType** puts each new item at the front of the list because that is the most efficient algorithm if the list is unordered. However, searching for an item requires that the entire list be searched in order to determine that an item is not in the list. If the list is ordered, the search can stop when the place is passed where the item would be if it were in the list. Specify an ordered list class. Fill in the following chart showing which algorithms can remain the same, which must change, and which can be changed to make them more efficient. Note that we have gone back to the original member functions defined for **ListType**.

Member Function	Not Changed	Must Be Changed	Could Be Changed
IsThere			
Insert			
Delete			
Print			
Length			
Constructor			
Destructor			

Exercise 2:   Write the implementation for the specification in Exercise 1. If you said that only member function **Insert** must to be changed, you are correct. However, **IsThere** and **Delete** can be made more efficient.

Exercise 3:   Write a driver program to test your new sorted list using file **Char.dat**.

Lesson 18-5: Debugging

Name _____   **Date** _____

Section _____

> **Exercise 1:**   Program **IntLis**t reads values into a linked list and prints the list. However, the list is always empty. Can you find the errors? Describe them, correct them, and rerun the program.

Postlab Activities

Exercise 1:   The Postlab for Chapter 16 required you to design and implement the ADT MusicCollection. You kept the recordings as an array-based list because that was the only list implementation structure that you knew. Now you realize that a linked list is a better structure to use because your collection is continuing to grow. Rewrite your program once again, changing the array-based list to a linked list.

Exercise 2:   Can you use the same test plan you used for the previous version? Explain.

Exercise 3:   The program to manipulate information about your music collection takes a long time to run. You decide to improve its performance by keeping the list ordered by title. Which operations have to be changed? Which ones do not?

Exercise 4:   Arrays and linked structures are two implementations of the abstract data type list. Can one implementation always be substituted for the other? Are there types of problems for which one is more efficient that the other? Discuss the relative merits of array-based lists and linked lists using concrete examples.

19

Recursion

OBJECTIVES

- To be able to write a recursive value-returning function to solve a problem involving simple variables.
- To be able to write a recursive void function to solve a problem involving simple variables.
- To be able to write a recursive value-returning function to solve a problem involving structured variables.
- To be able to write a recursive void function to solve a problem involving structured variables.

Chapter 19: Assignment Cover Sheet

Name _____   **Date** _____

Section _____

Fill in the following table showing which exercises have been assigned for each lesson and check what you are to submit: (1) lab sheets, (2) listings of output files, and/or (3) listings of programs. Your instructor or TA can use the Completed column for grading purposes.

Activities	Assigned: Check or list exercise numbers	Submit (1)	(2)	(3)	Completed
Prelab					
Review					
Prelab Assignment					
Inlab					
Lesson 19-1: Check Prelab Exercises					
Lesson 19-2: Simple Variables					
Lesson 19-3: Structured Variables					
Lesson 19-4: Debugging					
Postlab					

Prelab Activities

Review

When a function invokes itself, the call is known as *recursive*. *Recursion* —the ability of a function to call itself—is an alternative control structure to repetition (looping). Rather than use a While statement, Do-While statement, or For statement to execute a segment of code again, the program uses a selection statement (If or Switch statement) to determine whether to repeat the code by calling the function again or to stop the process.

Each recursive solution has at least two cases: the *base case* and the *general case*. The base case is the one to which we have an answer; the general case expresses the solution in terms of a call to itself with a smaller version of the problem. Because the general case solves a smaller and smaller version of the original problem, eventually the program reaches the base case where an answer is known and the recursion stops.

Simple Variables

Associated with each recursive problem is some measure of the size of the problem. The size must get smaller with each recursive call. The first step in any recursive solution is to determine the *size factor*. If the problem involves a numerical value, the size factor might be the value itself. For example, a classic recursive problem is the factorial. The factorial of a number is defined as the number times the product of all the numbers between itself and 0: $N! = N * (N-1)!$. The factorial of 0 is 1. The size factor is the number for which we are calculating the factorial. We have a base case, Factorial(0) is 1, and we have a general case, Factorial(N) is $N * $ Factorial(N-1). An If statement can evaluate N to see if it is 0 (the base case) or greater than 0 (the general case). Because N is clearly getting smaller with each call, the base case is reached.

```
long Factorial(long n)
// Pre:  n is not negative.
{
    if (n == 0)
        return 1;                        // base case
    else
        return n * Factorial(n-1);       // general case
}
```

What happens if **n** is a negative number? The function just keeps calling itself until the runtime support system runs out of memory. This situation is called infinite recursion and is equivalent to an infinite loop. If infinite recusion occurs, the program may crash with a message such as "RUN-TIME STACK OVERFLOW" or the program (and the screen) may just freeze.

Structured Variables

If we are working with structures rather than single values, the size is often the number of items in the structure. For example, if we want to count the number of items in a list, the base case is when the list is empty: there are no items in an empty list. In a nonempty list, the number of items is one plus the number of items in the rest of the list.

```
int  NumItems(NodePtr  listPtr)
{
    if (listPtr == NULL)
       return  0;
    else
       return  (1 + NumItems(listPtr->next));
}
```

When using recursion with structured variables, the base case can be a "do nothing" case. For example, the following function prints the values in a linked list in reverse order.

```
void  RevPrint(NodePtr  listPtr)
{
    if (listPtr != NULL)
    {
        RevPrint(listPtr -> next);
        cout  << listPtr -> component  << endl;
    }
}
```

Notice that there is no **else** branch. When **listPtr** is **NULL**, the function simply returns to the previous call.

Recursion is a very powerful and elegant tool. However, not all problems can easily be solved recursively, and not all problems that have an obvious recursive solution should be solved recursively. But there are many problems for which a recursive solution is preferable. If the problem statement logically falls into two cases, a base case and a general case, you should consider a recursive solution.

Chapter 19: Prelab Assignment

Name _____   **Date** _____

Section _____

Exercise 1:   Fill in the following chart showing the value of the variable **n** at the beginning of each execution of function **Factorial**, starting with the nonrecursive call **Factorial(5)**. Fill in the third column with the function value returned at the completion of the execution of that call.

Call	n	Function Value Returned
Nonrecursive Call		
1st Recursive Call		
2nd Recursive Call		
3rd Recursive Call		
4th Recursive Call		
5th Recursive Call		

Exercise 2:   Fill in the chart showing the value of the variable **listPtr** at the beginning of each execution of function **NumItems** where **listPtr** is as shown below. Refer to **listPtr** by an arrow to the value in the node. For example, → 3 refers to the node containing the value 3. Fill in the third column with the function value returned at the completion of the execution of that call.

listPtr

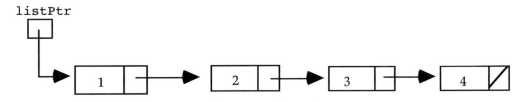

Call	listPtr	Function Value Returned
Nonrecursive Call		
1st Recursive Call		
2nd Recursive Call		
3rd Recursive Call		
4th Recursive Call		

Lesson 19-1: Check Prelab Exercises

Name _____   **Date** _____

Section _____

Exercise 1:

Call	n	Function Value Returned
Nonrecursive Call	5	120
1st Recursive Call	4	24
2nd Recursive Call	3	6
3rd Recursive Call	2	2
4th Recursive Call	1	1
5th Recursive Call	0	0

Exercise 2:

Call	listPtr	Function Value Returned
Nonrecursive Call	→ 1	4
1st Recursive Call	→ 2	3
2nd Recursive Call	→ 3	2
3rd Recursive Call	→ 4	1
4th Recursive Call	NIL	0

Note that the function return value gets assigned at the end of the execution of each call.

Lesson 19-2: Simple Variables

Name _____   **Date** _____

Section _____

Exercise 1:   C++ does not have an exponential operator. Write the recursive value-returning function, **Power**, that takes two parameters (**number** and **exponent**) and returns **number** multiplied by itself **exponent** times. That is, **Power** returns the result of number^{exponent}. Run a driver program that calls **Power(7, 3)** and prints the result.

What is printed?

Exercise 2:   The Fibonacci numbers are defined as the following sequence:

0 1 1 2 3 5 8 13 21 34 55 ...

Notice that except for the first two numbers, each number is the sum of the two preceding numbers. Write a recursive value-returning function, **Fib**, that returns the Nth Fibonacci number where N is a parameter. Test your program with **Fib(5), Fib(10)**, and **Fib(20)**.

Show your output.

Exercise 3:   Write an iterative version of function **Fib** and test it with the same values.

Exercise 4:   You have just demonstrated that the Fibonacci numbers can be generated recursively and iteratively. If you need them in a program, which version do you use? Justify your answer.

Lesson 19-3: Structured Variables

Name _____   **Date** _____

Section _____

Exercise 1:   Write a recursive void function that prints out the values in a linked list.

Exercise 2:   Is Exercise 1 a good use of recursion? In the chapter Review, we wrote a function to print the values in a linked list in reverse order. Was that a good use of recursion? Explain your answers.

Exercise 3:   Write a recursive **int** function that returns the position of a given value in a linked list. If the value is not in the list, return 0. For example, given the following list and a value of 4, the function would return 2.

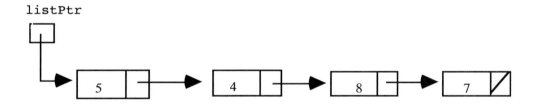

```
listPtr
```

Exercise 4:   Write a test driver for your function in Exercise 3. Use the list shown above. Run your driver asking for the position of 5, 4, 8, 7, and 10. Record the results.

Lesson 19-4: Debugging

Name _____   **Date** _____

Section _____

> **Exercise 1:**   In order to practice writing recursive processes, you decide to write a recursive function to sum the values in a file. Program **SumTest** is the result, but it isn't working. Debug it.
>
> List the errors found and what you did to correct them. (Hint: There are two.)

Postlab Activities

Exercise 1:   How many possible bridge hands are there?   This question is a specific case of the general question: how many combinations of X items can I make out of Y items? In the case of the bridge hand, X is 13 and Y is 52. The solution is given by the following formula:

Combinations(Y, X) =

Y	if $X = 1$
1	if $X = Y$
(Combinations(Y-1, X-1) + Combinations(Y-1, X))	if $Y > X > 1$

Write a recursive function that calculates the number of combinations of X items that can be made from Y items. Write a driver and answer the original questions.

Exercise 2:   Write a recursive void function that prints the contents of an array-based list in reverse order.

Exercise 3:   Write and implement a test plan for Exercise 2 above. Is Exercise 2 a good use of recursion? Justify your answer.

Exercise 4:   Write a recursive **Boolean** function, **IsThere**, that searches an array-based list for a value and returns **TRUE** if the value is there and **FALSE** otherwise. Use the binary search algorithm.

Exercise 5:   Write and implement a test plan for Exercise 4 above. Is Exercise 4 a good use of recursion? Justify your answer.

Appendixes

Appendix A   Reserved Words

The following identifiers are *reserved words*—identifiers with predefined meanings in the C++ language. The programmer cannot declare them for other uses in a C++ program.

asm	double	new	switch
auto	else	operator	template
break	enum	private	this
case	extern	protected	throw
catch	float	public	try
char	for	register	typedef
class	friend	return	union
const	goto	short	unsigned
continue	if	signed	virtual
default	inline	sizeof	void
delete	int	static	volatile
do	long	struct	while

Appendix B   Operator Precedence

The following is a complete list of the C++ operators, some of which are not covered in the manual. Operators are binary unless marked unary.

Operators	Associativity
::	Left to right
() [] -> .	Left to right
++ -- ~ ! + - & * **new** (unary)	Right to left
delete **(cast)** **sizeof** (unary)	Right to left
->* .*	Left to right
* / %	Left to right
+ -	Left to right
<< >>	Left to right
< <= > >=	Left to right
== !=	Left to right
&	Left to right
^	Left to right
|	Left to right
&&	Left to right
||	Left to right
? :	Right to left
= += -+ etc.	Right to left
, (the operator, not the separator)	Left to right

Appendix C   Description of Operators Covered in Manual

Type of Operator	Operator	Meaning
arithmetic	*	Unary plus
	–	Unary minus
	+	Addition
	–	Subtraction
	*	Multiplication
	/	Floating point operands: floating point result Integer operands: quotient Mixed operands: floating point result
	%	Modulus (remainder from integer division, operands must be integral)
	++	Increment by one; can be prefix or postfix
	– –	Decrement by one; can be prefix or postfix
	`sizeof`	returns the size in bytes of its operand
assignment	=	Assignment; evaluate expression on the right and store in variable named on the left
I/O	<<	Insertion; insert the characters (if a string) or the value (if a variable or constant) in the output stream named on the left of the first insertion operator
	>>	Extraction; extract the value from the input stream named on the left of the first extraction operator and store in the place named on the right
relational	==	Equal to
	!=	Not equal to
	>	Greater than
	<	Less than
	>=	Greater than or equal to
	<=	Less than or equal to
logical	&&	AND is a binary Boolean operator. If both operands are true, the result is true. Otherwise, the result is false.
	||	OR is a binary Boolean operator. If at least one of the operands is true, the result is true. Otherwise, the result is false.

logical (cont.)	!	NOT is a unary Boolean operator. NOT changes the value of its operand: if the operand is true, the result is false; if the operand is false, the result it true.
pointer related	*	(postfix on a type or prefix on a variable in a pointer variable declaration) Declare a variable that is a *pointer to* a place that can contain a variable of the type; must be dereferenced to access the place pointed to
	*	(prefix on a pointer variable in an expression) Dereferencing operator; accesses *place pointed to*
	&	(postfix on a type or prefix on a variable in a reference variable declaration) Declare a variable that is a *pointer to* a place that can contain a variable of the type; dereferenced automatically by the compiler
	&	(prefix on a variable) *Address of* a variable
	->	(infix between a pointer variable to **struct** or **class** and member name) Dereferences a pointer variable and accesses a member
	new	Returns the address of new space allocated for a dynamic variable of the type named on the right
	delete	Returns the space allocated for the dynamic variable on the right to the heap to be allocated again
selection	.	(infix: **struct** variable.member) Accesses the member field of the **struct** variable
	.	(infix: **class** variable.member) Accesses the member data or function of the **class** variable
	[ ]	(postfix: encloses an integral expression) Accesses a position within the array variable named on the left
scope resolution	::	(infix: **class** type::method) Associates a method with the **class** in which it is declared

Appendix D   C++ Library Routines and Constants

Header File `ctype.h`

`isalnum(ch)`	Returns true if **ch** is a letter or a digit; false otherwise.
`isalpha(ch)`	Returns true if **ch** is a letter; false otherwise.
`iscntrl(ch)`	Returns true if **ch** is a control character; false, otherwise.
`isdigit(ch)`	Returns true if **ch** is a digit; false otherwise.
`isgraph(ch)`	Returns true if **ch** is a nonblank printable character; false otherwise.
`islower(ch)`	Returns true if **ch** is lowercase; false otherwise.
`isprint(ch)`	Returns true if **ch** is a printable character; false otherwise.
`ispunct(ch)`	Returns true if **ch** is a nonblank printable character (i.e., not a letter or a digit); false otherwise.
`isspace(ch)`	Returns true if **ch** is a whitespace character; false otherwise.
`isupper(ch)`	Returns true if **ch** is an uppercase letter; false otherwise.
`toupper(ch)`	Returns **ch** in uppercase regardless of original case.
`tolower(ch)`	Returns **ch** in lowercase regardless of original case.

Header File `string.h`

`strcat(s1, s2)`	Returns the base address of **s1** with **s2** concatenated on the end.
`strcmp(s1, s2)`	Returns a negative integer if **s1** comes before **s2**; returns zero if **s1** is equal to **s2**; and returns a positive integer if **s2** comes before **s1**.
`strcpy(s1, s2)`	Returns the base address of **s1** with **s2** copied in it.
`strlen(s)`	Returns the number of characters in **s**.

Header File `stddef.h`

`NULL`	The system-dependent null pointer constant (usually 0).

Header File `float.h`

`FLT_DIG`	Approximate number of significant digits in a **float** value on your machine.
`FLT_MAX`	Maximum positive **float** value on your machine.
`FLT_MIN`	Minimum positive **float** value on your machine.
`DBL_DIG`	Approximate number of significant digits in a **double** value on your machine.
`DBL_MAX`	Maximum positive **double** value on your machine.
`DBL_MIN`	Minimum positive **double** value on your machine.
`LDBL_DIG`	Approximate number of significant digits in a **long double** value on your machine.
`LDBL_MAX`	Maximum positive **long double** value on your machine.
`LDBL_MIN`	Minimum positive **long double** value on your machine.

Header File **limits.h**

CHAR_BITS	Number of bits in a byte on your machine.
CHAR_MAX	Maximum **char** value on your machine.
CHAR_MIN	Minimum **char** value on your machine.
SHRT_MAX	Maximum **short** value on your machine.
SHRT_MIN	Minimum **short** value on your machine.
INT_MAX	Maximum **int** value on your machine.
INT_MIN	Minimum **int** value on your machine.
LONG_MAX	Maximum **long** value on your machine.
LONG_MIN	Minimum **long** value on your machine.
UCHAR_MAX	Maximum **unsigned char** value on your machine.
USHRT_MAX	Maximum **unsigned short** value on your machine.
UINT_MAX	Maximum **unsigned int** value on your machine.
ULONG_MAX	Maximum **unsigned long** value on your machine.

Appendix E   The Character Sets

The following charts show the ordering of the two most common character sets: ASCII (American Standard Code for Information Interchange) and EBCDIC (Extended Binary Coded Decimal Interchange Code). The internal representation for each character is shown in decimal. For example, the letter *A* is represented internally as the integer 65 in ASCII and as 193 in EBCDIC. The blank character is denoted by a " ▯ ".

					ASCII					
Left	*Right digit*									
Digit(s)	*0*	*1*	*2*	*3*	*4*	*5*	*6*	*7*	*8*	*9*
0	NUL	SOH	STX	ETX	EOT	ENQ	ACK	BEL	BS	HT
1	LF	VT	FF	CR	SO	SI	DLE	DC1	DC2	DC3
2	DC4	NAK	SYN	ETB	CAN	EM	SUB	ESC	FS	GS
3	RS	US	▯	!	"	#	$	%	&	´
4	(	)	*	+	,	−	.	/	0	1
5	2	3	4	5	6	7	8	9	:	;
6	<	=	>	?	@	A	B	C	D	E
7	F	G	H	I	J	K	L	M	N	O
8	P	Q	R	S	T	U	V	W	X	Y
9	Z	[	\	]	^	_	`	a	b	c
10	d	e	f	g	h	i	j	k	l	m
11	n	o	p	q	r	s	t	u	v	w
12	x	y	z	{	|	}	~	DEL		

Codes 00-31 and 127 are the following nonprintable control characters:

NUL	Null character		LF	Line feed
SOH	Start of header		VT	Vertical tab
STX	Start of text		FF	Form feed
ETX	End of text		CR	Carriage return
EOT	End of transmission		SI	Shift in
ENQ	Enquiry		DLE	Data link escape
ACK	Acknowledge		DC1	Device control one
BEL	Bell character (beep)		DC2	Device control two
BS	Back space		DC3	Device control three
HT	Horizontal tab		DC4	Device control four

(ASCII control characters cont.)

NAK	Negative acknowledge
SYN	Synchronous idle
ETB	End of transmitted block
CAN	Cancel
EM	End of medium
SUB	Substitute
ESC	Escape
FS	File separator
GS	Group separator
RS	Record separator
US	Unit separator
DEL	Delete

EBCDIC

Left Digit(s)	0	1	2	3	4	5	6	7	8	9
6										
7					¢	.	<	(	+	|
8	&									
9	!	$	*	)	;	¬	—	/		
10							^	,	%	_
11	>	?								
12		`	:	#	@	´	=	"		a
13	b	c	d	e	f	g	h	i		
14						j	k	l	m	n
15	o	p	q	r						
16		~	s	t	u	v	w	x	y	z
17								\	{	}
18	[	]								
19				A	B	C	D	E	F	G
20	H	I								J
21	K	L	M	N	O	P	Q	R		
22							S	T	U	V
23	W	X	Y	Z						
24	0	1	2	3	4	5	6	7	8	9

Nonprintable control characters—codes 00–63, 250–255, and those for which empty spaces appear in the chart—are not shown.

Glossary

abstract data type a class of data objects with a defined set of properties and a set of operations that process the data objects while maintaining the properties

abstraction the separation of the logical properties of data or actions from their implementation details

abstraction (in OOD) the essential characteristics of an object from the viewpoint of the user

abstract step an algorithmic step for which some implementation details remain unspecified

actual parameter a variable, constant, or expression listed in the call to a procedure

aggregate operation an operation on a data structure as a whole, as opposed to an operation on an individual component of the data structure.

algorithm a step-by-step procedure for solving a problem in a finite amount of time; a verbal or written description of a logical sequence of actions

ALU see *arithmetic/logic unit*

anonymous type a type defined in the VAR section of a program, so-called because it does not have an identifier (a name) associated with it

arithmetic/logic unit (ALU) the component of the central processing unit that performs arithmetic and logical operations

array data type a collection of components, all of the same type, ordered on N dimensions ($N >= 1$); the operations are whole array assignment and component access, each component is accessed by N indices, each of which represents the component's position within that dimension

assembler a program that translates an assembly language program into machine code

assembly language a low-level programming language in which a mnemonic represents each of the machine language instructions for a particular computer

assignment expression a C++ expression with a value and the side effect of storing the expression value into a memory location

assignment statement a statement that stores the value of an expression into a variable

atomic data type a data type that allows only a single value to be associated with an identifier of that type

automatic variable a variable for which memory is allocated and deallocated when control enters and exits the block in which it is declared

auxiliary storage device a device that stores data in encoded form outside the computer's memory

base address the memory address of the first element in an array

base case the case for which the solution can be stated nonrecursively

base class (superclass) the class being inherited from

batch processing a technique for entering data and executing programs without intermediate user interaction with the computer

binary expressed in terms of combinations of the numbers 1 and 0 only

binary search a search algorithm for sorted lists that involves dividing the list in half and determining, by value comparison, whether the item would be in the upper or lower half; the process is performed repeatedly until either the item is found or it is determined that an item is not on the list

bit short for binary digit; a single 1 or 0

block the declaration and statement sections of a program, procedure, or function

body the statement to be repeated within the loop

Boolean a data type consisting of only two values: True and False

Boolean expression an assertion that can be evaluated as being either True or False, the only values of the Boolean data type

Boolean operators operations applied to values of the type Boolean; in C++ these are the special symbols &&, ||, and !

booting the system the process of starting up a computer by loading the operating system into its main memory

branch see *selection control structure*

branching control structure see *selection control structure*

byte eight bits

call the point at which the computer begins following the instructions in a subprogram is referred to as the subprogram call

cancellation error a form of representational error that occurs when numbers of widely differing magnitudes are added or subtracted

central processing unit (CPU) the part of the computer that executes the instructions (program) stored in memory; consists of the arithmetic/logic unit and the control unit

char data type consisting of one alphanumeric character (letter, digit, or special symbol)

character set a standard set of alphanumeric characters with a given collating sequence and binary expression

class a structured type in a programming language that is used to represent an abstract data type

class member a component of a class. Class members may be either data or functions

class object (class instance) a variable of a class type

client software that declares and manipulates objects of a particular class

code coverage a testing procedure in which each branch of a program is executed at least once

code walk-through a verification process for a program in which each statement is examined to check that it faithfully implements the corresponding algorithmic step, and that the preconditions and postconditions of each module are preserved

coding translating an algorithm into a programming language; the process of assigning bit patterns to pieces of information

collating sequence the ordering of the elements of a set or series, such as the characters (values) in a character set

communication complexity a measure of the quantity of data passing through a module's interface

compiler a program that translates a high-level language (such as C++. Pascal, or FORTRAN) into machine code

compiler listing a copy of a program into which have been inserted messages from the compiler (indicating errors in the program that prevent its translation into machine language if appropriate)

complexity a measure of the effort expended by the computer in performing a computation, relative to the size of the computation

composite data type a data type that allows a collection of values to be associated with an identifier of that type

composition (containment) a mechanism by which the internal data (the state) of one class includes an object of another class

computer a programmable device that can store, retrieve, and process data

computer program a list of instructions to be performed by a computer

computer programming the process of planning a sequence of steps for a computer to follow

concrete step a step for which the implementation details are fully specified

conditional test the point at which the Boolean expression is evaluated and the decision is made to either begin a new iteration or skip to the first statement following the loop

constant an item in a program whose value is fixed at compile time and cannot be changed during execution

constant time an algorithm whose Big-O work expression is a constant

constructor an operation that builds new instances of an abstract data type (such as a list) or alters the state of an instance

control abstraction the separation of the logical properties of a control structure from its implementation

control structure a statement used to alter the normally sequential flow of control

control unit the component of the central processing unit that controls the action of other components so that instructions (the program) are executed in sequence

conversion function a function that converts a value of one type to another type so that it can be assigned to a variable of the second type; also called transfer function or type cast

count-controlled loop a loop that executes a predetermined number of times

counter a variable whose value is incremented to keep track of the number or times a process or event occurs

CPU see *central processing unit*

crash the cessation of a computer's operations as a result of the failure of one of its components; cessation of program execution to an error due to an error

cursor control keys a special set of keys on a computer keyboard that allow the user to move the cursor up, down, right, and left to any point on the screen

data information that has been put into a form a computer can use

data abstraction the separation of a data type's logical properties from its implementation

data coverage a testing procedure in which all allowable data values are tried without regard to the program code

data flow the flow of information from the calling code to a function and from the function back to the calling code

data representation the concrete form of data used to represent the abstract values of an abstract data type

data type the general form of a class of data items; a formal description of the set of values (called the domain) and the basic set of operations that can be applied to it

data validation a test added to a program or a procedure that checks for errors in the data

debugging the process by which errors are removed from a program so that it does exactly what it is supposed to do

decision see *selection control structure*

declaration a statement that associates an identifier with a process or object so that the user can refer to that process or object by name

deep copy an operation that not only copies one class object to another but also makes copies of any pointed-to data

delete a C++ operator that returns the space allocated for a dynamic variable back to the heap to be used again

delimiter a symbol or keyword that marks the beginning or end of a construct (e.g., statement, comment, declaration, and parameter list)

demotion (narrowing) the conversion of a value from a "higher" type to a "lower" type according to a programming language's precedence of data types. Demotion may cause loss of information

derived class (subclass) the class that inherits

development environment a single package containing all of the software required for developing a program

documentation the written text and comments that make a program easier for others to understand, use, and modify

down a descriptive term applied to a computer when it is not in a usable condition

driver a simple dummy main program that is used to call a procedure or function being tested

dynamic binding the runtime determination of which function to call for a particular object

dynamic data structure a data structure that can expand and contract during program execution

dynamic variable a variable created during execution of a program and hence not declared in the declaration section of a program.

echo printing printing the data values input to a program to verify that they are correct

editor an interactive program used to create and modify source programs or data

encapsulation the practice of hiding a module implementation in a separate block with a formally specified interface

encapsulation (in OOD) the bundling of data and actions in such a way that the logical properties of the data and actions are separated from the implementation details

enumeration data type a data type in which the formal description of the set of values is an ordered list of literal values; the basic operations on the data type are those common to all data types

enumerator one of the values in the domain of an enumeration type

event-controlled loop a loop that terminates when something happens inside the loop body to signal that the loop should be exited

event counter a variable that is incremented each time a particular event occurs

exception report a set of messages in a program that explains the actions taken when an invalid data item is encountered during execution

executing the action of a computer performing as instructed by a given program

execution summary a computer-generated list of all commands processed and any system messages generated during batch processing

execution trace a testing procedure that involves simulating by hand the computer executing a program

expression an arrangement of identifiers, literals, and operators that can be evaluated to compute a value of a given type

expression statement a statement formed by appending a semicolon to an expression

external file a file that is used to communicate with people or programs and is stored externally to the program

external pointer a named pointer variable that references the first node in a linked list

external representation the printable (character) form of a data value

fetch-execute cycle the sequence of steps performed by the central processing unit for each machine language instruction

field a group of character positions in a line of output

field identifier (member in C++) the name of a component in a record

field of a record a component of a record data type

field selector the expression used to access components of a record variable; formed by using the record variable name and the field identifier, separated by a period

file a named area in the computer's memory that is used to hold a collection of data; the collection of data itself

finite state machine an idealized model of a simple computer consisting of a set of states, the rules that specify when states are changed, and a set of actions that are performed when changing states

flag a Boolean variable that is set in one part of the program and tested in another to control the logical flow of a program

flat implementation the hierarchical structure of a solution written as one long sequence of steps; also called inline implementation

floating point number the value stored in a type **float** variable, so called because part of the memory location holds the exponent and the balance of the location the mantissa, with the decimal point floating as necessary among the significant digits

flow of control the order or execution of the statements in a program

formal parameter a variable declared in a procedure heading

formal parameter declaration the code that associates a formal parameter identifier with a data type and a passing mechanism

formatting the planned positioning of statements or declarations and blanks on a line of a program; the arranging of program output so that it is neatly spaced and aligned

free store (heap) a pool of memory locations reserved for allocation and deallocation of dynamic data

function a subprogram in C++

functional cohesion a property of a module in which all concrete steps are directed toward solving just one problem, and any significant subproblems are written as abstract steps

functional equivalence a property of a module that performs exactly the same operation as the abstract step it defines, or when one module performs exactly the same operation as another module

functional modules in top-down design, the structured tasks and subtasks that are solved individually to create an effective program

functional problem description a description that clearly states what a program is to do

function call an expression in the main program requiring the computer to execute a function subprogram

function definition that portion of a function subprogram appearing in a declaration section

function prototype a function declaration without the body of the function

function result the value computed by the function subprogram and then returned to the main program; often just called the result

function result type the data type of the result value returned by a function; often referred to simply as function type

function type see *function result type*

general case in a recursive definition, the case for which the solution is expressed in terms of a smaller version of itself; also called recursive case

global a descriptive term applied to any identifier declared in the main program, so-called because it is accessible to everything that follows it

global declaration an identifier declared before the **main** function, which is accessible to everything that follows it

hardware the physical components of a computer

heuristics assorted problem-solving strategies

hierarchical implementation a process in which a modular solution is implemented by subprograms that duplicate the hierarchical structure of the solution

hierarchical records   records in which at least one of the fields is itself a record

hierarchy (in OOD)   structuring of abstractions in which a descendant object inherits the characteristics of its ancestors

high-level programming language   any programming language in which a single statement translates into one or more machine language instructions

homogeneous   a descriptive term applied to structures in which all components are of the same data type (such as an array)

identifier   a name associated with a process or object and used to refer to that process or object

implementation phase   the second set of steps in programming a computer: translating (coding) the algorithm into a programming language; testing the resulting program by running it on a computer, checking for accuracy, and making any necessary corrections; using the program

implementing   coding and testing an algorithm

implicit matching   see *positional matching*

index   a value that selects a component of an array

infinite loop   a loop whose termination condition is never reached and which therefore is never exited without intervention from outside of the program

infinite recursion   the situation in which a subprogram calls itself over and over continuously

information   any knowledge that can be communicated

information hiding   the programming techniques of hiding the details of data or actions from other parts of the program

inheritance   a mechanism for automatically sharing data and methods among members of a class and its subclasses

inline implementation   see *flat implementation*

in place   describes a kind of sorting algorithm in which the components in an array are sorted without the use of a second array

input   the process of placing values from an outside data set into variables in a program; the data may come from either an input device (terminal keyboard) or an auxiliary storage device (disk or tape)

input/output (I/O) devices   the parts of a computer that accept data to be processed (input) and present the results of that processing (output)

input prompts   messages printed by an interactive program, explaining what data is to be entered

input transformation   an operation that takes input values and converts them to the abstract data type representation

insertion sort   a sorting algorithm in which values are placed one at a time into their proper position within a list that was originally empty

integer number   a positive or negative whole number made up of a sign and digits (when the sign is omitted, a positive sign is assumed)

interactive system   a system that allows direct communication between the user and the computer

interface   a connecting link (such as a computer terminal) at a shared boundary that allows independent systems (such as the user and the computer) to meet and act on or communicate with each other; the formal definition of the function of a subprogram and the mechanism for communicating with it

internal file   a file that is created but not saved; also called a scratch file

interpreter   a program that inputs a program in a high-level language and directs the computer to perform the actions specified in each statement; unlike a compiler, an interpreter does not produce a machine-language version of the program

invoke   to call on a subprogram, causing the subprogram to execute before control is returned to the statement following the call

iteration   an individual pass through, or repetition of, the body of a loop

iteration counter   a counter variable that is incremented with each iteration of a loop

iterator   an operation that allows us to process all the components in an abstract data type sequentially

length   the actual number of values stored in a list or string

lifetime   the period of time during program execution when an identifier has memory allocated to it

linear time   for an algorithm, when the Big-O work expression can be expressed in terms of a constant times N, where N is the number of values in a data set

linked list   a list in which the order of the components is determined by an explicit link field in each node, rather than by the sequential order of the components in memory

listing   a copy of a source program, output by a compiler, containing messages to the programmer

literal value   any constant value written in a program

local variable   a variable declared within a block that is not accessible outside of that block

logarithmic order   for an algorithm, when the Big-O work expression can be expressed in terms of the logarithm of N, where N is the number of values in a data set

logging off   informing a computer—usually through a simple command—that no further commands will follow

logging on   taking the preliminary steps necessary to identify yourself to a computer so that it will accept one's commands

logical order   the order in which the user wants the statements in the program to be executed, which may differ from the physical order in which they appear

loop   a method of structuring statements so that they are repeated while certain conditions are met

loop control variable (LCV)   a variable whose value is used to determine whether the loop executes another iteration or exit

loop entry   the point at which the flow of control first passes to a statement inside a loop

loop exit   that point when the repetition of the loop body ends and control passes to the first statement following the loop

loop invariant   assertions about the characteristics of a loop that must always be true for a loop to execute properly; the assertions are true on loop entry, at the start of each loop iteration, and on exit from the loop, but are not necessarily true at each point in the body of the loop

loop test   the point at which the loop expression is evaluated and the decision is made either to begin a new iteration or skip to the statement immediately following the loop

machine language   the language, made up of binary-coded instructions, that is used directly by the computer

mainframe   a large computing system designed for high-volume processing or for use by many people at once

maintenance   the modification of a program, after it has been completed, in order to meet changing requirements or to take care of any errors that show up

maintenance phase   period during which maintenance occurs

mantissa   with respect to floating point representation of real numbers, the digits representing a number itself and not its exponent

member selector   the expression used to access components of a **struct** or **class** variable. It is formed by using the variable name and the member, separated by a dot (period)

memory leak   the loss of available memory space that occurs when dynamic data is allocated but never deallocated

memory unit   internal data storage in a computer

metalanguage   a language that is used to write the syntax rules for another language

method   a procedure or function declared as a field of an object type

microcomputer   see *personal computer*

minicomputer   a computer system larger than a personal computer but smaller than a mainframe; sometimes called an entry-level mainframe

mixed mode expression   an expression that contains operands of different data types

modularity (in OOD)   meaningful packaging of objects

modular programming   see *top-down design*

module   a self-contained collection of steps that solves a problem or subproblem; can contain both concrete and abstract steps

module nesting chart   a chart that depicts the nesting structure of modules and shows calls among them

named constant   a location in memory, referenced by an identifier, where a data value that cannot be changed is stored

named matching   see *explicit matching*

named type   a typed defined in the TYPE section of a program, procedure, or function

name precedence   the priority treatment accorded a local identifier in a block over a global identifier with the same spelling in any references that the block makes to that identifier

nested control structure a program structure consisting of one control statement (selection, iteration, or procedure) embedded within another control statement

nested If an If statement that is nested within another If statement

nested loop a loop that is within another loop

new a C++ operator that returns the address of new space allocated for a dynamic variable

nodes the building blocks of dynamic structures, each made up of a component (the data) and a pointer (the link) to the next node

nonlocal a descriptive term applied to any identifier declared outside of a given block

nonlocal access access to any identifier declared outside of its own block

null statement an empty statement

nybble four bits; half of a byte

object variables and constants

object-based programming language a programming language that supports abstraction, encapsulation, and inheritance but not virtual methods (i.e., not polymorphism)

object-oriented design a building-block design technique that incorporates abstraction, encapsulation, modularity, and hierarchy

object-oriented programming a method of implementation in which programs are organized as cooperative collections of objects, each of which represents an instance of some class, and whose classes are all members of a hierarchy or classes united via inheritance relationships

object program the machine-language version of a source program

observer an operation that allows us to observe the state of an abstract data type without changing it

one-dimensional array a structured collection of components of the same type given a single name; operations are whole array assignment and component access; each component is accessed by an index that indicates its position within the collection

operating system a set of programs that manages all of the computer's resources

out-of-bounds array index an index value that, in C++, is either less than zero or greater than the array size minus one

overriding reimplementing a member function inherited from a parent class

output transformation an operation that takes an instance of an abstract data type and converts it to a representation that can be output

overflow the condition that arises when the value of a calculation is too large to be represented

parameter a literal, constant, or variable, or an expression used for communicating values to or from a subprogram

parameter list a mechanism by which functions communicate with each other

pass by address a parameter-passing mechanism in which the memory address of the actual parameter is passed to the formal parameter; also called pass by reference

pass by name a parameter-passing mechanism in which the actual parameter is passed to a procedure as a literal character string and interpreted by a thunk

pass by reference see *pass by address*

pass by value a parameter-passing mechanism in which a copy of an actual parameter's value is passed to the formal parameter

password a unique series of letters assigned to a user (and known only by that user) by which that user identifies himself or herself to a computer during the logging-on procedure; a password system protects information stored in a computer from being tampered with or destroyed

PC see *personal computer*

peripheral device an input, output, or auxiliary storage device attached to a computer

persistent variable a variable declared in the outermost scope within an abstract data type implementation and used to hold values between calls to the operations that comprise the abstract data type

personal computer (PC) a small computer system (usually intended to fit on a desktop) that is designed to be used primarily by a single person

pointer a simple data type consisting of an unbounded set of values, each of which addresses or otherwise indicates the location of a variable of a given type; operations defined on pointer variables are assignment and test for equality

polymorphic operation   an operation that has multiple meanings depending on the type of the object to which it is bound at run time

polymorphism   the ability to overload the name of an action so that it is possible to determine at either compile time or runtime which action is appropriate for a particular instance variable

positional matching   a method of matching actual and formal parameters by their relative positions in the two parameter lists; also called relative or implicit matching

postconditions   assertions that must be true after a module is executed

postfix operator   an operator that follows its operand

precision   a maximum number of significant digits

preconditions   assertions that must be true before a module begins execution

prefix operator   an operator that precedes its operand

priming read   an initial reading of a set of data values before entry into an event-controlled loop in order to establish values for the variables

problem-solving phase   the first set of steps in programming a computer: analyzing the problem; developing an algorithm; testing the algorithm for accuracy

procedural abstraction   the separation of the logical properties of an action from its implementation

programming   planning, scheduling, or performing a task or an event; see also *computer programming*

programming language   a set of rules, symbols, and special words used to construct a program

pseudocode   a mixture of English statements and C++-like control structures that can easily by translated into a programming language

range of values   the interval within which values must fall, specified in terms of the largest and smallest allowable values

real number   a number that has a whole and a fractional part and no imaginary part

record data type   a composite data type with a fixed number of components called fields; the operations are whole record assignment and selection of individual fields by name

recursion   the situation in which a subprogram calls itself

recursive algorithm   a solution that is expressed in terms of (a) smaller instances of itself and (b) a base case

recursive call   a subprogram call in which the subprogram being called is the same as the one making the call

recursive case   see *general case*

recursive definition   a definition in which something is defined in terms of a smaller version of itself

referenced variable   a variable created and accessed not by a name but by a pointer variable; a dynamic variable

reference parameter   a formal parameter that receives the location (memory address) of the caller's actual parameter

reference type   a simple data type consisting of an unbounded set of values, each of which is the address of a variable of a given type. The only operation defined on a reference variable is initialization, after which every appearance of the variable is implicitly dereferenced

refinement   in top-down design, the expansion of a module specification to form a new module that solves a major step in the computer solution of a problem

relational operators   operators that state that a relationship exists between two values; in C++, symbols that cause the computer to perform operations to verify whether or not the indicated relationship exists

relative matching   see *positional matching*

representational error   arithmetic error caused by the fact that the precision of the true result of arithmetic operations is greater than the precision of the machine

reserved word   a word that has special meaning in a programming language; it cannot be used as an identifier

result   see *function result*

return   the point at which the computer comes back from executing a function

right-justified   placed as far to the right as possible within a fixed number of character positions

robust   a descriptive term for a program that can recover from erroneous inputs and keep running

scope   the region of program code where it is legal to reference (use) an identifier

scope rules   the rules that determine where in a program a given identifier may be accessed, given the point at which the identifier is declared

scratch file   see *internal file*

secondary storage device   see *auxiliary storage device*

selection control structure   a form of program structure allowing the computer to select one among possible actions to perform based on given circumstances; also called a branching control structure

self   the instance object (class) used in the invocation of a method

self-documenting code   a program containing meaningful identifiers as well as judiciously used clarifying comments

semantics   the set of rules that gives the meaning of instruction written in a programming language

semihierarchical implementation   a modular solution implemented by procedures and functions in a manner that preserves the hierarchical design, except that a subprogram used by multiple modules is implemented once, outside of the hierarchy, and called in each place it is needed

sentinel   a special data value used in certain event-controlled loops as a signal that the loop should be exited

sequence   a structure in which statements are executed one after another

shallow copy   an operation that copies one class object to another without copying any pointed-to data

side effect   any effect of one function on another that is not part of the explicitly defined interface between them

significant digits   those digits from the first nonzero digit on the left to the last nonzero digit on the right (plus any zero digits that are exact)

simulation   a problem solution that has been arrived at through the application of an algorithm designed to model the behavior or physical systems, materials, or processes

size (of an array)   the physical space reserved for an array

software   the computer programs; the set of all programs available on a computer

software engineering   the application of traditional engineering methodologies and techniques to the development of software

software life cycle   the phases in the life of a large software project including requirements analysis, specification, design, implementation, testing, and maintenance

software piracy   the unauthorized copying of software for either personal use or use by others

sorting   arranging the components of a list in order (for instance, words in alphabetical order, numbers in ascending or descending order)

source program   a program written in a high-level programming language

standardized   made uniform; most high-level languages are standardized, as official descriptions of them exist

static binding   the compile-time determination of which function to call for a particular object

static variable   a variable for which memory remains allocated throughout the execution of the entire program

stepwise design   see *top-down design*

stepwise refinement   see *top-down design*

string   a collection of characters that is interpreted as a single data item; in C++, a null-terminated sequence of characters stored in a **char** array

stub   a dummy function that assists in testing part of a program; it has the same function that would actually be called by the part of the program being tested, but is usually much simpler

style   the individual manner in which computer programmers translate algorithms into a programming language

subprogram   see *function*

supercomputer   the most powerful class of computers

switch expression   the expression whose value determines which switch label is selected. It cannot be a floating point expression

syntax   the formal rules governing how valid instruction (constructs) are written in a programming language

system software   a set of programs—including the compiler, the operating system, and the editor—that improves the efficiency and convenience of the computer's processing

tail recursion   a recursive algorithm in which no statements are executed after the return from the recursive call

team programming   the use of two or more programmers to design a program that would take one programmer too long to complete

temporary file   a file that exists only during the execution of a program

termination condition   the condition that causes a loop to be exited

testing   checking a program's output by comparing it to hand-calculated results; running a program with data sets designed to discover any errors

testing the state of a stream   the act of using a C++ stream variable in a logical expression as if it were a Boolean variable; the result is true if the last I/O operation on that stream succeeded, and false otherwise

test plan   a document that specifies how a program is to be tested

test plan implementation   using the test cases specified in a test plan to verify that a program outputs the predicted results

text file   a file in which each component is a character; each numeric digit is represented by its code in the collating sequence

top-down design   a technique for developing a program in which the problem is divided into more easily handled subprograms, the solutions of which create a solution to the overall problem; also called stepwise refinement and modular programming

transfer function   see *conversion function*

transformer   an operation that builds a new value of an ADT, given one or more previous values of the type

traverse a list   to access the components of a list one at a time from the beginning of the list to the end

two-dimensional array   a collection of components, all of the same type, structured in two dimensions; each component is accessed by a pair of indices that represent the component's position within each dimension

type cast   see *conversion function*

type coercion   an automatic assignment of a value of one type to a variable of another type

type definition   the association of a type identifier with the definition of a new data type

unary operator   an operator that has just one operand

underflow   the condition that arises when the value of a calculation is too small to be represented

unstructured data type   a collection consisting of components that are not organized with respect to one another

user name   the name by which a computer recognizes the user, and which must be entered to log on to a machine

value parameter   a formal parameter that receives a copy of the contents of the corresponding actual parameter

variable   a location in memory, referenced by an identifier, in which a data value that can be changed is stored

value-returning function   a function that returns a single value to its caller and is invoked from within an expression

virtual method   a method in which each invocation cannot be matched with the proper code until run time

virus   a computer program that replicates itself, often with the goal of spreading to other computers without authorization, possibly with the intent of doing harm

visible   accessible; a term used in describing a scope of access

void function (procedure)   a function that does not return a function value to its caller and is invoked as a separate statement

word   groups of 16, 32, or 64 bits; a group of bits processed by the arithmetic-logic unit in a single instruction

work   a measure of the effort expended by the computer in performing a computation

workstation   a minicomputer designed to be used primarily by one person at a time